TEXT AND TRADITION

THE SOCIETY OF BIBLICAL LITERATURE
SEMEIA STUDIES
Edward L. Greenstein, Editor

TEXT AND TRADITION
The Hebrew Bible and Folklore

Edited, with Introductions
by
Susan Niditch

Scholars Press
Atlanta, Georgia

BS
1196
.T49
1990

TEXT AND TRADITION
The Hebrew Bible and Folklore

© 1990
The Society of Biblical Literature

Library of Congress Cataloging in Publication Data

Text and tradition : the Hebrew Bible and folklore, Amherst College /
    Susan Niditch, editor.
    p. cm.
    Proceedings from the Conference on the Hebrew Bible and Folklore
    held Apr. 28-May 1, 1988 at Amherst College.
    Includes bibliographical references.
    ISBN 1-55540-440-5 (alk. paper). -- ISBN 1-55540-441-3 (pbk. :
    alk. paper)
    1. Folklore in the Bible--Congresses. 2. Bible. O.T.--Criticism,
interpretation, etc.--Congresses. I. Niditch, Susan.
II. Conference on the Hebrew Bible and Folklore (1988 : Amherst
College)
BS1196.T49 1990
398.2--dc20   89-77402
                                                 CIP

Printed in the United States of America
on acid-free paper

TABLE OF CONTENTS

PREFACE

On April 28–May 1, 1988 a group of colleagues gathered at Amherst College to participate in a Conference on the Hebrew Bible and Folklore. The Conference, sponsored by the Willis Wood Fund and the Georges Lurcy Trust, allowed scholars in a broad spectrum of disciplines ranging from folklore, anthropology, and comparative literature to biblical and Near Eastern studies to share ideas, debate concepts, and assess the state of one another's fields—all by focusing together on particular texts and problems in the Hebrew Scriptures. The pattern of presentations was arranged so that the response to the biblical scholar was prepared by someone whose scholarship rests under the umbrella of folklore studies and vice versa. A round-robin discussion was held on the final day of the conference.

This book contains the proceedings of our meetings, including papers, responses, and contributions from each panelist based on their impromptu comments during the meetings. I have altered slightly the original order of the papers to draw out implicit thematic connections between certain essays that emerged after they were presented but have left intact the "oral" quality of these beautifully polished presentations. My only additions have been an introduction and transitions, which provide continuity and allow me to include insights gleaned from the discussions that followed each set of papers and responses. The essays include a number of very kind statements about myself as organizer of the conference. I want to thank my colleagues for their graciousness and for all that I learned from them. I thank Professor Edward L. Greenstein for working through the final draft with such care and sensitivity. Thanks go also to my husband, Robert Doran, for his tremendous support, and to Diane Beck, Daniel Byman, Alexander Solomita, and Jody Shapiro who helped in organizing and hosting the conference. I hope that the readers of our work will themselves become participants in the valuable, enjoyable, and on-going dialogue between students of folklore and the Bible.

INTRODUCTION
Susan Niditch

The essays in this volume explore connections between biblical and nonbiblical traditional literatures and test and discuss what may be learned from such a comparative and cross-cultural enterprise. The charge to contributors was to consider 1) the presence and significance of patterned repetition in the language, content, and structures of traditional creations—the boundary where biblical form-criticism meets the folklorist's study of formulicity and folk genres; 2) the study of context, the boundary where the Bible scholar's *Sitz im Leben* or life-setting meets the folklorist's emphasis on culture both as broadly defined and as immediately defined in the communication between authors and audiences in the context of performance; 3) an understanding of the workings of tradition and "the traditional" that allows for dynamism, freshness, and capacity to change along with a certain conservatism, changelessness, and archetypal quality. Questions of text and texture, culture, context and performance, tradition and the traditional all of which are relevant to the study of folklore and the Bible.

An anthology on the Hebrew Bible and folklore and the conference which produced it necessarily evoke the work of Hermann Gunkel, the great innovative Bible scholar of the early 20th century who recognized the importance of folklore, as understood in his times, to the study of the Bible. Gunkel may be criticized for an all-too-romantic notion of the story-telling process, with his emphasis on pastoralism and the poetic. Nevertheless, he remains the honorary forebearer of those who consider the discipline and the material of folklore relevant and important for the study of the Hebrew Scriptures. It is therefore with amusement that one reads the apology with which Gunkel seeks to justify his work in the book *The Folktale in the Old Testament* (33).

However—and the reader will have certainly long since asked the question—what has the Bible to do with folktales? Is it not an attack on the

prestige on the holy book to seek in it products of the imagination? And
how can the lofty religion of Israel—to say nothing of the New Testament—contain material filled with what may be creative, yet nevertheless entirely subordinate, belief? These questions must be answered,
first, by saying that the Bible hardly contains a folktale anywhere. The
elevated and rigorous spirit of biblical religion tolerated the folktale as
such at almost no point and this near total eradication from the holy
tradition is one of the great acts of biblical religion.

If I might paraphrase: the Bible must be appreciated in the light of
non-biblical traditional literature, but thank God none of the poi-
sonous stuff remains in unadulterated form in the Bible. Elsewhere in
this book Gunkel states, "The history of Yahwism is to a certain extent also the history of the struggle against the folktale" (176).

The debate concerning the relevance of folklore for the study of
the Hebrew Scriptures continues in this volume in a healthy spirit of
discussion and dialogue. A recurring issue faced by contributors is
the very defining of folklore itself. Is folk literature only that which is
orally and extemporaneously composed and therefore not at all relevant to understanding the edited and now canonical compositions of
the Bible? Is folk literature a relic of the Hebrew Bible's pre-history
and not recoverable or are interests in orally composed works lying
behind the Bible the wrong interests altogether? Should we concern
ourselves less with differentiating oral from written, earlier versions
from later canonical, preserved versions than with recognizing and
studying what is "traditional" in the Hebrew Scriptures in its current
form? To approach traditional literature is to appreciate a style, a poetic, a rhetoric that evidences recurring patterns in language, content,
and structure, patterns shared by the creators of the literature and
audiences who receive them, a matter of narrative expectations,
forged by shared group identity and history. To study the
"traditional" is to explore a communicative form that falls into patterns as well-worn as the rhythms of speech itself. During the conference, A. B. Lord spoke eloquently to the issue of the "traditional,"
suggesting, in fact, that whether or not creators and receivers of particular compositions could read and write may be irrelevant for understanding their special literary qualities and the ethos behind their
composition. Evidence of participation in a tradition, and not the literacy of composers and audiences, is what is essential to the special
oral character of certain works, for written works may well share in
the "traditional" or oral-seeming mode.

Questions concerning traditional style, whether in orally composed or written literature, versus non-traditional style and concerning the more specific contrast between orally composed and performed works versus written works are important and recurring
threads in the essays of this volume and in the discussion that took

place during the conference. What happens when nonrecursible, orally composed material is set in writing? What are the roles played by ideology, censorship, and aesthetic choices in the transformation of oral compositions into written-down texts?

One of the most interesting features of discussions following the papers, not overtly represented in the essays and responses themselves, has to do with aesthetics. What constitutes a good piece of oral or traditional-style narration? Is leaving a key feature of the story as an afterthought at the end of tale (e.g., "Oh by the way, I forgot to tell you about . . .") a sign of a disorganized and poor story-teller? Not all bards, after all, are Homer. As David Bynum pointed out during the conference, the Milman Parry collection of Serbo-Croatian tales presents a fine range of story-telling techniques and skills from the singer who may not know many songs and whose tales have a rote, wooden style to the advanced singer with a rich repertoire who combines formulas in fresh and imaginative ways to suit the nuances of the particular scenes, moments, and emotions he seeks to portray. And yet, as readers of biblical traditional-style literature, we often delight in biblical "silences" and find deep reasons for delayed revelations of narrative content. Are we justified in these reader responses or are we sometimes too desperate to find aesthetic order and skill whereas narrative decisions really have been made on grounds other than aesthetics? Can we who are cultures and centuries away from the world of the Hebrew Scriptures make judgments about the literary quality of this or that piece of literature?

In addition to raising these important questions about quality of narration, contributors frequently return to the contrast between traditional style and non-traditional style literatures to ask how the orally composed or traditional-style work creates meanings in contrast to the written, non-traditional work. Can we define these two poetics? A recurring message from conference participants was that while we are challenged to delineate and contrast these two poetics, oral and traditional-style literature is not to be equated with unsophisticated and less artistic work, written literature with creations of nuance and depth. Each variety of literature may be sophisticated or not, artistic or not.

In discussing the trajectory from oral to written literature, one final theme of the conference and this volume should be mentioned, the interest in post-biblical continuations of the canonical tradition in oral traditions which are then sometimes themselves written down in the various midrashic collections. The relevance of midrash for the study of folklore and the Bible became an important sub-theme of the conference. Midrash may well preserve early oral traditions that were not included in the canon. In its pre-written form or in current Jewish material collected in Israel and elsewhere, midrash shows what happens when written literature becomes a source for oral literature. Midrash also provides a repository of variants for biblical tales, the better to understand the various ways in which tales about an Eve or a Cain may have gone, the better to illuminate the particular choices made by biblical composers.

These issues of traditional versus non-traditional, oral versus written, the movement from oral to written, and the trajectory from written to oral, the aesthetics, poetics, and quality of oral, traditional, and non-traditional works, are some of the theoretical and methodological problems addressed by this volume. Many more specific problems in the Hebrew Scriptures and folklore, of course, are explored by the essays themselves. We turn to them now in the hope of raising new questions and providing fresh insights into the meanings and messages of Scripture, studying the ways in which such messages are composed and conveyed, the ways they function and are preserved in traditional cultures, with our ultimate goal an ever-deepening appreciation for the literature, its creators, and their world.

WORKS CONSULTED

Gunkel, Hermann
1987   *The Folktale in the Old Testament* trans. Michael D. Rutter. Sheffield: Almond Press. Originally published in 1917/ 1921 as *Das Märchen im alten Testament*. Tübingen: J.C.B. Mohr.

The Milman Parry Collection, housed in the Harvard Center for the Study of Oral Literature, Cambridge, Massachusetts, is a collection of over 12,500 texts on phonograph discs and in dictation. The texts include epic and lyric songs and conversations with singers collected by Parry in Yugoslavia in 1934 and 1935.

A. Biblical Narrative

The papers and responses presented under the heading biblical narrative exhibit shared interests, one of the most basic being the collecting and comparing of narrative patterns recurring within the Hebrew Scriptures (Lord; Gunn; Culley; Ben-Amos; Zakovitch; Alter) and which the Hebrew Bible shares with the oral and traditional-style literatures of other cultures (Lord; Ben-Amos; Bynum). Important debates and disagreements also emerge in the essays, varying nuances in the interpretation of specific texts and broader differences over essential methodological issues.

David Gunn's response does not take issue with the major thematic thrusts of Albert Lord's essay, but employs Professor Lord's examination of the lives of biblical heroes and pairs of heroes as a point of departure in a study of the recurring patterns of family violence and rupture that characterize the Hebrew Scriptures. Gunn asks a trenchant question, echoed by several of the panelists: Does a reliable narrator lie behind the tales of the Hebrew Scriptures, a narrator who, on some level, is implied and required by Professor Lord's insightful tracing of narrative patterns? Sometimes, redactional gaps have to be admitted. Thus Gunn asks, "Who slew Goliath, David or Elhanan?"

Robert Culley, like A. B. Lord, uncovers a recurring pattern, that of the punishment tale, a common-denominator set of action motifs which is specified with particular nuances in each instance where it is found. Culley works composition-critically, describing each appearance of the pattern as it stands in the Hebrew Scriptures, then asking how the patterns as found operate to create coherence in the complex text that is the canonical Hebrew Bible. Dan Ben-Amos, however, responds to Culley's composition-criticism, redaction-critically, his interest being in the process by which oral tales are transformed into written Scripture. Ben-Amos suggests that the current forms and themes of the punishment tales strongly reflect the ideological and theological bent of the preservers of the tales, writers concerned to emphasize God's just control over human action and natural events. Ben-Amos discusses the possible forms of oral versions of the tales that have been subjected to ideological "flattening" in the process of becoming Scripture. Implicitly he suggests that to appreciate the current form of these biblical tales of punishment, it is more important to understand how a tale is transformed through writing than to take note of the tales' underlying orality or traditional style. The essays of Robert Culley, the Bible scholar, and of Dan Ben-Amos, the folklorist, lead in interesting conceptual ways to that of the literary critic Robert Alter.

Alter like Culley deals with his text, the narrative of Samson (Judges 13-16), as it is and like Ben-Amos sees the poetics of writers as more important to its full appreciation than "folklore." Alter, alone among the contributors, however, implies that oral or traditional-seeming features of the Samson narrative are merely the primitive stuff out of which a talented author produced an aesthetically sophisticated and psychoanalytically rich narrative. Important to this narrative are the repetition of key words and the intertextual play between it and other narratives in the Hebrew Scriptures. Alter is taken to task by the panelists for lacking a true understanding of traditional-style narrative and narrators; the very techniques he uncovers are the purview of traditional as well as non-traditional composers (Nagy; Mills [this volume]). David Bynum's seminal response suggests that one cannot fully understand Samson without "folklore," that is without placing that hero in the context of other comparable characterizations in the traditional literatures of a wide range of cultures. Bynum's comparative work with classical Greek material is particularly helpful for a deeper understanding of Judges 13–16, but his methodological presuppositions and techniques have great relevance for those of us who work with classical texts that have a long written history and nevertheless resonate with qualities of oral/traditional literatures.

A stark and spirited contrast in methodology and presuppositions is represented by treatments of the tale of Rahab (Joshua 2) by Yair Zakovitch and Frank Moore Cross. Zakovitch's approach like Alter's is strongly intertextual, and like that of Ben-Amos emphasizes the changes that take place in a narrative when oral narrative becomes written literature. His approach compares the tale of Rahab with similar biblical and extra-biblical tales to delineate the building blocks and genesis of Joshua 2. Zakovitch's essay is enriched by resources as diverse as feminist criticism and Jewish medieval commentaries.

Cross offers text- and source-critical criticisms of Zakovitch's essay, suggesting ultimately that Zakovitch reads too much into Joshua 2 through his comparisons with other tales and hypothetical or idealized traditional "types."

Zakovitch's presentation and the lively debate which surrounded it challenge us to ask how much we can bring to the biblical text from other texts—biblical and non-biblical—to examine our own presuppositions in interpreting texts, and to question whether and how folkloristic interests in variants may go hand in hand with more typical historical-critical concerns and with redactional analysis.

1. Patterns of Lives of the Patriarchs from Abraham to Samson and Samuel

Albert B. Lord

ABSTRACT

This paper attempts to suggest an approach to the oral traditional character of some parts of the Old Testament through the appearance of repeated narrative patterns and elements associated with the lives of the patriarchs.

God communicated personally first with Cain and secondly with Noah, in both cases establishing a covenant. His next communication initiated a pattern of the lives of the patriarchs, and eventually a covenant with Abram to whom He promised offspring and a nation. The pattern begins with a prophecy of a miraculous birth and includes a genealogy of the parents. This birth is sometimes associated with that of a "twin," who may be opposite in temperament or calling from his brother. The first examples are Isaac and Ishmael in the first generation and Jacob and Esau in the second. The "miraculous birth" pattern was used for the succession from Isaac to Jacob, and on to Joseph. With it were associated elements of "annunciation," of "marriage," of "divine pairs," and possibly even of "childhood deeds."

Before the pattern of miraculous birth returns after Genesis with the story of Samson, there are two examples of "calling." The first is that of Moses in Exodus 3 in which God speaks to him from the burning bush. The second, that of Gideon in Judges 6. In these parallel multiforms we observe oral traditional patterns of narrative used to relate the calling of a deliverer for Israel.

Samson's miraculous birth is the first after that of Joseph in Genesis. In the pattern of Samson's life, however, the element of a "divine pair," which was so strong in earlier lives, is missing. Samson was a loner. The last of the miraculous births in our series is that of Samuel, whom his mother gave "on loan" to the Lord, even as Samson was dedicated as a Nazirite.

The Old Testament is a splendid tapestry of traditional stories interwoven with history. Its traditional tales link it with other traditions such as the neighboring ones in the Near East and in the Greek-speaking world. Through understanding the way in which the Old

Testament is constructed our experience of its depth of meaning is enriched.

Introduction

In this paper I should like, as a number of scholars have already done, to comment on the repeated patterns in the lives of the patriarchs and others in the Bible, which I believe were probably originally patterns of the lives of gods, then of demi-gods, then of divinely-called human beings.[1]

In the Old Testament God sometimes spoke to men directly and sometimes through angels or other forms, such as a burning bush or a whirlwind, and He sometimes intervened personally, as it were, in the lives of the great leaders, foreshadowing their glorious destiny, even before they were born. After the generations of Adam and Eve and their sons Cain, Abel, and Seth, God first talked, without intermediary, to Seth's direct descendant, Noah (Gen 5:1–29). We have no account of Noah's birth, beyond his naming by his father Lamech. The action of the flood drama begins with Gen 6:12–13: "And God saw the earth, and behold, it was corrupt; for all flesh had corrupted their way upon the earth. And God said to Noah: 'I have determined to make an end of all flesh.'" Thus began the Lord's instructions to Noah concerning the building of the Ark, the first recorded direct speech of God to man since His conversation with Cain after the slaying of Abel, in which He established a covenant with the guilty brother promising that he would not be slain by any who met him (Gen 4:13–15).

The next confidant of the Lord in Genesis was Abram, a direct descendant of Noah's son Shem. We know nothing of the details of

---

[1]It was a special pleasure and honor for me to participate in this conference organized by Professor Susan Niditch, whose work has added much to the fields of both Old Testament studies and folklore. The first form of this paper was a public lecture delivered at Amherst College. When writing that lecture, there were several books and articles of which I was not aware, and should have been, notably David Gunn's articles on Judges and Samuel (1974) and on the "Succession Narrative" (1976) in *Vetus Testamentum;* Robert C. Culley's *Studies in the Structure of Hebrew Narrative (Semeia* Supp., 1976;) and Robert Alter's *The Art of Biblical Narrative* (1981). Since that time Robert Alter's *The Art of Biblical Poetry* (1985) has appeared; Professor Niditch has published *From Chaos to Cosmos* and *Underdogs and Tricksters* (1987); Ronald Hendel has given us *The Epic of the Patriarch* (1987); and Robert Alter and Frank Kermode have contributed their monumental *The Literary Guide to the Bible* (1987).

It has been necessary for me in what follows to ignore the several redactions of Genesis by J, E, and P. I realize that this is a serious matter, but since I am not essentially a biblical scholar but one concerned with oral traditional narrative, for the purposes of this paper I must accept the given text as having been formed by traditional tellers.

Abram's birth, but we are told that his father was Terah and that Abram had two brothers, Nahor and Haran. I quote: "and Haran was the father of Lot. . . . And Abram and Nahor took wives; the name of Abram's wife was Sarai, and the name of Nahor's wife, Milcah, the daughter of Haran . . . Now Sarai was barren; she had no child" (Gen 11:27–30).

Here at last we embark on the first element in the full pattern of the lives of the patriarchs—or anyone else—namely, their births. Up to this point there has been nothing special about the births of any of the descendants of Adam and Eve. The descendants of Adam's and Eve's sons peopled the earth; the descendants of Noah's sons repeopled it; the descendants of Terah's and Sarai's sons were to form a new nation. For peopling and repeopling ordinary reproduction sufficed, but for the founding of that nation and for its survival a series of a special kind of leader was required. The life-pattern for such extraordinary leaders of men who could be the repesentatives of divinity on earth was an old one, a traditional one of theogony among several of the peoples of the Near East, and elsewhere as well.

I am thinking of its manifestations in the Babylonian *Enuma elish*, with its account of the birth of Marduk, and Hesiod's genealogy of Zeus in his *Theogony*. It was a sacred pattern. Ronald S. Hendel's work on Jacob cites many parallels with Canaanite traditional literature (Hendel; cf. Cross 1973).

The element of birth, naturally enough, first concerns itself with the parents of the patriarchs and their families. If, as I assume, the life-pattern "originally" told of the birth of a god or divine being, in time it became applied as well to beings who were part god and part man, in other words, part immortal and part mortal. This application became deeply associated, inextricably intertwined, with narratives about the mortality of humankind. Figures like Gilgamesh and Achilleus come immediately to mind; their stories revolve around their mortality. This may be the kind of being alluded to in Gen 6:4. Be that as it may, one might suggest that the monotheism of the Old Testament, together with its essential historicism and concern for humanity, transformed the traditional sacred or partly sacred parentage in the pattern to human parentage under the special sacred care of the Lord God. The concern of divinity gave rise to the importance of unusual birth in the life-pattern, which may be considered as having two parts, an annunciation and the birth itself.

As Hendel (1987) has pointed out, it takes the narrator of Genesis a long time to get even to the annunciation of the first miraculous birth. After the statement that Sarai was barren, a number of incidents intervene before the wonderful scene in which the visiting angels tell Abram that Sarai will bear him a son. First of all, the family moved. They set out for Canaan, but when they came to

Haran they settled there, and there Terah died (Gen 11:31–32). In Gen12:1–2 the Lord spoke to Abram for the first time, saying to him: "Go from your country and your kindred and your father's house to the land that I will show you. And I will make of you a great nation, and I will bless you, and make your name great, so that you will be a blessing." With his wife Sarai and—for some unstated reason—his nephew Lot, Abram left Haran and settled in Canaan. When Abram came to the oak of Moreh in Shechem, the Lord appeared to him and again spoke to him, saying: "To your descendants I will give this land." And Abram built an altar there "to the Lord who had appeared to him" (Gen 12:6–7). They journeyed further, more altars were set up; they went to Egypt, where the strange incident of Sarai and the pharaoh occurred; Abram separated amicably from Lot; and military action took place with the king of Sodom, in the course of which Abram rescued his nephew from captivity. Finally, the Lord spoke again to Abram in a vision, saying: "Fear not, Abram, I am your shield; your reward will be very great." Only at this point did Abram remind the Lord: "Lord God, what wilt Thou give me, for I continue childless, and the heir of my house is Eliezer of Damascus?" And behold, the word of the Lord came to him, "This man shall not be your heir; your own son shall be your heir" (Gen 15:1–4). And God entered into a covenant with Abram concerning the land for him and his descendants (Gen 15:5–17).

The birth of the hero is somtimes duplicated in traditional narrative, that is to say that it may involve also the birth or appearance of a "twin." I have wondered why Lot was so important in the story of Abram. Although the life-pattern of Abraham may lack a miraculous birth, I wonder if we may have in Lot a vestige of a "twin" for him, even if the "twin" be of a different generation? At any rate, the uncle-nephew relationship is a special one in traditional narrative in many cultures. Herakles had both a fully mortal twin, Iphicles, and a mortal nephew Iolaus, both of whom played a part in his life; Iolaus, for example, helped him in killing the Lernaean Hydra. As Abram's story develops, his life is intertwined with that of Lot. Lot was captured in the war with Chedorlaomer and rescued by Abraham, and later Abraham saved his nephew and his family from the fate of the cities of the valley, Sodom and Gomorrah. The Lord cared for Lot and for his descendants.

The birth of Ishmael from the handmaid Hagar comes before the miraculous birth of Isaac. The Lord, speaking to Hagar by an angel, foretold that the child she was carrying was destined to be "a wild ass of a man," who will "dwell over against all his kinsmen" (Gen 16:12). Later, when Hagar and Ishmael, driven out by Sarah, had fled to the wilderness and the child cried out from thirst, "God heard the voice of the lad; and the angel of God called to Hagar from heaven, and said to her, '. . . Arise, lift up the lad, and hold him fast with your hand; for I will make him a great nation.' And God was with the lad, and he grew up; he lived in the wilderness, and became an expert with the bow" (Gen 21: 17–21). Here the traditional element of the birth of a "twin" and opposite for the divine child interrupts the god-pattern, if I may call it that for the moment. One is reminded of John the Baptist, also a man of the wilderness, whose birth preceded that of Jesus.

But not even now do we reach the birth of Isaac. One more element had to be added, namely the covenant with the Lord that Abram would be father of a multitude of nations and that he and his descendants would possess the land of Canaan, and that the Lord would be their God. The covenant was sealed by the rite of circumcision. Abram's name was changed to Abraham, and Sarai's to Sarah.

At this point the strange episode of passing a wife off as a sister appears for the first time, when Abram, in Egypt because of famine, tells the Pharaoh that Sarah is his sister. The three multiforms of the wife-sister incident in Genesis (chaps. 12, 20, and 26) have been brilliantly treated by Niditch (1987:23-69) from the point of view of the folklorist. It is clearly a significant incident, or it would not be in this highly important part of Genesis, nor would it be repeated, once again in connection with Abraham and once in connection with Isaac.

As God repeated his promises to Abram and as cult sites were established, the need for an heir became more pressing, as Hendel has pointed out in his discussion of the birth of Jacob in relation to the other parallels, including that of Isaac. One can understand the necessity also of the intervening actions: the need to mark out territory, the need to set places of cult and to inaugurate essentials of rite. One can understand also the importance of gaining wealth in livestock and servants. When all that was accomplished, the stage was set for the birth of Abraham's successor, Isaac, who was given his name in advance by the Lord, as, indeed, was Ishmael in Gen16:11. Beginning with the story of Isaac's birth, a pattern of miraculous birth, sometimes associated with a "twin," followed by a precocious childhood, or at least some account of childhood deeds, often marriage, and a divine mission emerges in the Old Testament, and its tradition carries over into two of the gospels of the New Testament, Matthew and Luke.

The marriage of Isaac with Rebekah, and later that of Jacob with Rachel, was elaborately narrated, as was fitting, because these were to be the parents of the next generation of divinely chosen leaders. The process of finding a wife was governed by the will of God. Abraham made his servant swear that he would not take a wife for Isaac from among the Canaanite women but from his kindred, saying to the servant: "The Lord God of heaven . . . will send his angel before you, and you shall take a wife for my son from there (Gen 24:7). When the servant came with his camels to the city of Nahor, Abraham's brother, he stopped at a well to water them and prayed that the maiden who would give him to drink from the well and water his camels would be the one appointed. And so it befell, as you know, for Rebekah, who did as the servant had prayed, was the daughter of Bethuel, the son of Milcah, the wife of Nahor. The servant gave Rebekah a ring and bracelets and went home with her, where he was questioned by her brother Laban. When he, Laban, learned that it was the will of the Lord, the family consented, and Isaac married his kinswoman.

The element of the divine pair for a third time, counting Abraham and Lot as an example of it, or a fourth, if one counts Cain and Abel, appears again with the birth of Isaac's real twin sons, Jacob and Esau. On one level, which we might call the historical, these pairs may represent the divisions of peoples, or nations, as well as of families, but on the mythic level of the pattern we encounter the concept of binary oppositions; Abraham was the chosen leader rather than Lot, Isaac was favored over Ishmael, Jacob was also given the advantage over Esau and gained his birthright and his father Isaac's blessing, although Esau was the older. It is interesting to note in passing that Esau, like Ishmael, was a hunter. The differentiation between the two also reminds one of that between Cain and Abel. The similarity to those earlier pairs is heightened when we remember that Isaac told Esau that he would dwell "away from the fatness of the land," and "away from the dew of heaven on earth. By your sword you shall live, and you shall serve your brother." Adam was driven from the Garden of Eden, Cain was sent into exile, Ishmael escaped to the wilderness, and now Esau too was destined to live apart. But, even as the Lord assured Cain that he would not be slain, so Isaac told Esau that when he broke loose, he would break his brother's yoke from his neck (Gen 27:39–40) The sentence was mitigated.

After the birth of the twins comes the incident of Esau selling his birthright for some pottage, which may be considered as a "childhood deed." This is followed by the wife-sister episode with Abimelech, and a repetition of the quarrels between Abraham and Abimelech over wells, only this time the dispute is between Isaac and Abimelech. It ended with the establishment of peace, because Abimelech realized that the Lord was with Isaac. Jacob then gained his father's blessing, taking it away from Esau. But when Esau sought a blessing from Isaac, his father gave him a negative blessing, as noted above.

Esau's murderous hatred of Jacob caused Rebekah to send her younger son to her brother Laban to dwell until Esau's anger should cool. Thus began Jacob's journey for a bride. As Hendel has noted, Jacob encountered divinity at Bethel on his way to Haran and once again on the return journey, after gaining Rachel, when he encountered the angel of the Lord and wrestled with him. Hendel finds a significant parallel to these episodes in the life of Moses, who also encountered divinity at the start of his journey and had an adversarial meeting with the Lord as he was returning home. These are obviously very important incidents in both lives, yet they are also enigmatic.

The positioning of these events in the pattern has led me to wonder if they represent vestiges of the dangers that the hero faces when crossing the mythic boundary between one world and another, between the world of men and that of the sacred. In Jacob's case, the vision of a ladder reaching from earth to heaven with angels going and coming on it seems to welcome him onto sacred territory, with God as his guide. On his return journey Jacob wrestled with an angel, who, as it were, sought to keep him in the sacred land. When he had been given a new identity in the form of a new, and, if you will a magic, name, he passed the boundary back into the world of men. In the experience between those two episodes he had not only gained a bride but he had also been transformed by contact with the divine in the sacred world. Together with a new name, he had a mission, as symbolized by it and by its donor. The implication about his bride is that she is from the sacred world! In fact, there was something special about Rachel, as there was, of course, about Joseph, the first son of the wife whom he had really wanted to marry!

The birth of Joseph comes after an elaborate maneuvering by Jacob, his two wives and two handmaids. He is the last born in the "other world." Only Benjamin was born after the return to Canaan. In all this multitude of brothers and half-brothers what has become of the element of the "divine pair?" Perhaps Benjamin fulfills this role, although he and Joseph are not opposites. I assume that the earlier maneuvering had to do with tribal origins and had historical significance. At any rate, after the births of sons and daughters, and after negotiations—and trickery, as Niditch has shown—to gain wealth in livestock, Jacob left Laban secretly, who pursued him—as he was ritually obliged to do in a bride-stealing sequence—and ultimately came to a settlement with his father-in-law and departed from his territory. It was as he was about to meet his twin Esau, uncertain as to how he would be received, that Jacob wrestled with the angel, on the boundary, perhaps, between worlds. The structure is sensible, and the reconciliation with Esau brings the story full circle.

In Chapter 35 Jacob settled in Bethel, as directed in God's words to him, and then He appeared to Jacob and changed his name to Israel, in a typical duplication of the naming by the angel with whom Jacob wrestled. The death of Rachel, associated with the birth of Benjamin, and then the demise of Isaac, with accompanying genealogies, mark the end of one portion of Jacob's life and lead to the beginning of the Joseph story and of the Egyptian exile.

With Joseph the miraculous births cease for a time. The next important leader, the monumental and magnificent figure of Moses, does not come into the world as the result of a miraculous birth, but he is "called," as were Noah and Abraham. Yet there is a kind of substitute for the miraculous birth. After all, the miraculous birth is a birth from barrenness, life from non-life. Moses' exposure and escape, or being saved, from death, might possibly be thought to form symbolically a rebirth from extinction. In his case, a "special child" is "called" when he grows up. And Moses too is one of a pair, the other member of it being his brother Aaron. Yet once again the brothers are not opposites in virtue, although they do complement one another in their abilities.

The "miraculous birth" pattern was used for the succession from Isaac to Jacob to Joseph. With it were associated elements of "annunciation," of "divine pairs," and possibly even of "childhood deeds." Before this pattern returns with the story of Samson, there are two examples of "calling" that we must mention.

The first is that of Moses in Exodus 3 in which God speaks to him from the burning bush. In verse 10 God says: "Come, I will send you to Pharaoh that you may bring forth my people, the sons of Israel, out of Egypt." But Moses said to God, "Who am I that I should go to Pharaoh, and bring the sons of Israel out of Egypt?" And God said, "But I will be with you . . ." And after a comparatively long speech by the Lord, Moses continued, "But behold, they will not believe me or listen to my voice, for they will say the Lord did not appear to you." And, as you recall, God gave Moses three signs: the rod that became a serpent, the leprous hand cured, and the water of the Nile turned to blood.

This story has a multiform in the lovely tale of Gideon, which begins in the first verse of Judges 6, "The people of Israel did what was evil in the sight of the Lord; and the Lord gave them into the hand of Midian seven years." (For studies of Judges and Samuel, see Gunn, 1974 and 1976, and Alter and Kermode [102-21].) This is a repeated "formula," of course. Israel cried out to the Lord for deliverance and He sent a prophet who upbraided them. The angel of the Lord appeared to Gideon, son of Joash, and sat down under a sacred tree, which belonged to Joash. And the angel said to Gideon, "The Lord is with you, you mighty man of valor." And Gideon, who was quick to see an inconsistency, said, "If the Lord is with us, why has all this befallen us? Where are all His wonderful deeds which our fathers recounted to us?" And the Lord said to him: "Go in this might of yours and deliver Israel from the hand of Midian; do I not send you?"

But Gideon persisted and said, "Pray, Lord, how can I deliver Israel? Behold, my clan is the weakest in Manasseh, and I am the least in my family?" But the Lord said, "But I will be with you and you shall smite the Midianites as one man." Gideon made the Lord's angel wait while he brought a gift, a kid and unleavened cakes and flour. He put the meat in a basket and the broth in a pot, and brought them under the tree where the angel was sitting. This was not a voice from an invisible being, but an honest to goodness angel sitting under the tree, although he must have looked like a man. And the angel told him to put the meat and the cakes on a rock and pour the broth over them. "Then the angel of the Lord reached out the tip of the staff that was in his hand and touched the meat and the unleavened cakes; and there sprang up fire from the rock and consumed the flesh and the unleavened cakes; and the angel of the Lord vanished from his sight." And Gideon was afraid that he would die because he had "seen the angel of the Lord face to face." But the Lord told him that he would not, and Gideon built an altar there.

In these parallel multiforms we observe oral traditional patterns of narrative used to relate the calling of a deliverer for Israel, be it Moses leading the Israelites out of Egypt, or Gideon saving them from the oppression of the Midianites. (Noah also was a kind of deliverer.) After a number of other episodes in this series, a sort of annotated catalogue of judges, we come in Judges 13 to the story of Samson, a story of a miraculous birth, with the added element of the dedication of the child to the Lord as a Nazirite, whose head no razor should cut. One notes that there is an annunciation by an angel of the Lord to Samson's mother, who tells her husband Manoah what has happened. As Samson grew with the Lord's blessing, he began his childhood deeds, the first of which was the killing of a lion on his way to Timnah to find a woman whom he had seen and asked his father for. "And behold a young lion roared against him, and the Spirit of the Lord came mightily upon him, and he tore the lion asunder as one tears a kid and he had nothing in his hand. But he did not tell his father or his mother what he had done" (Judg 14:5–6). Here we are fully in the heroic pattern, with parallels in other heroic literature. One thinks of Digenis Akritas and of Herakles, for example. But there is an added dimension of betrayal in Samson's story. Thinking of the honey which he had later found in the body of the lion, he proposed a riddle, "Out of the eater came something to eat, Out of the strong came something sweet" (Judg 14:14). Samson's wife-to-be tricked him into letting her know the answer, thus betraying him to her countrymen, and she was given to his best man. The element of betrayal was perhaps duplicated later when Samson was bound by the men of Lehi and delivered to the Philistines. "And the spirit of the Lord came mightily upon him, and the ropes which were on his arms became as flax that has caught fire, and his bonds melted off his hands. And he found a fresh jawbone of an ass, and put out his hand and seized it, and with it slew a thousand men" (Judg 15:14–15). I need not go into all his deeds. He was a man of might, but he was finally betrayed by Delilah into the hands of his enemies and killed; he had judged Israel for twenty years.

Samson's is the first "miraculous birth" since that of Joseph in Genesis. In the pattern of Samson's life, however, the element of a "divine pair," which was so strong in earlier lives, is missing. Samson was a loner.

The "miraculous birth" of Samuel, whose mother Hannah, Elkanah's barren wife, prayed, silently moving her lips, before the priest Eli in the temple, occurs at the beginning of the sequence of events leading to the establishment of the kingdom. For it happened that for a long time Israel had been without a king and had had only judges.

Hannah presented Samuel "on loan" to the Lord as long as he lived, and her prayer in 1 Sam 2:1–10 is sometimes compared to the *magnificat* in the gospel of Luke. The boy grew, and Hannah asked the Lord to give her children for the loan of Samuel, and she bore three more sons and two daughters. The motif of replacing children reminds one of the birth of Seth to take the place of the murdered Abel, except that in his case one might suggest that Seth was possibly reconstituting a broken "divine pair." Yet Samuel, like Samson, had no "twin." Samuel, however, was not a hero in the ordinary sense of the word; he had no real childhood deeds, unless one were to count as such the momentous event of his "calling."

I might digress a moment on the calibre of childhood deeds. They seem to be appropriate to the character and role of the person involved. Samson was a man of might, a Herakles, associated with wild beasts, and his killing of a lion was appropriate to him. Jacob was a clever man, and obtaining his brother's birthright was perhaps an appropriate action for him, although the selling of it by Esau is more the point of the story. In fact, the deed was characteristic of Esau, Jacob's twin, who was also of "miraculous birth." Samuel's "calling" was appropriate to him, the boy in the temple. We are reminded of another boy of miraculous birth talking wisely with the learned men in the temple while his parents sought him elsewhere. That childhood incident as it is related in the gospel of Luke also suited the special character of Jesus.

There are other childhood deeds in 1 Samuel, but they are not Samuel's. The book contains a "divine pair," perhaps two, but Samuel is not in either of them. Eli had two sons and so did Samuel himself, but they were rejected by the Lord which was not the case, you will remember, with Ishmael or Esau. Eli's sons were killed in battle with the Philistines, and at the news of their death Eli fell over backwards and was killed. Samuel made his sons judges, but they strayed from their father's path and the elders of Israel sought a king. I hesitate to see in either of these pairs of sons the equivalent of a "divine pair." The book, however, seems to spawn duplicates on many levels, which I do not have time to consider further here.

It may be stretching a point, but I should like to suggest that the element of the twin, as it is found in other examples of the life-pattern we have been investigating, is satisfied by the two kings anointed by Samuel, Saul and David. Both Saul and David are unlike Samuel, but they are also unlike one another. David and Jonathan, of course, form another, more recognizeable and more famous, "divine pair." One might, indeed, discern here several overlapping pairs.

If the "divine pair" element is associated with the pattern of miraculous birth, so too is that of childhood deeds. In the case of David these deeds are connected with his two introductions to the court of Saul, themselves duplicates, or multiforms. First, David was brought to Saul to play the lyre to him when the evil spirit was on the king. And Saul kept him in his house. This incident is appropriate for David, the psalmist. The second incident is the slaying of the giant Goliath by young David. Here is a fitting childhood deed for a mighty man. As he came back from the field carrying Goliath's head, he was brought before Saul, and Saul asked whose son he was, and David told him. Saul took him that day and would not let him return to his father's house. But a great enmity arose between Saul and David, because David eclipsed Saul. And here we must stop our story.

I have been able only to suggest an approach to the oral traditional character of some parts of the Old Testament through the appearance of repeated narrative patterns and elements associated with the lives of the patriarchs. The Old Testament is a splendid tapestry of traditional stories interwoven with history. Its traditional tales link it with other traditions such as the neighboring ones in the Near East and in the Greek-speaking world. Through understanding the way in which the Old Testament is constructed our experience of its depth of meaning is enriched.

WORKS CONSULTED

Alter, Robert
 1981 *The Art of Biblical Narrative.* New York: Basic.
 1985 *The Art of Biblical Poetry.* New York: Basic.

Alter, Robert and Frank Kermode, eds.
1987   *The Literary Guide to the Bible.* Cambridge: Belknap Press of Harvard University Press.

Cross, Frank M., Jr.
1973   *Canaanite Myth and Hebrew Epic: Essays in the History of the Religion of Israel.* Cambridge: Harvard University Press.

Culley, Robert C.
1976   *Studies in the Structure of Hebrew Narrative.* Philadelphia: Fortress/Missoula: Scholars.

Gunn, David M.
1974   "Narrative Patterns and Oral Tradition in Judges and Samuel," *VT* 24:286–317.

1976   "Traditional Narrative Composition in the 'Succession Narrative'," *VT* 26:214–29.

Hendel, Ronald S.
1987   *The Epic of the Patriarch. The Jacob Cycle and the Narrative Traditions of Canaan and Israel.* Harvard Semitic Monographs 42. Atlanta: Scholars.

Niditch, Susan
1984   *Chaos to Cosmos: Studies in Biblical Patterns of Creation.* Atlanta: Scholars.

1987   *Underdogs and Tricksters. A Prelude to Biblical Folklore.* San Francisco: Harper and Row.

2. "THREADING THE LABYRINTH": A RESPONSE TO ALBERT B. LORD

David M. Gunn

It is an honor, and a particularly delightful one, for me to be asked to respond to Professor Lord's paper. And I'm not just speaking in terms of my recognition of a scholar whose work has touched more corners of the academic world than I can begin to contemplate let alone count. My interest in Professor Lord happens to be more precisely defined than that.

Twenty-five years ago I was a beardless youth reading English Literature and Greek at the University of Melbourne, Australia. A friend in the Classics Department said to me: "You should read this book. It's fascinating." I read it, and it changed my life. (Fair dinkum—as my mate, Crocodile Dundee, might say.) And no, it wasn't the Bible. It was—you've guessed, of course—Albert Lord's *The Singer of Tales.* My friend was right. It was fascinating. I quit reading Aeschylus and started reading Homer. I bought a little book on How-to-Get-By-in-Serbo-Croat—especially useful for people not wanting to read Serbo-Croatian heroic songs—wrote off to Black-well's in Oxford for the first two volumes of the Parry collection, and settled down to wait the twelve weeks or so for the books to wend their way past the Rock of Gibraltar, through the Suez Canal and across the Indian Ocean. I was hooked, utterly hooked. This book was dynamite. I read Homer, Beowulf, The Song of Roland, all through the lenses of *The Singer of Tales.*

I put off going on to theological school and wrote instead a Master's thesis on composition by "theme" (typical scene) in Homer and Southslavic Heroic Songs and the question of Homeric authorship (see Gunn, 1971). After theology, I took ship to Britain and went on to postgraduate work in Old Testament—but on Albert Lord's terms, so to speak. I wanted to work on oral tradition, and especially I wanted to use the concept of thematic composition as a criterion for determining whether Old Testament narrative in its present form was a product of oral traditional composition. That seemed to me a potentially fruitful path through the forests of assertion about oral tradition in ancient Israel—much of it singularly ill-informed, so it seemed to me. Indeed, I must confess that the thought did more than once occur to me (with the arrogance that so becomes an aspiring researcher) that only two people in the world really knew what was what about the Old Testament and oral tradition. Which is to say, that only two people in Hebrew Bible studies had really read and understood Lord—myself and Robert Culley. Culley (1963), I read as a classics student before ever I got near studying the Old Testament.

In any event it never worked out as neatly as I had hoped. I was able to define (to my own satisfaction at any rate!) features in the narratives that were strikingly reminiscent of Lord's "themes" as well as more broadly conceived stereotypes or motifs suggestive of traditional composition (see Gunn, 1978: chap. 3). Such definition seemed possible, even in a text—the so-called "Succession Narrative" or "Court History of David" in 2 Samuel and 1 Kings 1–2—which was usually (and mistakenly, in my view then) classed as "literary" as opposed to "oral traditional" and designated "history-writing" as opposed to categories such as "saga" or "legend" or whatever was then the going fashion for oral genres. Yet how *precisely* our texts stood in relation to a living oral narrative tradition seemed to me impossible to determine. Some fifteen years later that still seems to me to be the case.

As difficulties in determining the actual mechanics of composition compounded, so my interest grew in the way one read and interpreted these texts. That, of course, was a debate that raged initially in Homeric studies in the sixties. It intrigued me then and still does. As an undergraduate I wrote an annual paper attempting to outline a theory of how a reader/listener might be expected to respond to oral traditional formulas and themes depending on their degree of stereotyping. What relationships exist between compositional techniques on the one hand and aesthetics and interpretation on the other? It was this issue that made me for many years respond cautiously, over-cautiously I would now say, to finding significance in the nuances of variation within repetition in the way that Alter (1981) has so delightfully taught us.

Now Professor Lord's paper wisely skirts the compositional question as it might once have been asked—in terms of genre, for example, or verbatim as opposed to fluid composition, transitional texts, oral dictation, etc. Yet his present account of patterning in the "primary story" strongly elicited from me once again questions about aesthetics, poetics, and interpretation. How are we to read such patterned story? His own reading reminded me again of how richly repetitive, redundant even, is so much of that story from Genesis to 2 Kings—though rarely is the repetition or redundancy precisely that.

His own interpretive response is (characteristically perhaps?) towards a mythic reading. Narrative patterning as the vestige of myth, or myth transformed. The journey to the other land, framed by the meeting and struggle with divinity, as the hero-transforming journey to the underworld. That is an intriguing reading. In principle, at least, Deutero-Isaiah would have approved, I think. The prophet's reading likewise found a mythic multiform in the primary story (Isa 51:9–11):

> Was it not you who cut Rahab in pieces,
> Who pierced the dragon?
> Was it not you who dried up the sea,
> The waters of the great deep?
> Who made the depths of the sea a path
> For the redeemed to pass over?

From the myth of dragon slaying, the prophet tracks a story of order out of chaos through creation, flood, exodus, and the crossing of the Jordan into the land.

More often, perhaps, the narrative provides its own templates. That is to say, we may neglect the extra-intertextual in favor of the intra-intertextual. The primary story begins with an account of God's gift of a home (a garden) to humankind and their subsequent expulsion for disobedience. Already, therefore, we have the seeds of the whole story, which tells of the gift of a home, a land, and its loss. Or to take an intratextual template on what seems initially to be a micro scale but which, on reflection, may assume macro proportions: the story of Jephthah begins with his rejection by his own people of Gilead and then their demand for his return—when they are desperately in need of his help. When we recognize that this is precisely the formula that has typified the people's relationship to God in Judges, our reading cannot avoid constructing the one as a kind of multiform of the other—so terribly the same and yet different as the outcast in turn casts out his innocent daughter in order to shore up his own restoration. Humanity as a subtle perversion of divinity.

The story of expulsion from Eden gives place to Cain's killing of Abel. Violence: brother against brother, brother against sister, father against daughter, son against father—the variety extraordinary but the sameness numbingly apparent. Simply to take the story of Jephthah again: it ends with brother slaughtering brother as tribe slaughters tribe. And while Cain rages against an arbitrary rejection, the Ephraimites and Gileadites have nothing but pride and pique to fight over. By the end of Judges the nation is again torn by civil war, invoked to settle a case of rape—a civil war which leads to mass rape in order to settle the consequences of civil war. Lord takes us to the beginning of David's story. At the heart of that story is, of course, David's taking of Bathsheba and murder of her husband, hard on the heels of which comes the story of violence within his own family. Amnon rapes his sister Tamar and is murdered in turn by his brother Absalom (by proxy, aping, as a good son should, his father with Uriah). "Absalom is Cain *redivivus* who just as decisively, if less impetuously, ruptures the fabric of family," as Long (30) has nicely put it. That story is capped by Solomon's judicial murder of his brother Adonijah, and Solomon's story by the rupture of the whole country, north from south.

A family divided. Lord's focus upon the motif of "twins" or "pairs" I found stimulating. Perhaps one reason this mythic vestige permeates our story is that twins are emblematic of the intimate bond between people that humankind so desperately craves and so readily destroys.

Such patterning can lead us to formulate notions about theme or theology. It can also lead us to fill particular gaps in the one text by comparison or contrast with another—when we "twin" the text. That is essentially the strategy Alter adopts (chap. 3) with his "type scenes." The sacrifice of Jephthah's daughter, his "only child," resonates, of course, with Genesis 22 and Isaac, but in due course the story will also resonate with 1 Samuel 14, where Jonathan is rescued by the people from paying with his life for his father, Saul's, vow. Depending where we stand as readers will depend on how we respond to those resonances. We might, for example, ask, Why is it that the young woman dies, the young men are spared? We might ask, Why is the daughter so alone? Where was Sarah, or Jephthah's daughter's mother? And when we pair this text with the account of Miriam's reception of Moses at the defeat of Pharaoh, or with David's reception by the women of Bethlehem on his return from victory over Goliath, our question has a way of reduplicating itself: it can take the form, Did Jephthah, after all, *expect* his daughter?

Let us take another case. The rape of Tamar (2 Samuel 13) conjures the rape of Dinah (Genesis 34). Amnon, Tamar's brother, "loves" her, invites her into his home, rapes her, hates her, and casts her out. "No, my brother," she says, ". . . I pray you, speak to the king [her father]; for he will not withhold me from you." "No, my brother, for this wrong in sending me away is greater than the other which you did to me." For her part, Dinah goes out to visit the daughters of the land, is raped by Shechem, loved by him, taken into his home, and asked in marriage of her father. In the name of her honor (or is it their own?) her brothers slaughter Shechem, pillage his people, and take Tamar from his house. Both Tamar and Dinah are destined to live out their lives, dishonored, in their brother's keeping. Read Dinah's story and you may neglect to hear her voice; you may triumph with the brothers in their imposition of poetic justice (cf. Sternberg:445–75) Re-read Dinah's story as you read Tamar's, and you may, surprisingly, hear her weep for the dead Shechem, and, as her brothers berate their father, lament for the pillaged daughters of the land.

Another kind of "pairing" of texts can evoke yet another effect on a reader. Lord ends his paper with the childhood deeds of David. "The deeds are connected with the two introductions of David to the court of Saul, themselves duplicates, or multiforms." David soothes Saul with his music; David slays the Philistine Goliath. Of the many multiforms these two mesh less well than most. May that not disturb our confidence in the narrator? It certainly has done that for generations of historical critics! Yet the narrator does not stop here. For the slaying of Goliath is itself a duplicate. By the end of 2 Samuel we have been faced with another account, of Elhanan slaying Goliath. Who slew Goliath? That's not really the question that I ask. Rather it is, Can I always trust this narrator to tell me as it is? What has happened to the "reliable narrator" the theorists of biblical poetics have been telling me to believe in? (see further, Gunn, 1987:70–72).

So I start with traditional patterns and I end with a question of poetics and interpretation. That's not altogether surprising since in another sense I started with the question of poetics and interpretation. I read Lord's essay out of that concern. He not only stirs me to read the text once more with an eye to patterns and shapes that will give form to my reading and clues to my understanding; he also presses me to explore again the connection between composition and interpretation, between the making and the reading of a text.

Reading and listening to his paper has been a great pleasure. It has prompted me to look back and to pick up threads that I had dropped, to find new ones, and to look forward to where they might be taking me. Whether I shall ever make it out of the labyrinth I'm not sure—but then I don't think I mind very much whether I ever do: wandering through the highways and byways of the Bible and its criticism is for me rather like being stuck in the labyrinth of Minos— without the minotaur and with Ariadne.

WORKS CONSULTED

Alter, Robert
    1981   *The Art of Biblical Narrative*. New York: Basic.

Culley, Robert C.
    1963   "An Approach to the Problem of Oral Tradition," *VT* 13:114–25.

Gunn, David M.
   1971   "Thematic Composition and Homeric Authorship." *Harvard Studies in Classical Philology* 75:1–31.

   1978   *The Story of King David: Genre and Interpretation.* JSOT Supplement Series, 6. Sheffield, JSOT.

   1987   "New Directions in the Study of Biblical Hebrew Narrative." *JSOT* 39:65–75.

Long, Burke O.
   1981   "Wounded Beginnings: David and Two Sons." Pp. 26–34 in *Images of Man and God: Old Testament Short Stories in Literary Focus.* Ed. Burke O. Long. Sheffield: Almond.

Lord, Albert B.
   1960   *The Singer of Tales.* Cambridge, MA: Harvard University Press.

Sternberg, Meir
   1985   *The Poetics of Biblical Narrative: Ideological Literature and the Drama of Reading.* Indiana Literary Biblical Series. Bloomington: Indiana University Press.

3. FIVE TALES OF PUNISHMENT IN THE BOOK OF NUMBERS

Robert C. Culley

ABSTRACT

Speaking about the Talmud, a scholar recently commented: "A decisive element in the literary analysis of a text, particularly an ancient and unfamiliar one, is the metaphor chosen to describe the text and the method of its exegesis" (Neusner:39). That scholar inclined toward the metaphor of the web of the loom in order to capture the peculiar nature of the Talmudic text with its "stages of agglutination and conglomeration." Whether or not this metaphor is apt for the Talmud, it is true that our perception of a text, the way we conceive and picture it, shapes our critical response. The problem of how best to grasp the nature of the biblical text, in all its complexity, lies behind this essay and gives it direction, although I will be limiting myself to narrative. In this regard, the study of folklore may be of some help in that it draws to our attention some features of literature which need to be kept in mind when reflecting on ancient texts. I will make some general comments about two aspects of folklore and then consider five stories from the book of Numbers.

Folklore and Biblical Narrative

As a biblical scholar, I have developed a modest acquaintance with two topics which folklorists as well as comparativists discuss, namely, oral tradition and narrative structure. This interest has influenced in some measure the way I look at the biblical text. My comments on these two topics will be brief. I simply wish to recall some of the important features of the long and complex discussion surrounding these matters. This will provide a background against which to discuss the stories in Numbers, and thereby biblical narrative and the biblical text itself.

First oral tradition. "Oral" usually means performance before an audience, and the relationship between performer and audience is vital. Performers are preservers of the common heritage of a community, presenting the known and familiar, but they are also artists who can do this creatively and well. Since the performed stories and poems are closely related to a group or community, they may work in many ways, including aesthetic, religious, ideological, social, and cultural mixing entertainment, inculcation, persuasion, ritual, and the like. There also seem to be literary types frequently associated with oral tradition, such as those stories usually labelled myth and legend. Furthermore, texts from oral tradition appear to display a high degree of redundancy or repetition at various levels of the text: words, phrases, typical outlines, including narrative patterns.

This brings me to the subject of narrative structure which, in the sense of narrative action or emplotment, is part of the redundancy characteristic of oral tradition but also more than this. All narrative, oral and written, is patterned and repeats patterns since this is fundamental to telling stories. At any rate, folklorists and other students of oral narrative have played an important role in the investigation of narrative structure. Whatever the lasting merit of the work of Lévi-Strauss and Propp, they have drawn attention to the role of the repeated yet ever varying narrative patterning of traditional narrative. Indeed, it was the work of these two scholars that first stimulated my interest in narrative structure, and it was Propp who set me thinking about the kinds of repetition and variation we can find in biblical narrative.

Of course, biblical narrative is a written text and not oral tradition, not a bundle of transcripts of oral performances. Indeed, it is very difficult to identify material which may be very close to oral performance. On the other hand, biblical narrative is not a written text in our sense of the term. Based on my general impressions of the nature of oral and written literature, it seems to me that some of the material, at least, is like oral tradition and some of it is like a written text, suggesting that biblical narrative is in varying degrees some kind of "oral-derived" text (Foley:5). I will call biblical narrative "traditional" (Niditch:xiii) to indicate that it seems to contain a significant amount of traditional material which continues to reflect in its form and content something from an earlier oral stage of composition and transmission so that even newer material added in writing may still be composed under the influence of traditional oral styles.

When I speak of features that suggest an oral background or derivation, I am thinking of things like the anonymity of the material. For most biblical narrative, authors are not identified, and this could mean that the authors were seen primarily as custodians of common tradition, however creative they were and however much they contributed something from their own perspective. Then, too, many of the stories in biblical narrative bear some resemblance to what many call legends or sacred legends (Jason:34). The action of biblical narrative normally works on the human plane and bases its action in events and persons from the past. Running alongside this, however, is another dimension of reality, the supernatural or divine, which frequently intersects with the human plane. This presence is regularly implicit in the flow of narrative and often explicit in the form of miracle, direct intervention bringing both good and bad effects to human participants.

While we sense that we can identify stories in biblical narrative that are like folklore, these are now elements in a larger story framework recounting the history of Israel from the creation to the return from the exile. In other words, the material has undergone a process of ordering and arranging along a chronological line. Whether this composition occurred through a lengthy and complex process of tradition or a shorter activity of early historiography (Van Seters), the act of arranging smaller stories into larger narrative units, at least on the scale seen in the Bible, suggests that the advantages of writing are being exploited to record the past and to arrange the traditions of the past along a chronological line.

In the end, we get a body of narrative with a substantial measure of coherence but with significant indications of its composite nature. Most recognize this but few have deliberately considered how one might read or interpret a composed or composite text (but see Alter, Greenstein, and Damrosch). The notion composite text usually leads in one of two directions. One may stress the word "composite" as historical criticism has done and seek to reconstruct the stages of development. Or one may stress the word "text," assuming a certain notion or convention of unity so that readings which feature coherence are favored over those which recognize tensions.

Is it possible to take seriously both the idea of "composite" and the idea of "text" thus taking into account the kind of coherence and tensions this double perception implies? If our composite text is also a traditional text, may we then explore the notion of varied repetition of narrative structure discussed above within such a text? In a composite narrative text, repetition of similar stories may be sufficiently striking that one may consider them paradigmatically, linking like to like, as well as syntagmatically, in their linear ordering. After all, if the narrative material was tradition, and therefore familiar to listeners or readers, it did not need to be read as a whole or in order. A composite text invites this kind of use, since stories are not tightly bound to surrounding material. Linear ordering in a given stretch of text may not produce a strong subordination of individual stories to that ordering. There is certainly a natural pull toward reading the text in its present order, but there may also be a pull toward reading out of order, since the mind associates like stories in different parts of the text.

Five Stories in Numbers

The stories in Numbers are the following: Num 11:1–3, punishment by fire; Num 11:4–35, punishment by quails, along with help to Moses; Numbers 12, punishment of Miriam by leprosy; Num 20:1–13, punishment of Moses and Aaron; and finally Num 21:4–9, punishment by serpents. There are actually two more punishment stories, the spies in Numbers 13–14 and Korah, Dathan and Abiram in Numbers 16, which I am leaving out for reasons of time and space. The five stories all recount a pattern of punishment yet each story does so differently (for general studies, see Noth and Coats; for an interesting structural analysis, see Jobling).

These stories are stages in the desert journey, which provides a chronological framework. The stories are also bound together by constants: the deity, Moses, the people, and the wilderness. Yet, the stories are not tightly linked in a continuous narrative movement. There may be good reasons for the present order, and these would need to be examined. But rather than the chronological ordering of the stories which is not terribly obvious here, I would like to consider the stories as a set in which one may reflect on similarity and difference. The redundancy or repetition of the same punishment pattern in similar stories creates a sense of coherence, but variation among the stories introduces certain tensions, which produce a measure of complexity and subtlety as the possibilities of the pattern are explored (for another view of these patterns, see Childs:258–64).

Let us, then, look at these five stories to note how each is similar to yet different from the others.

1. Num 11:1–3 tells of a punishment by fire. The people complain. Yahweh hears and becomes angry. The fire of Yahweh consumes the edges of the camp. The people appeal of Moses who prays to Yahweh so that the fire subsides. The mitigation is a rescue pattern.

This story is remarkable because it is so terse. The action is reduced to a minimum, which records the basic steps necessary to the move from wrong to punishment and then the mitigation which moves from difficult situation to rescue. The pattern of wrong/punishment stands out sharply and clearly without complexity or subtlety.

While the story is complete, the whole flies by so rapidly that there is little time to become involved in the narrative. Perhaps this is the brevity of a chronicler simply noting what happened at a particular time and place, but there is a certain elegance to this minimal statement as in some styles of drawing where two or three lines may suggest a face or a figure. The terseness creates a distance and objectivity in which one contemplates the pattern rather than the particular story it states. The pattern is simple and clear: wrong brings punishment, yet there can be mitigation.

2. Num 11:4–35 relates a punishment by quails, and that sums up its unusual feature, a kind of reversal. The bringing of quails suggests a positive response to an appeal for help but here it means punishment. Intertwined with this punishment pattern is a rescue pattern in which Moses is freed from the difficulty of having to bear the responsibility of leading the people all by himself.

The story begins with a complaint uttered by the rabble and picked up by the people. What they demand is not basic food for survival, the manna has provided that, but they desire meat, a luxury they remember from Egypt. This kind of complaint is, of course, the so-called "murmuring motif" (see Coats) which, when used, calls into question the whole enterprise of leaving Egypt. Although this complaint does not always provoke Yahweh's anger, here it does, and so we have the first part of a punishment pattern: people have done wrong and angered the deity.

At this point, Moses laments his lot and complains that Yahweh wronged him in placing on him the burden of this people, particularly with the demand for meat, and he asks to be killed on the spot. While this in its own way challenges Yahweh's plans, Yahweh does not take exception to Moses' complaint but regards it as a genuine problem which merits help, a difficulty from which Moses needs to be rescued, and so we have a rescue pattern.

Steps are taken to settle both problems. First, the spirit which rests on Moses will be shared with seventy elders who will help bear the burden. Second, the punishment of the people is announced. The announcement starts off on a good note as though a positive answer to their complaint will be forthcoming. They are to prepare themselves to eat meat on the following day. But suddenly the tone changes. The people will eat it until it comes out their noses, for they have rejected Yahweh. A wind from Yahweh brings quail and while they are consuming the meat, Yahweh flares out against them in anger and strikes them with a great plague.

Thus two patterns, a punishment of the people and a rescue of Moses, are intertwined with both flowing from the same incident, the complaint of the people. The punishment pattern still asserts that wrong brings punishment but a certain complication, even blurring, occurs with the use of an apparent rescue by quails to achieve a punishment. Further blurring comes from the fact that the sharp complaint of Moses is met with help.

3. Numbers 12 tells of a punishment by leprosy and a rescue or mitigation. What is remarkable about this story is the fact that it is not

the people who are the cause of the trouble but persons close to Moses. A further puzzle is that only one of them gets punished, Miriam, the woman.

The story opens with Miriam and Aaron speaking against the Cushite woman Moses had taken, about whom we know nothing and who will not be mentioned again. Next, these two claim that Yahweh speaks through them as well as Moses. This matter is settled through a meeting at the tent, where Yahweh confirms Moses' special position in the strongest terms: Yahweh speaks with Moses, his servant, face to face, and so Miriam and Aaron should have been afraid to speak against him. While both are reprimanded, and through Aaron admit their sin, only Miriam is struck with leprosy in a sudden and miraculous intervention. Mitigation or rescue comes through Aaron's appeal. It may be that a coming together of different traditions in the present condensed text is responsible for the loose ends in the story. But the result produces ambiguity. Wrong brings punishment but not always.

4. Num 20:1–13 also recounts a punishment but the remarkable, if not shocking, feature of this story is that it is Moses and Aaron who are punished. Intertwined with this punishment pattern is a rescue. The people lack water and quarrel with Moses, asserting that they were brought to the wilderness to die. One might anticipate that the people would be punished and Moses vindicated but the opposite happens. Moses is instructed to take his staff, gather the community and Aaron, and speak to the rock. He does so. But then he addresses the people calling them rebels and asks "Shall we bring forth water from this rock for you?" It is not clear what this means. He strikes the rock twice and water flows out for the people. Yahweh charges Moses and Aaron with not believing him, not acknowledging his holiness before the people. Now, whether this was for what Moses said to the people, or for striking the rock instead of speaking to it, or both is not clear (but see Margaliot, Milgrom, and Sakenfeld). A wrong is declared and a punishment is announced: Moses and Aaron will not lead the people into the land.

That a punishment was administered is clear but disturbing. Moses, the faithful leader who bore the burden alone until given help, received constant abuse, advised Yahweh wisely, bore a special spirit, and who alone spoke to Yahweh face to face is the one punished. What he did wrong, and even this is not clear, does not seem to merit the punishment, and this is not to mention Aaron who seems to be an innocent bystander in the whole affair.

5. Num 21:4–9, the last story, tells about a punishment by serpents followed by a rescue or mitigation. The people spoke against the deity and Moses, once again charging that they had been brought out here to die. Their complaint is that they lack food and water.

Yahweh sent fiery serpents which bit the people so that a large number died. Confessing that they have sinned, the people appeal to Moses to intervene. In response to his prayer, Yahweh instructed that a bronze serpent be made so that people bitten can look at it and live and this happens.

The striking thing about this story is perhaps that the rescue seems to draw more attention than the punishment. Punishment comes but so does an even more remarkable rescue.

Conclusion

The five stories all repeat a punishment pattern (wrong/punishment) but we have seen how the roles change. Punishment by fire (Num 11:1–3), by quails (Num 11:4–35), and by serpents (Num 21:4–9) all concerned a wrong by the people in which they complained and thus challenged the journey to the promised land, although in the first and last cases there was a mitigation or rescue from the punishment. Yet in the story of the quails (Num 11:4–35) Moses also complains bitterly but is delivered from his difficulty rather than punished. Then again in the story about the lack of water (Numbers 20) the people complain but are rescued from their difficulty, while Moses and Aaron are charged with doing something wrong (although it is not clear what) and are punished severely with no mitigation. Finally, Miriam and Aaron challenge Moses and are shown to be in the wrong, but Miriam alone is punished while Aaron is not. In the punishment by serpents the punishment seems to be subordinated to the rescue.

It is likely that different sources, both oral and written, lie behind much of this variety, not to mention the tensions noticeable in several of the individual stories. However, rather than trying to follow the individual threads back to the different settings, which is one way of accounting for the different perspectives in the material, I have tried to consider what happens when these perspectives are brought together in the present biblical text. Regarding the punishment pattern, its repetition appears to reinforce the notion that Yahweh may not be crossed or provoked. He will punish, even though there may be a rescue afterwards. On the other hand, the remarkable variation produces a kind of blurring of this general notion: punishment comes but is less clear when, why, to whom.

I have not arrived at a metaphor that would grasp the peculiar nature of biblical text, but this limited study of five stories may suggest one significant aspect of the depth and complexity of the composite biblical text, at least in the narrative tradition.

WORKS CONSULTED

Abrahams, Roger D.
1972   "Folklore and Literature as Performance." *Journal of Folklore Institute* 9:75–94.

Alter, Robert
1981   *The Art of Biblical Narrative.* New York: Basic.

Bauman, Richard
1975   "Verbal Art as Performance." *American Anthropologist* 77:290–311.

Ben-Amos, Dan
1971   "Toward a Definition of Folklore in Context." *Journal of American Folklore* 84:3–15.

Childs, Brevard S.
1974   *The Book of Exodus: A Critical, Theological Commentary.* OTL. Philadelphia: Westminster.

Coats, George W.
1968   *Rebellion in the Wilderness.* Nashville: Abingdon.

Culley, Robert C.
1984   "Stories of the Conquest: Joshua 2,6,7 and 8." *Hebrew Annual Review* 8:25–44.

1985   "Exploring New Directions." Pp. 167–200 in *The Hebrew Bible and its Modern Interpreters.* Ed. Douglas A. Knight and Gene M. Tucker. Philadelphia: Fortress/Chico: Scholars.

1986   "Oral Tradition and Biblical Studies." *Oral Tradition* 1:30–65.

Damrosch, David
1987   *The Narrative Covenant: Transformations of Genre in the Growth of Biblical Literature.* San Francisco: Harper and Row.

Foley, John Miles
1986   "Introduction." Pp. 1–17 in *Oral Tradition in Literature: Interpretation in Context.* Ed. John Miles Foley. Columbia: University of Missouri Press.

Greenstein, Edward L.
1982 "An Equivocal Reading of the Sale of Joseph." Pp. 114–25 in *Literary Interpretations of Biblical Narratives, Volume II.* Ed. Kenneth R. R. Gros Louis with James Ackerman. Nashville: Abingdon.

Jason, Heda
1977 *Ethnopoetry.* Forum Theologiae Linguisticae. Bonn: Linguistica Biblica.

Jason, Heda and Dimitri Segal
1977 *Patterns in Oral Literature.* World Anthropology. The Hague: Mouton.

Jobling, David
1978 "A Structural Analysis of Numbers 11–12." Pp. 26–62 in *The Sense of Biblical Narrative. JSOTSup* 7. Sheffield: JSOT.

Margaliot, M.
1983 "The Transgression of Moses and Aaron—Num 20:1–3." *JQR* 74:196–228.

Milgrom, Jacob
1983 "Magic, Monotheism and the Sin of Moses." Pp. 251–65 in *The Quest For the Kingdom of God: Studies in Honor of George E. Mendenhall.* Ed. H. B. Huffmon, F. A. Spina, and A. R. W. Green. Winona Lake, IN: Eisenbrauns.

Neusner, Jacob
1983 "I. Introduction: Metaphor and Exegesis." *Semeia* 27:39–44.

Niditch, Susan
1987 *Underdogs and Tricksters: A Prelude to Biblical Folklore.* New Voices in Biblical Studies. San Francisco: Harper & Row.

Noth, Martin
1968 *Numbers: A Commentary. OTL.* Philadelphia: Westminster.

Olson, Dennis T.
1985 *The Death of the Old and the Birth of the New.* Brown Judaic Studies 71. Chico, CA: Scholars.

Overholt, Thomas W.
    1986   *Prophecy in Cross-Cultural Perspective*. SBL Sources for Biblical Study 17. Atlanta: Scholars.

Sakenfeld, Katharine Doob
    1985   "Theological and Redactional Problems in Numbers 20:2–13." Pp. 133–54 in *Understanding the Word. JSOTSup* 37. Ed. James T. Butler, Edgar W. Conrad, and Ben C. Ollenburger. Sheffield: Department of Biblical Studies, University of Sheffield.

Van Seters, John
    1983   *In Search of History*. New Haven: Yale University Press.

4. COMMENTS ON ROBERT C. CULLEY'S "FIVE TALES OF PUNISHMENT IN THE BOOK OF NUMBERS"

Dan Ben-Amos

Allow me to begin with a personal note. Twenty five years ago, as I was wandering among the library shelves, I chanced upon a volume of the journal *Vetus Testamentum*. Thumbing through its pages, I came across an article entitled "An Approach to the Problem of Oral Tradition." The author was unknown to me, but I was pleased to find among modern biblical scholars a renewed interest in the issues surrounding oral tradition and the biblical text. At that time, xeroxing was an expensive novelty, particularly for students, and instead of simply copying the essay I took, what at the time seemed to me, a daring step, and requested an offprint from the author. I received it by return mail.

With this act of kindness, Robert Culley initiated me into the community of scholars in which ideas are exchanged and cross their disciplinary boundaries through the United States (and Canadian) mail service. Ever since then, as I have been plowing the furrows of the field of folklore, I have been glancing over the fence, trying to glimpse any new movements and emerging trends that engage scholars of biblical studies. Obviously, any indications of convergence of interests between folklore and biblical studies have been heartening.

As Professor Culley has pointed out, formulaic and structural analyses have been the two major trends in folklore research that have made an effective contribution to biblical studies. In a variety of writings he has applied these methods to the study of the biblical text (Culley 1963, 1967, 1974, 1975, 1976, 1984, 1986), and, together with other modern scholars, has furthered the exposition of the oral literary foundations of the Hebrew Bible (see surveys and bibliographies in Culley 1986, Kirkpatrick 1988, Niditch 1987). Formulaic analysis has enabled Culley and others to trace the effects of oral performance in poetic genres, whereas structural analysis has revealed traditional patterns in prose narratives. These methods have helped biblical scholars to reach beyond the text, delineating literary and rhetorical elements that have survived the transformation from oral to scriptural verbal forms.

As much as these discoveries have been rewarding, once their novelty has waned, it has become apparent that they have not described the transformation of oral into written literature in full. Mostly they uncovered oral textual survivals in the written text, as if removing its scriptural patina, and allowing the oral layer to shine through. Insufficient as they are, these new insights have demonstrated the need to examine not only the oral residue in the written text, but the very process of transformation from oral to written literature. This is not an involuntary but a deliberate process, often subject to its own principles and social constraints. The commitment of oral literature to script, and later to print, forces upon the text distinct social restrictions that emanate from the cultural conceptions of writing and the idea of cultural centrality that a scriptural canon implies.

Unfortunately, the two preeminent scholars of orality and literacy, Walter Ong (1967, 1971, 1977, 1982) and Jack Goody (1968, 1977, 1986, 1987), conceive of them as two respective processes that are independent of society and individuals. For Ong and Goody orality and literacy are primary forces that subject all to submit to their inherent laws and principles. They are forces with a superorganic independent power. They create movements that transform society and human beings, but remain independent of them. Walter Ong and Jack Goody complement each other. While the former focuses on the verbal, the latter concentrates upon the cognitive and psychological manifestations of orality and literacy. Yet, both regard them as processes *sui generis* acting upon and not activated by the people. Brian Street (1985) criticizes Goody, in particular, for constructing a theory of "the great divide" between orality and literacy, a divide that may exist in theory but not in reality.

However, not only is "the great divide" a theoretical construct; so is also the abstract idea of independent forces of orality and literacy themselves. In reality both are tools for the attainment of specific social goals; both are subject to human will, wish, and belief. Oral and literate performances are dependent not only upon the technical limits inherent in each of these modes of communication, but also upon the cultural attitudes toward them. Hence the transformation of texts from oral to written literature is not merely a technical shift in modes of wording, nor is it only a cognitive turn from one mode of thought to another. Once the potentiality of script is an available socio-cultural option, it is dependent upon values and attributes which a particular society accords to writing.

The Pentateuch offers a clear illustration of the dependency of this process upon the intention, goals, and beliefs of the scribes and editors who have carried out this transformation. No matter what explanation is offered for the monotheistic tendency of the Pentateuch, whether it is an expression of an inherent monotheism of desert tribes (Kaufmann; see also Weinfeld:459–60), or a result of deliberate demythologization (Bentzen:241), by the time scribes and editors composed the oral and written fragments that were available to them into a continuous narrative, they fostered the text to express the ideology and the theology to which they subscribed (Zakovitch:31).

In doing so they garnered all narratives and metaphors to serve their religious ideals, justifying God's judgment of His people. Consequently, the text that they created obliterated the chorus of dissenting voices, debates, and conflicting ideas that are an integral part of any oral tradition that concerns past leaders and events. In their historical narration the scribes and editors strove to validate beliefs and ideas that attained a central position at least in their time and religious circles if not the society at large.

On the basis of these assumptions I would like to suggest that the pattern of "punishment narratives" that Robert Culley has exposed serves scribal ideology rather than reflects oral tradition. It is a narrative pattern that upholds *a posteriori* a religious ideology that justifies the ways of God to His people, and vindicates the actions of Moses regardless of their actual effects in human terms. Consequently, the "punishment pattern" silences contrasting voices that could be heard again only by rhetorical analysis of these very passages.

Such an analysis requires not only a morphological account of the sequence of actions that together form a cohesive narrative. Rather it must admit a range of alternative narrative functions that serve the same purpose. Furthermore, it is necessary to admit into the analysis the speaker's voice, realizing that within the act of narration the same story can serve the purposes of different parties, and achieve conflicting goals when told by different people. In short, the same story has the potentiality of being a voice for antagonistic speakers.

The "punishment pattern" that Culley has exposed in these five narratives depends not just on the sequence of episodes but mostly on the speaker's point of view. Each tale is told to uphold the belief in God's just control over human actions and natural events. From a different ideological perspective, most of the tales could have been disaster stories, reporting one kind of mishap or another. For example, the first tale is a fire report.

> And the people were as murmurers, speaking evil in the ears of the Lord; and when the Lord heard it, anger was kindled; and the fire of the Lord burnt among them, and devoured in the uttermost part of the camp. And the people cried unto Moses; and Moses prayed unto the

Lord, and the fire abated. And the name of that place was called
Taberah, because the fire of the Lord burnt among them (Num 11:1–3).

The restructuring of a disaster account as a punishment tale is in
accord with a world view that assumes a divine rule in human
affairs. Under the control of the Lord, the world is in balance. When
order is disrupted, the cause could not be divine but human. Thus the
narrator lodges the responsibility for the disaster with the murmurers
who doubted the efficacy of divine rule. The establishment of causal
relations between the murmurers and the fire completely depends on
the theological views of the biblical writers. There is no other basis for
connecting words with flames. Fire could strike due to natural
causes, or human errors. The particular timing of a disaster gives
room for religious speculation and divine causation, enabling a writer
to transform a disaster report into a cohesive, motivated story,
patterned as a punishment narrative. If a disaster has a divine cause,
it follows that it is possible to abate it only by appealing to its
supernatural primary cause. The restoration of balance into nature
and society is the function of the charismatic personality, the miracle
worker, and in this account Moses functions in this role (see also
Tiede:178–206). The use of the verb "prayed," or as in the fifth tale's
"prayed for the people" (Num 21:7), underscores his mediating function in bringing about miracles.

Moreover, Moses' position as a singular miracle worker, like the
pattern of punishment itself, is more likely to reflect a literary-theo-
logical, rather than an oral narrative, pattern. In oral tradition, miracle tales often rhetorically establish the position of as yet unrecog-
nized charismatic leader. In fact, the miracle stories themselves are
part of the cultural rhetoric that consolidates his position. It is possible to surmise that in the pre-biblical oral tradition there were tales
about miracle workers, but by the time the text was committed to
writing the centrality of Moses in Israelite tradition had been completely solidified. Then there was no need to counter any dissenting
voices that vied for the support of an alternative cultural hero.

Finally, as a fire report, the episode is also a naming story. The
narrative coda establishes a connection between an event and a local-
ity. This is a rather common feature of disaster narratives. Through
names language mediates between time and place and commemorates an occurrence in a particular locale. This feature appears in
three of the "punishment narratives" that Culley analyzes. In the first
tale the place is Taberah, in the second Kibroth-hattaavah (Num
11:34) and the fourth is placed spatially at the Waters of Meribah
(Num 20:13).

In the second punishment tale (Num 11:4–35) an anti-Mosaic
trend is even more pronounced. This is an account of a medical disaster. The people ate, rather overate, meat, and many died from some

stomach ailment. Considering the poor conditions for the preservation of organic food in the desert, the disaster is hardly a medical surprise. Yet, while initially the narrator's causal explanation for the tragedy suggests that the "rabble" is responsible for its own ill-fated end, an anti-Mosaic sentiment runs throughout the story. Moses becomes a murmurer himself.

> And Moses said unto the Lord: "Wherefore hast Thou dealt ill with Thy servant? and wherefore have I not found favour in Thy sight, that Thou layest the burden of all this people upon me? Have I conceived all this people? have I brought them forth, that Thou shouldest say unto me: Carry them in thy bosom, as a nursing-father carrieth the sucking child, unto the land which Thou didst swear unto their fathers? Whence should I have flesh to give unto all this people? for they trouble me with their weeping, saying: Give us flesh, that we may eat. I am not able to bear all this people myself alone, because it is too heavy for me. And if Thou deal thus with me, kill me, I pray Thee, out of hand, if I have found favor in Thy sight; and let me not look upon my wretchedness" (Num 11:11–15).

By providing the people with meat, Moses performs a vindictive miracle of aggression, supplying them with the food they desire and then turning it into poison. Thus this is a miracle that has turned into disaster, deliberately, rather than saving the community from hardship.

The narrator is continuously trying the absolve Moses from his responsibility for the disaster. The rabble is blamed for initiating the chain of events by their inappropriate desire for meat. Such a designation of part of the congregation reflects social rift and diverse narrative voices. "Rabble" is a denigrating designation that is applied to a social class from a vantage point of an assumed superiority. Had we been able to learn the account of this event as told by relatives of those who died in the disaster, Moses rather than a human mass would have been to blame.

As told, however, Moses is protected by the narrator from assuming the sole responsibility for the disaster. He does not perform the miracle by himself but shares the event with seventy elders of the community. If the oral tradition once had diversified voices, expressing views of various segments of the society, the scribes and the editors of the biblical text have made them conform to a single perspective, turning a disaster into a punishment, and blaming the victims for their own fate.

In the third "punishment narrative" (Numbers 12) the anti-Mosaic voice turns directly to personal affairs. This is an account of Miriam's punishment for her slandering remarks against Moses' Cushite wife. Moses overreacts. As a charismatic personality who can resort to supernatural means in managing his affairs, he inflicts upon his sister a dangerous disease, a socially excluding sickness, commensurate with her own attempt to exclude a person.

Before the burning bush not only does Moses receive the mission to redeem the Israelites; he is also endowed with the ability to employ three magical transformations: turning his rod into a snake and reversing the process; inflicting leprosy and curing the disease; and changing the Nile water into blood (Exod 4:1–9). While the rod has become Moses' magical companion (Exod 4:17; 4:20; 7:8–12, 15–17, 19–20; 8:12; 14:16; 17:9; Num 20:8–11), and the transformation of water to blood is the first of the ten plagues (Exod 7:17–21), the power to inflict and cure leprosy is employed only once, as Miriam's punishment. The same metaphor "leprous as white as snow" occurs in both scenes of magical endowment and punishment, respectively (Exod 4:6; Num 12:10).

Structurally the punishment is appropriate, following principles of reversibility and binary opposition. Miriam slanders a black person and for it she turns white, sickly white. She alone is punished while Aaron remains unafflicted although he clearly participates in the slander as much as she does. Culley puzzles over this injustice, but the structural method can offer a clue. Wife and sister are in binary opposition to each other: the first is sexually accessible, the second is sexually prohibited. Hence, it is the sister and not the brother who is punished for slandering the wife.

However, the severity of the punishment that Moses inflicts upon his sister does not speak well for his character. His action portrays him as a vindictive and cruel person. The scribes and editors that incorporate the story into the scriptures come to his defense. Before telling about Miriam's punishment, the narrator digresses, describing Moses as "very meek, above all the men that were upon the face of the earth" (Num 12:3). This is the only scriptural attribution of meekness to Moses and for that matter to any other individual in the Hebrew Bible. The insertion of this character description just before one of his more cruel acts is a clear form of a literary defense. Even so, the editors find it insufficient and introduce the voice of God to offer an additional character testimony on behalf of Moses:

> And He said: 'Hear now My words: if there be a prophet among you, I the Lord do make Myself known unto him in a vision, I do speak with him in a dream. My servant Moses is not so; he is trusted in all my house; with him do I speak mouth to mouth, even manifestly, and not in dark speeches; and the similitude of the Lord doth he behold . . .' (Num 12:6–8).

The punishment itself, definitely one that Moses is equipped to inflict magically, is delivered, as if, directly by God Himself. Moses is passive; the narrator makes him active only to make an appeal for a cure on behalf of his sister (Num 12:13). Such a three-fold defense, through the narrator's character description, divine character testimony, and a role reversal of a prosecutor turned into an advocate, is necessary to quiet loud, accusing voices, blaming Moses for the abuse of magic.

The fourth "punishment narrative" (Num 20:1–13) is, as Culley has already pointed out, a unique tale because Moses and Aaron themselves are the subjects of punishment. This is a story about death. It begins with an account of Miriam's demise (Num 20:1), continues with the people's complaint that they would rather perish (vv. 3–4), and concludes with information about the future demise of Moses and his brother.

The death of a charismatic personality is problematic because it must resolve a paradox: how to account for the death of a healer and miracle worker who so many times has overcome disease and death. In later traditions this narrative dilemma has been resolved by incorporating references to historical events, making the miracle worker and the prophet a martyr as well (Agus:89–114, esp. 91; Fischel). Death by an evil force could be acceptable because it does not detract from the strength of the supernatural forces with which the charismatic personality is in contact. But when this element is historically absent, how would it be possible to terminate a life that has virtual control over death. Punishment could be a narrative solution.

At the same time, such a solution could draw upon traditional voices that cast doubt about the range of magical abilities of Moses. Can he produce water by hitting the rock with his rod? Can he better that feat? Literary scribes and editors must homogenize such traditional voices, turning the doubt in Moses' supernatural power into causal factor in his demise, a cause which otherwise would have been the missing element in his biographical narrative as a charismatic personality. In that sense the scribes and editors achieve narrative cohesion by establishing a sequence that starts with the motifeme "wrong" and concludes with a punishment that in this case is natural death. However, by itself death is not Moses' and Aaron's punishment; preventing them from entering into the land of Canaan is. The known and named location of their sin, Meribah, substitutes for the missing location of Moses' burial place.

The fifth "punishment narrative" (Num 21:4–9) is similar in pattern to the first tale. Both proceed from Complaint to Punishment and conclude with Rescue. However, in this account snake bites are substituted for the fire that occurs in the first story. Not accidentally, in these two tales Moses prays for the people (Num 11:2; 21:7), as befits a miracle worker. However, in this tale prayer is insufficient. The restoration of health offers legitimacy to the incorporation of the symbol of a healing snake cult into the monotheistic Israelite religious symbolism. The snake was a therapeutic symbol in Egyptian magic

(Jacq:145–149), and possibly Midianite (Rothenberg:89, 100) religion. Their worship is obviously contradictory to the monotheistic theology of the biblical scribes and editors. However, the attribution of its ritualistic-magical use to God's own command to Moses offers the necessary religious and social legitimacy.

Structural analysis and the discoveries of narrative patterns have been instrumental in exposing biblical layers of oral tradition that the written text has often obscured. Such works have and will contribute to further understanding of the relations between folklore and the biblical text. However, in the Israelite society in which orality dominated communication, and literacy was only in a state of emergence (Haran), structural analysis of parallel themes and forms offers only a static view of the relations between oral and written literatures. A more dynamic perspective of these relations as a process of historical transformation would become apparent when it is possible to account for the ideology and theology of the scribes and editors of the text. From such a vantage point the "punishment pattern" is not part of the oral tradition, but to the contrary, part of the effort of scribes and editors to harness the diversity of perspectives, themes, and figures that is available in oral tradition to the specific point of view that the Pentateuch upholds. The punishment pattern is a literary construction of narratives that in oral tradition circulated as miracle tales. The intent and purpose of their narration in society had been either the promotion or the denigration of charismatic figures. In the literate phase of the monotheistic religion of the Israelites, Moses emerges as the sole prophet of this religion, but in earlier periods, in oral tradition, he could have been one of several charismatic figures about whom rival stories have circulated.

Although the available and extant tradition upholds the superiority of Moses to all other prophets (Num 12:6–8; Deut 34:10), this very emphasis is a clear indication of possible similar traditions about other prophets. The image of Moses that these tales project is not that of hero (Coats), but that of a miracle worker and a cult leader who began to attract people by performing his miracles through magic, and to whom later generations attributed political, judicial, and religious leadership.

WORKS CONSULTED

Agus, Aharon (Ronald E.)
   1988   *The Binding of Isaac & Messiah: Law, Martyrdom, and Deliverance in Early Rabbinic Religiosity.* Albany: State University of New York Press.

Bentzen, Aage
   1967   *Introduction to the Old Testament.* Vol. 1. 7th ed. Copen-
          hagen: G. E. C. Gad.

Coats, George W.
   1988   *Moses: Heroic Man, Man of God. JSOTSup* 57. Sheffield: Sh-
          effield Academic Press.

Culley, Robert C.
   1963   "An Approach to the Problem of Oral Tradition," *V T*
          13:113–25.

   1967   *Oral Formulaic Language in the Biblical Psalms.* Toronto:
          University of Toronto Press.

   1974   "Structural Analysis: Is it Done with Mirrors?" *Int* 28:165–
          81.

   1975   "Themes and Variations in Three Groups of OT Narra-
          tives," *Semeia* 3:3–13.

   1976   "Oral Tradition and the OT: Some Recent Discussions,"
          Semeia 5:1–34.

   1984   "Stories of the Conquest: Joshua 2,6,7, and 8," *HAR* 8:5–
          44.

   1986   "Oral Tradition and Biblical Studies," *Oral Tradition* 1:30–
          65.

Fischel, Henry A.
   1947   "Martyr and Prophet," *JQR* 37:265–80, 363–86.

Goody, Jack, ed.
   1968   *Literacy in Traditional Societies.* Cambridge: Cambridge
          University Press.

   1977   *The Domestication of the Savage Mind.* Cambridge: Cam-
          bridge University Press.

   1986   *The Logic of Writing and the Organization of Society.* Cam-
          bridge: Cambridge University Press.

   1987   *The Interface between the Written and the Oral.* Cambridge:
          Cambridge University Press.

Haran, Menahem
   1988   "On the Diffusion of Literacy and Schools in Ancient Is-
          rael." Pp. 81–95 in *Congress Volume, Jerusalem 1986.* Ed.
          J.A. Emerton. *VTSup* 40. Leiden: E. J. Brill.

Jacq, Christian
    1985   *Egyptian Magic.* Trans. Janet M. Davis. Chicago: Bolchazy-Carducci.

Kaufmann, Yehezkel.
    1960   *The Religion of Israel: From Its Beginnings to the Babylonian Exile.* Trans. Moshe Greenberg. Chicago: University of Chicago Press.

Kirkpatrick, Patricia G.
    1988   *The Old Testament and Folklore Study. JSOTSup* 62. Sheffield: Sheffield Academic Press.

Niditch, Susan
    1987   *Underdogs and Tricksters: A Prelude to Biblical Folklore.* New York: Harper & Row.

Ong, Walter J.
    1967   *The Presence of the Word: Some Prolegomena for Cultural and Religious History.* New Haven: Yale University Press.

    1971   *Rhetoric, Romance and Technology: Studies in the Interaction of Expression and Culture.* Ithaca: Cornell University Press.

    1977   *The Interfaces of the Word: Studies in the Evolution of Consciousness and Culture.* Ithaca: Cornell University Press.

    1982   *Orality and Literacy: The Technologizing of the Word.* New York: Methuen.

Rothenberg, Beno
    1983–   "The Timna Mining Sanctuary." Pp. 85–122 in *Israel*
    1984   *—People and Land: Haaretz Museum Yearbook.* Ed. Rechavam Zeevy. N. S. Vol. 1. Tel-Aviv: Haaretz Museum [Hebrew].

Street, Brian V.
    1985   *Literacy in Theory and Practice.* Cambridge: Cambridge University Press

Tiede, David Lenz
    1972   *The Charismatic Figure as Miracle Worker. SBLDS* 1. Missoula, MT: Society of Biblical Literature.

Weinfeld, Moshe
    1987   "The Traditions about Moses and Jethro at the Mount of God," *Tarbiz* 56:449–60 [Hebrew].

Zakovitch, Yair
    1981   "From Oral to Written Tale in the Bible," *Jerusalem Studies in Jewish Folklore* 1:9–43 [Hebrew].

5. SAMSON WITHOUT FOLKLORE
Robert Alter

ABSTRACT

The Samson story abounds in folkloric motifs and patterns, but an awareness of the folkloric backgrounds of the biblical text should not deflect us from attending to the subtlety with which traditional materials have been given literary articulation. The use of thematic key-words, variation in near-verbatim repetition, and nuanced dialogue are prime instances of such articulation. This literary recasting is not merely a matter of giving aesthetic finish to folkloric materials but of redefining their meanings. The writer's treatment of the term "time" (pa‘am) is especially instructive in this regard, for what it amounts to is a deliberate, thematically purposeful foregrounding of the folktale pattern of three repetitions followed by a reversal.

The story of Samson is, of course, one of the most conspicuously folkloric narratives in the Hebrew Bible. It abounds in motifs and even formulaic patterns that have notable analogues elsewhere in folktales and myth. Samson is the only strongman-hero in the Bible, and as early as the Church Fathers parallels were drawn between the story of this powerful figure who takes constant risks and performs impossible tasks and the Greek demigod-hero Hercules. More recent commentators have proposed correspondences with the Akkadian Enkidu and with Gilgamesh himself, while others have pursued the path of ethnopoetic analogies as far afield as the Scandinavian sagas. The patterning as well as the plot and protagonist of the Samson story has suggested to many a background of folklore: the prominence of riddles and secrets, the elaborate use of literal repetition deployed in sequences of three or three plus one, the flaunting of the formulaic numbers three and seven, and the introduction of stichomythia in the dialogue (the wedding guests solve the riddle by saying, "What is sweeter than honey,/and what is stronger than a lion?" and Samson responds in answering verse, "Had you not

plowed with my heifer,/you would not have found out my riddle"
[2:18]).

It would be foolish to ignore this abundance of folkloric elements.
Indeed, a thematic concern that often appears in folklore but is not
generally characteristic of biblical narrative is at the heart of our
story, as Mieke Bal (37–67), in her often wild-and-woolly psychoana-
lytic reading, has persuasively argued: the archetypal confrontation
of man by woman, predicated on male fear of the mystery and the
consuming power of female sexuality (sweeter than honey, stronger
than a lion). The common hypothesis that there were various Sam-
son-tales in oral circulation which were eventually drawn together in
Judges 13–16 seems plausible enough. The marking of the conclusion
of chapter 15, after the victory with the ass's jawbone, by the formula,
"And he judged Israel in the days of the Philistines twenty years,"
does look suspiciously, as scholars have proposed, like the end of a
once independent narrative unit. In attempting, however, to consider
Samson without folklore, or at any rate Samson beyond folklore, I
would argue that what requires crucial attention here, as elsewhere in
biblical narrative, is not the conjectural penumbra of Ur-text or pre-
text but the illuminated details of the text itself. Perhaps there are bits
and pieces of the story that were taken over verbatim from oral tradition, but there are scant grounds for concluding which these might
be, and the nice literary formulation of all antecedent materials is in
most respects decisive.

Thus, the initial narrative sequence of Samson's marriage to the
woman at Timnah, his trick with the fox-tails and torches, her death
by fire, and the battle at Ein-hakore, may not have been originally at-
tached to the subsequent two episodes, but in the articulated structure of the story as we have it, the three episodes fit together with an
almost architectonic tightness. Samson passes through a series of
three women who mark the spectrum of female sexual partners—
wife, whore, and mistress (see Vickery).[1] The narrative configuration
of the three episodes takes the form of ABA—long, short, long; two
protracted involvements sandwiching a one-night stand,[2] with the
common denominators of the foreign woman, the threat of danger,
and betrayal. The symmetry of numerical progression in the first
episode is picked up in the third, and presupposes the three women
as its arithmetic base: 30 wedding-guests and 30 garments are trans-

---

[1]Crenshaw (65) offers a related perception about the sequence of three women,
to which he adds the intriguing proposal that the story as a whole is "a sort of
midrash on the astute observation in Genesis 2:24 ('Therefore a man leaves his father and his mother and cleaves to his wife, and they become one flesh')."

[2]Soggin (256) makes the interesting suggestion that "after his disappointments
in chapters 14 and 15, Samson . . . is . . . content with a transaction of a commer-
cial kind."

lated by Samson into 300 dead Philistines, after which he is confronted by 3,000 men of Judah, who deliver him to the Philistines, of whom he slays 1,000. The reduction by 300% represented in this last number is no doubt to save the full tally of vengeance for the grand climax of the story, when there will be 3,000 Philistine men and women in the temple of Dagon that Samson brings crashing down.

One might object that such quantitative patterning is a rather schematic kind of shaping of narrative materials and thus offers thin evidence of literary elaboration. It behooves us therefore to focus more closely on the verbal texture of the story and to try to see how here, as throughout biblical narrative, particular word-choices prove to be anything but formulaic, exhibiting a fine local expressive power as well as a capacity through reiteration to give thematic definition to the story as a whole. Let me begin with the verb used at the end of chapter 13, immediately after the annunciation story, to designate the inception of Samson's career: "And the spirit of the Lord began to drive him in the encampment of Dan, between Zorah and Eshtaol" (13:25). The usual verb for the descent of the spirit on a judge—a verb which in fact will be applied to Samson at 14:19—is ṣālaḥ. Only here do we have the verb pāʿēm, and, indeed, only here in the entire Bible is that verb used in a transitive (pīʿēl) form. The basic meaning of the root, from a term for "foot," is to stamp or pound (thus the sundry modern translations that render it here as "to move" are rather weak). Two common nouns associated with the root are paʿam, time (because times were counted by a stamping of the foot), and paʿămôn, bell. Samson, then, is not a judge who is merely taken possession of by the spirit of the Lord but a man in whom it pounds, like the clapper of a bell, a man driven by inward energy in a series of pulsating motions, like the movements of violence, like sexuality itself. Instructively, the only other times that the root pāʿam occurs in the Bible as a verb are to indicate the inner turmoil of a dreamer waking from a disturbing dream—first Pharaoh (Gen 41:8) and then, with a likely allusion to the earlier text in Genesis, Nebuchadnezzar (Dan 2:1 and 3). In both instances the verb is used in a passive form in conjunction with "spirit" ("and his spirit was troubled"). The author of the Samson story, then, is almost certainly playing on a familiar locution. Here it is not the character's spirit or inward state that is troubled (wattippāʿēm) or churned up, but the spirit of the Lord that pounds in him, impels him. Perhaps such access to the spirit as is vouchsafed to a figure like Samson can be nothing but inner unrest, the explosive or spasmodic enactment of dark dreams of desire and violence leading to catastrophe.

If such suggestive possibilities of imagining the distinctive career of the hero are intimated in the unique verb used to mark its beginning, it is characteristic of biblical narrative that the denouement should punningly anchor those implications in a flaunted repetition of the very same root. We have already observed that the story freely deploys the folktale device of repetitions keyed on three. At the end, Delilah asks Samson three times to reveal the secret of his strength and is given three false answers in exchanges that also incorporate refrain-like repetition; then, on the third time plus one, he at last divulges the secret. What should be noted, however, is that the folktale procedure is explicitly "foregrounded"—that is, the artifice of the device is pointedly exposed—in the dialogue assigned to both characters. After her third frustration, Delilah rebukes Samson, "How could you say, 'I love you,' when your heart is not with me? It is now three times (*pĕʿāmîm*) that you have mocked me . . ." (16:15). Once she has extorted the secret from him—the early rabbis imagined she did it by maddeningly slipping out from under him in the heat of intercourse (cf. TB *Sota* 9b)—she frames her urgent message to the Philistine chieftains in the following terms: "Come up, for this time (*happaʿam*) he has told me his whole heart" (16:18). When the shorn Samson is roused from his fatal slumber by the already thrice-repeated cry, "The Philistines are upon you, Samson," his first words are, "I will go out this time as the previous times (*kĕpaʿam bĕpaʿam*) and shake loose" (16:20). But even with this climactic fourth time after the three recurrences that precede it, we are not quite done with the counting of times. When the blinded Samson leans against the supporting pillars of the temple of Dagon, he entreats God, "O give me strength just this time (*ʾak happaʿam hazzeh*)" (16:28).

What happens through all this is that the seemingly conventional multiplication of times is transformed into a thematic and, indeed, psychological datum of the story. Samson is a figure in the grip of what psychoanalysis would call a repetition compulsion, signalled from the beginning by the inner pounding of the verb *pāʿem*. He is repeatedly drawn by desire to alien women with whom he must bed down in alien places. The alien sexual partner and location are no doubt political figurations of the alluring otherness of the female body, but the hidden heart of the attraction for Samson seems to be the constant presence of danger, his scooping the honeyed pleasure of sex (for the metaphor, see Song 5:1) from the fierce mouth, not the bleached carcass, of the lion. Thus each of the three desired women is surrounded by a crowd of kinsmen, clansmen, plotting chieftains whose intentions toward the muscular Danite are hostile and sinister. The appeal of the game of love for Samson is precisely that it is playing with fire. That idiom itself is not biblical, but the Samson story abounds in fire images—the flame in which the announcing angel ascends to heaven, the fire that consumes Samson's wife and her father's house, the torches bound to the fox-tails that carry conflagration through the Philistine fields, the cords binding Samson that snap

like flax in flame—so that fire is at once associated with the power-
fully destructive energy he exerts and with the destruction he courts.
Time and time again (*kĕpaʿam bĕpaʿam*) he succeeds in playing with
fire—with the wife at Timnah, with the whore at Gaza, with Delilah
at Nahal-sorek, but when he thrice thwarts Delilah, she announces
that three times are as many as she will bear, and she finally contrives
to break the pattern, triumphantly telling her Philistine employers
that this time is different from all the others. The roused Samson
wants to declare that this time is just like the past times. Cruelly dis-
abused of this illusion, blinded and enslaved, he asks the Lord to
grant him just one more time—not to repeat the old compulsive pattern of taking honey where lions wait to pounce, but himself to play
the part once more of the ravening lion, an eyeless instrument of
vengeance forever beyond the beguilements of desire.

I am of course not suggesting that the whole literary art of the
Samson story is comprehended in its cunning use of this single word
paʿam. There are other carefully marked thematic words that define
the unfolding of the plot and set the context for the crucial moments
of dialogue. It is hardly surprising that the most prominent of these
should be "woman," *ʾiššāh*. Many readers have wondered why Samson's mother is given no name. This seems especially peculiar because she, after all, is the active and sensible one in the whole annunciation type-scene (chap. 13), while her husband Manoah, who is ac-
corded the dignity of a name, merely drags after her and seems rather
foolish by comparison (cf. Alter, 1983). But if we see chapter 13 as a
thematic prologue to the three chapters that follow it, what is surprising is not that the mother should be nameless but that Delilah should
be named at the end. Beyond the fact that she is the climax-with-re-
versal of the series of three, it is hard to know why she alone of the
women of the story is given a name because there is no certainty
about what her name means. The once popular identification of
Delilah with a root that suggests dangling hair or tresses has little to
substantiate it. Some have proposed that it is a truncated form of a
pagan theophoric name, Dalil-ishtar. The association of Delilah with a
love goddess has an attractive thematic logic, but the evidence for
this derivation is unfortunately inconclusive. With the anonymity,
however, of the other three women in the story, we are on firmer
ground.

The namelessness of Samson's mother is beautifully convenient
because every time she is involved in speech or action she can be referred to as "the woman." The angel of the Lord appears to the
woman (13:3); the woman then comes to tell the news to her man
(13:6). The man-woman, *ʾiš-ʾiššāh*, opposition is verbally reinforced
because they think he is a man of God, not an angel, and so he is referred to, in both their speech and in narrator's language that incor-

porates their point of view, as "the man." One can see how insistently these terms are repeated by recalling the sentence that reports how Manoah joins in on the second revelation of the angel, which again has been to the woman: "And Manoah arose and went after his woman and came to the man and said to him, 'Are you the man who spoke to the woman?' And he said, 'I am'" (13:11). This episode participates in a larger pattern in Judges, as at the beginning of the Deborah story, chapter 4, and the end of the Abimelech story, chapter 9, whereby the terms man and woman are flaunted as the roles they designate are tested and reversed in the narrative. Manoah's arising and going after the woman—to be sure, for divinely sanctioned purposes—is a bit of choreographed movement that will come to stand as an emblem for the career of his son.

The first verb of which Samson is the subject in the story indicates the first in the series of geographical displacements that will have fatal consequences, "And Samson went down to Timnah" (14:1). This is immediately followed by "and he saw a woman at Timnah." After the going down, the seeing, with "woman" as the first direct object of an action performed by Samson. Paired with the annunciation narrative, this clause is an odd inversion of the very lexical materials used to report the first epiphany: "And an angel of the Lord appeared [literally, was seen] unto the woman" (13:3). Samson's very first words of dialogue pick up this same grammatical object and this same verb, pointedly putting the woman first: "A woman have I seen," *ʾiššāh rāʾîtî* (14:2). When Samson goes off to Gaza in his second recorded liaison, once again we are told, "And he saw there a whorewoman" (16:1). (The Hebrew word-order is actually "a woman, a whore." In any case, the presence of the otherwise superfluous "woman" in this phrase shows that our author is carefully drawing together through repetition of terms the thematic threads of his different episodes.) At this juncture, the move from desirous seeing to the fulfillment of desire, probably because a professional is involved, is conveyed with brutal abruptness: "And he saw there a whorewoman and came into her [or, coupled with her]." No seeing is indicated, but perhaps by now it may be implied, at the beginning of the Delilah episode, only the fact of Samson's falling in love, though the object of this love or lust (in the story of Amnon and Tamar, the same verb seems to mean the latter) is first referred to as "woman" and then designated by proper name (16:4). The maiming to which she will lead him, the gouging out of his eyes, is of course in orthodox Freudian terms an image of castration, but in the story it is more explicitly aligned with the repeated activity of seeing fair female flesh that has gotten Samson into all this trouble. At the end forever deprived of such sight, he can still make his body a lethal weapon against his enemies.

The sequence of four scenes between Samson and Delilah may look naive or schematic, but it has powerful psychological resonance as a kind of climactic recapitulation of the whole Samson story. The Philistine chieftains hire Delilah (for a king's ransom, each offers 1100 silver shekels) to "seduce" Samson into allowing her to "see" the secret of his strength (16:5). Interestingly, what they seek is not to kill their formidable enemy, which would have made much more sense strategically, but to tie him up and torture him: "By what means may we prevail over him, to bind him and afflict him" (16:5). An odd intimation of sadistic fantasy hovers over the story, especially in this last episode. Samson has already been bound once, by the men of Judah, and it seems more important for the Philistines to have him bound in order to be their plaything than actually to destroy him. Only at first thought is it a violation of verisimilitude for Delilah to repeat openly the insidious aim of the Philistines in her first words to Samson, "In what lies your great strength,/and by what may you be bound to be afflicted?" (16:6). (This crucial last verb, *ʿinnâ*, has a range of meanings that includes affliction, torture, general miserable treatment, and also rape.) She drops the term of torment from her next two speeches, but I think both she and her lover tacitly understand that this is what is at stake. Her daring invocation of torture at the beginning is not a gesture of naïveté either on her part or on that of any putative folk-tradition behind the words of the story but flows from her shrewd intuition of what has impelled Samson all along. The glint of the dagger in the velvet hand of love is what has excited him from Timnah onward. Samson and Delilah are playing a game of psychological brinkmanship, Samson enticed by the threat of danger which he feels confident that in the crisis he will always be able to ward off. The three false answers he gives Delilah all elaborate on the project of binding that she has revealed to him, while the actual secret of his strength of course is unrelated to instruments of binding. As many commentators have observed along varying lines of interpretation, the three answers inch closer and closer to divulging the real secret: from the wet sinew-bowstrings, with their too-obvious association with warfare; to the new cords with which no labor has been performed, obliquely intimating the intactness of Samson's Nazirite condition; to the weaving of his seven tresses into the loom, which touches the very stuff of his essential Nazirite vow, entangling it in a proverbial woman's instrument, and thus providing a kind of emblem for the whole story.[3] When Samson finally succumbs to Delilah's relentless pestering and gives her the secret, he is caused before the actual having to regress to the ultimate condition of male

---

[3]Bal (54), with an excessively cinematic vividness, states that "The weaving represents the interlacement of the hair of both lovers in sleep."

powerlessness vis-à-vis woman—infant with mother—as Delilah lulls him to sleep on her knees (16:19). If the Masoretic text is accurate at this point, though Delilah calls to a man with a razor, she takes it from him to perform the act herself, for the verb "shaved" has a feminine subject, and the initiator of the process of torture is Delilah (apparently, she, too, likes to play with lions)—which is in perfect keeping with her flaunting of the prospect of bondage and discipline at the beginning.

The revelation of the secret—what the text repeatedly calls "his whole heart"—is one of the most striking illustrations in the story of the writer's exquisite control over the minute verbal means of the narrative: "No razor has touched my head, for I have been a Nazirite to God from my mother's womb. If I were shorn, my strength would leave me, and I would be weak and become like any other man" (16:17). The first of these two sentences is a verbatim repetition of the angel's words to Samson's mother in 13:5, with the verbs transposed by the necessity of the speaker's location from the angel's jussive to what amounts to a present perfect, and the possessive "my mother" added to the angel's "from the womb." The second sentence about the loss of power after shaving the head appears nowhere in the annunciatory directions in chapter 13, and it is an open question whether Samson's mother has instructed him in this wise or whether it is an inference he has drawn, and perhaps even a false inference, a merely magical construal of his Nazirite condition. But did the "woman" of the annunciation scene in fact have the taboo on shaving the head firmly in mind? The angel breaks his message to her into two discrete segments. At the end of 13:3, he tells her, "you will conceive and bear a son." Then he enjoins Nazirite restrictions which, exceptionally, fall on her during the pregnancy and, only implicitly, on the son after birth: "And so, watch yourself, and drink no wine or liquor, and eat nothing impure" (13:4). At this point, the birth-annunciation is oddly repeated, as though it were meant to serve as the heading for a quasi-independent second injunction: "For you are to conceive and will bear a son, and no razor will touch his head, for the lad will be a Nazirite to God from the womb, and he will begin to save Israel from the hand of the Philistines" (13:5).

In keeping with the general biblical practice of using changes in near-verbatim repetition for the definition of the new speaker's stance and the advancement of theme, when the woman repeats these words to her husband, she drops the clause about beginning to save Israel and, rather ominously, as I have noted elsewhere (Alter, 1981:101), she substitutes for it the curt phrase, "Till his dying day." (The whole story concludes not only with Samson's spectacular death but with a little explosion of repetitions of the root *m-w-t*, "die," five times in two verses.) Her other deletion may be even more significant. She begins her quotation of the angel with the words of the promised conception and birth, as a barren wife most plausibly would do, but then she entirely suppresses the second injunction, against shaving the boy's head (13:7). Still more curiously, when in the second encounter with the angel Manoah insists that the already perfectly explicit instructions be repeated, the angel, as if taking his cue from the woman's version of his own words (which he could not have heard, except by supernatural agency not intimated in the narrative), also deletes the clause about the razor. An elaborate game of revelation and concealment is going on here, though it is not easy to know what to make of it. Perhaps the sheer secretness of the vow against hair-cutting is meant to be conveyed through its double suppression at the beginning of the story, as though neither the woman nor the angel wanted to let Manoah in on it. Foreshadowing is also involved, for the woman refrains from uttering the crucial detail that Samson one day will be badgered into uttering to a woman, who will use it to destroy him. One must of course infer that Samson's mother duly noted the prohibition and raised her son to observe it. Though no mention whatever of Samson's hair is made until the denouement, his climactic declaration to Delilah and his immediately preceding reference to his seven tresses would make no sense if he had not been reared to observe the strict terms of the angel's ban. A secret so potent that wife was not willing to divulge it to husband, with an angel seconding her in her reticence, is now fatally revealed by the harried lover to his mistress. How does she know that at last Samson has told her his whole heart? Perhaps by his tone and affect, about which the text tells us nothing, except possibly for the additional words, "my strength would leave me," which do not occur in his refrain-like statements at the end of the three false leads he gives her. But unlike his progressively richer inventions of magical binding materials, this last confession is underwritten by observable fact: Samson does bear evidence dangling from his head that he has given all barbers a wide berth, but this striking fact of appearance has not been noted earlier in the narrative—not until the last of the false answers—because there was not yet an occasion for it in the plot.

One could multiply examples of the literary principle I am articulating—that beyond any archetypal configurations of the story, the choice of phrase, the choice of single word, the nuance of difference in the seeming repetition, are everything. As we ponder Samson's final revelation of the secret, we begin to wonder whether there is a disturbing thematic counterpoint between the last clause of the angel's annunciation and the negative clause with which it is replaced in Samson's words to Delilah. The angel promised the mother a future for the son as at least partial liberator of Israel from the

Philistines, without any indication of negative consequences if the vow were broken. Against the upbeat prophetic movement of those words, Samson poses a negative conditional clause, "If I were shorn, my strength would leave me and I would be weak and become like any other man." The weakness, at least causally if not actually, sets in with the confession of the secret, not with the shaving of the head: Delilah has no difficulty rocking Samson to sleep on her knees, already a babe made ready for the maiming. It is by no means necessary to conclude that the writer wants to replace supernatural categories with psychological and moral ones. But the fine adumbrations of motive, relationship, and theme through the minute management of verbal formulation bear striking evidence to the recasting of folkloric and legendary materials into an exacting, subtly discriminating art.

WORKS CONSULTED

Alter, Robert
  1981   *The Art of Biblical Narrative.* New York: Basic.
  1983   "How Convention Helps Us Read: The Annunciation Type-Scene in the Bible," *Prooftexts* 3:115-130.

Bal, Mieke
  1987   *Lethal Love: Feminist Literary Readings of Biblical Love Stories.* Bloomington and Indianapolis: Indiana University Press.

Crenshaw, James L.
  1977   *Samson.* Atlanta: John Knox.

Soggin, Alberto
  1981   *Judges: A Commentary.* Philadelphia: Westminster.

Vickery, John B.
  1981   "In Strange Ways: The Story of Samson." Pp. 58–73 in *Images of Man and God.* Ed. Burke O. Long. Sheffield: Almond.

6. SAMSON AS A BIBLICAL φὴρ ὀρεσκῷος
David E. Bynum

Preliminary Remarks

My admiration for Robert Alter's portrait of Samson-shorn-of-folklore is complete. It would obviously be a task beyond me to attempt any dialogue at all with him in regard to the matters which he has so skillfully set forth; indeed I should prefer to say nothing myself and hear instead the reply of some other actual authority on his subject. I am able for my part to comment only on those things mentioned marginally in Alter's exposition about which I have any experience at all.

Alter's somewhat alarming title, "Samson without Folklore," seems at first blush to fly provocatively in the face of an apparent historical reality—the reality, namely, that the four Samson stories somehow entered into the Book of Judges from an oral tradition older than the surviving Hebrew texts or "versions." But his title stands above a paper that is not actually about literary history or the traditional narrative at all, and that does not therefore attempt further to illuminate, much less to deny, the still murky historical provenance—or perhaps we ought to call it the *prehistory*—of the Samson stories. His paper consists, on the contrary, of a literary-critical essay in a contemporary vein, concerned with appreciation of the Hebrew story-teller's *manner of telling* the Samson saga and not with explanation of the stories *per se.* Correspondingly Alter's title is, grammatically speaking, in the optative rather than the indicative mood. Neither the title nor the paper under it asserts indicatively that the Samson stories were actually written independently of folklore (which would have been impossible), or that they were free of it in any part of their content (also obviously impossible). Instead of that, Alter only wishes yearningly: "would that the Samson stories were not folklore," or, "let us pretend [contrary-to-fact condition], in order to give free play to our modern powers of critical appreciation, that the oral traditional provenience of the Samson stories does not matter as either a curb or a guide to us in how we understand them three thousand years after their composition." And so, having simply avoided the question of history and of origins, and by that means gained for himself the critical elbow-room he wants, Alter has ably explained how the Hebrew text still speaks with refined and poignant sensibilities despite an interval of some three millennia elapsed between the ancient writing and a modern reading, just as the oral Homer does in Greek. It is good to be informed of this in such detail, and I am grateful, while at the same time I am unable to put aside so entirely as Alter would have me do either the question about the prehistory of the Samson saga or another, more general problem which has also troubled me about Samson for as long as I can remember.

Brought up in an old-fashioned family where a child must read something meaty from the Bible every day without fail, I learned to read my native English mostly not in school, but rather by making out the words of the Old and New Testaments at home each evening throughout my childhood. There was never any particular doctrine meant to be inculcated by such an exercise in my family, but the exercise itself was *de rigueur*. The reading was obviously a good thing, yet no one was ever able to explain to me in my youth how I was supposed to understand the bald narrative facts of what happened to Samson (and to many another biblical character as well). To this day, I have never heard a confident, straightforward explanation for the most obvious actions described in the Samson stories: his killing so many people with a bone from a dead donkey; his fascination with grossly duplicitous and greedy prostitutes; why Manoah's wife had to go outdoors to get herself pregnant with little Samson; why Samson mustn't go to the barber; why he never married a proper wife; why he went to all that trouble chasing down three hundred foxes (of all things) merely to set a fire. I haven't understood all the simplest, most down-to-earth, obvious and fundamental peculiarities in the stories of Samson. It is not that I find them obscure; what happens in the Samson stories is perfectly apparent. The problem is how to understand such intrinsically strange events in any language.

I had hoped Alter might at last explain some of these things, but he has on this occasion chosen other subjects. And I find that learning from him about the artful subtleties of the original Hebrew—which he teaches so well—just is not helpful with my more basic problem of even the simplest comprehension, a problem which I (and most other lay readers too, I am sure) really must solve before I even begin to reckon with the kinds of things Alter has explained. I am very confident, moreover, that neither he nor any other interpreter of the Samson saga will be able to satisfy this quite elementary critical need without a thorough, direct, and frontal examination of the Samson saga's dependency on oral narrative tradition.

I wouldn't think of trying to tell Professor Alter or any other Hebraist how to do that. But I do want in my following remarks to try to clarify exactly what it is that has all my life been hard for me to understand about Samson, and what it is that I therefore earnestly desire someone—I don't know who—to find some way of explaining.

I think it preferable from the outset to omit from discussion of Samson both the vague word "folklore" and the amorphous concept which it represents, since in my experience they both pose unnecessary quandaries that have no orderly exits. The word "folklore" is very often used, namely, by those who do not know exactly where to locate or how to define the specific texts which they need to examine and to rely upon as authority when they aver that some idea or other, or the traditional phrasing of that idea, is "folklore." Those, on the other hand, who are precisely knowledgeable about the texts pertaining to their subjects, and about the germane *loci* in the texts, commonly prefer to speak more scrupulously of *oral tradition*, or about literary borrowing or literary imitation of oral tradition, thus avoiding altogether the imprecision of the idea in the word "folklore."

In that sense, I am very willing—indeed, I was eager before this—to purge folklore from the study of Samson, and to dispel with it also the fog which it exhales upon the historical facts about oral tradition, and upon the rightful power which an accurate knowledge of those facts must exercise over an optimally comprehensive interpretation as well as an optimally liberated appreciative criticism of any "folkloristic" text, including certainly the Samson saga in the Old Testament Book of Judges.

One obvious historical fact is that the four Samson stories are not epic, ballad, or folktale. They are patently annalistic, and that much more in the manner of Diodorus Siculus' *Bibliotheke Historike*, as seen, let us say, in Diodorus' account of the Aloads—more like that than like anything in Herodotus' *Historiae*, for example. Whatever traces of oral traditional diction might subsist in them have therefore surely entered the Hebrew text through the agency of a literary retailer rather than by dictation from an oral traditional *raconteur*. I come to this opinion not via narrow stylistic evaluation of the presence or absence of a certain kind of formulary diction in the Hebrew text (which I cannot read), but on quite different and equally valid grounds. There simply are not a sufficient number of impenetrable obscurities in the Samson stories which only other texts of other narratives in the same oral tradition could explain. Such obscurities are a hallmark everywhere of true oral traditional dictated narratives. But the Samson stories as we have them have been systematically cleansed of such obscurities. That is what literary retailers of oral traditional tales have always done, and for obvious reasons. As one goes about ascertaining the matrix of oral narrative tradition from which the biblical reteller(s) of the Samson saga derived the four stories, one may reasonably expect therefore to discover some things in the tradition, and perhaps even in the four stories themselves, which the writer(s) of the texts in Judges 13–16 may not have known or understood.

No collections of certainly oral dictated texts from narrative tradition have been left lying about in the Near East since the Bronze Age to help us discern the exact shape of the oral tradition before its entrance by literary retelling into the biblical Samson saga. Yet that makes little difference for the present purpose, since the types of the Samson stories are so very common in the later and fuller records of actual oral traditions amongst a great diversity of peoples throughout Eurasia and in the pre-Columbian cultures of North America. These very numerous articles of comparative evidence make it apparent that whatever other wonderfully distinctive things the Hebrew reteller(s) of the biblical Samson stories may have introduced by choice of words or emphasis upon details of episode, nothing in their narrative substance was an Israelite or Canaanite invention; it was all certainly much older than that.

Examining them against the background of comparative evidence, I see four stories in Judges 13–16 arranged symmetrically in two pairs. The first pair (Judges 13 and Judges 14–15)—one short story and one longer one—concern Samson's own origin and his attempt thereafter to exploit persons of an alien ethnicity for the furtherance of his own and his parents' ambition to establish a family (i.e., to originate a lineage). In this cause—his own and his parents' progenerative cause—Samson is a spectacular failure. There follows a second pair of stories (Judg 16:1–3 and Judg 16:4–31)—again one short tale followed by a longer one—concerning Samson's maturity. In this second stage of his life the tables are turned, and aliens try to exploit him for *their* purposes. But in their cause too, just as he was earlier in his own cause, Samson is again a spectacular failure. Each of the two short stories anticipates and clarifies (by exemplifying it in another form) what the central principle of Samson's character will be in the more complicated succeeding story.

Samson's mother, wife of the obscure man Manoah, poor woman, is not able to conceive a child in the modestly discrete way women everywhere generally prefer to manage that particular business of life, namely by a secluded act of sex pudently concealed against observation (not to mention actual intrusion) of any third parties within the private shelter of a husband's and a wife's own dwelling. Instead this woman, Samson's justly nameless mother-to-be, has to go outdoors and meet another man who is not her husband in an open field under the full, unobstructed gaze of heaven not once but repeatedly in order to achieve her desired pregnancy. A proper wife still, she yet finds a way to draw her wedded husband into the matter (by inducing him too to go outdoors), if only as her future son's adoptive, cultural father. But no lineage of biological descent is obtained for Manoah through his adoption of a child who is so irregularly vouchsafed to his wife by a messenger from heaven, and accordingly no male offspring of his in later generations will ever hark back to either Samson or Manoah as agnatic ancestor in a society where the principle of agnation was certainly the paramount expression of meaningful kinship, and hence of inherited personal identity and worth. Samson is a social dead-end, a thing to be used, and completely used up, entirely within his own lifetime. A character located rigidly out-of-doors from his very inception, he remains lifelong a strictly extra-genealogical person too. The traditional connection between "house" and "lineage" was profound.

Within his brief lifespan (but a fleeting moment in the annals of the people to whom he is born), Samson's reason-for-being is to push a flourishing species of alien occupiers—the Philistines—out of a land which ought to be domesticated entirely for the use of his own people. Originating in an open field, he is throughout his youth an habitué of the ground and of outdoor haunts. His first, still juvenile movements (one is tempted to call them *vernal*)[1] are the tremors as of feet stamping on the earth, as Alter has insightfully recognized in the Hebrew expression of Judges 13:24–25 (numerous light chthonic tremors in anticipation surely of the more violent single concussion at the end of his life). Then, having reached breeding age, Samson goes about handling and manhandling all manner of earth's outdoor excrescences: wild bees and their honey, vineyards, lions, foxes, olive trees, sheaves and standing grain, even the carcasses of a rapt raptor and an abandoned beast of burden that have been left to rot away on the earth's surface; and not least, those other growths nourished by the same ground, the Philistines, whom he destroys together with all the other earthy things on it. Thus Samson extirpates Philistines of agrarian habits.

The manner of his destructiveness must be significant. He *tears apart* joint from joint with his bare hands both living animals (the lion at Timnah) and carrion (the dead lion and the dead donkey); or else by the same crude means he ties live wild animals together (the fire-foxes). He tears apart his own hair out of Delilah's weaving. He *strikes* (with the jawbone of the ass); he *bursts asunder* (the bonds put upon him at the Rock of Etam and again by Delilah); he *ignites* and burns (the ripe fields and orchards of the Philistines, and thereby

---

[1]Concerning other vernal customs of striking the earth, see Pausanias, VIII, 15:3, and an interpretation of that passage by Nilsson (1957:478 and plate 39, figs. 1 and 2). See further Nilsson (1961:53–4). Considered in this light, the burial of Samson at the end of Judges 16 may have been something more than a merely prosaic detail in the original oral tradition.

consequently also the Philistine family of the ripe woman at Timnah); he *strips* (honey from inside the dead lion and clothes from off the corpses of the thirty men whom he kills, surely by *bludgeoning* or fatal *diastrophy*, at Ashkelon); he *uproots* (the gates of Gaza); and he *pushes* and *pulls* irresistibly (the pillars in the building of the Philistines).

In all of this his powers of ravagement are coextensive with the terrifying primal destructive techniques of great nature itself; indeed there is only a single imaginable method of devastation that he does not employ, which indeed he never even attempts, and which we should therefore probably judge to be beyond him. It is, moreover, the sole variety of damage that can diminish Samson himself: he cannot hew, cut, or sever, nor can he bear to be hewn, cut, or severed. And uniquely amidst the litany of methods for destroying and dismembering things in the Samson saga, only this one technique—hewing and cutting—is a strictly human accomplishment, a power due exclusively to the culture of cutting tools and weapons, and a power unavailable therefore to any so elemental, uncultured form of life as Samson, the "man" of open fields and the great outdoors.

Thus Samson seems not really a man at all—I have no difficulty imagining him as a quadruped (how does he run down three hundred foxes if he isn't a kind of centaur?)—or at most an exceedingly deficient man who cannot hew, cut, and continue his line by the usual means of sexual reproduction *indoors*. For that is the second thing which poor Samson, like his pitiable mother, can never do. He can never simply go indoors, enter a wife, and there conjure up a male heir to continue his own kind in an adaptable new form. Men who cannot hew and bear hewing are of course not fit for that. To be sure, he tries to do this unattainable thing time and again, but the Timnite woman's bedroom remains by cultural barriers impenetrably closed to him, and the best this miserable fellow can do, who began his own existence on an open field under no roof but heaven itself, is to go to ground again in a cave at the Rock of Etam like seed sown in the earth from which no truly neoteric, newly educable and culturally malleable being but only more of himself can ever emerge. And like the processes of cutting and hewing, buildings and houses too (i.e., the culturally devised artifacts and products of cutting and hewing) remain together with the very concept of *indoors* foreign and inimical to Samson all his life, but especially so throughout the first pair of stories about his youth, the pair of stories that tell of his origin and of his own failed attempt in turn to originate progeny by marriage.

Samson is not alone in his inefficacy. The Philistine policy towards him in the first pair of tales is equally a ruinous failure for them. They try hard and ingeniously to *keep him out*: out of the Timnite woman's bedroom and out of his cave in the Rock of Etam. It seems, after all, the most logical policy, given Samson's own so de-

cidedly exoteric nature. But the Philistines gain no respite from his fe-
rocious energies by that means. And so, like good men of culture everywhere—i.e., like good folktale tricksters—they exactly reverse
their failed former policy and try instead a new plan not of *exclusion*
but rather of close *containment* in the second pair of Samson tales,
when Samson has matured. Well acculturated men who are used to
hewing and to containment are thus also able to learn something new
and to change their ways when there is need; feral creatures like
Samson cannot.

Whores contain and tame the ravaging powers of an unbridled
outdoor nature repeatedly in ancient Near Eastern traditions; so for
example the whore who urbanizes the dangerous wild thing Enkidu
in the Epic of Gilgamesh. (This correspondence is real, though it does
not mean that Samson is just a Jewish Enkidu.) But the woman in the
first of the second pair of Samson stories is no longer an object of
Samson's acquisitive ambition or his hope of progenerative profit as
the Timnite woman was. This second woman is only bait in the
Philistine stratagem to acquire Samson and to profit from containing
him. The bait works, and in the little preliminary tale of Judg 16:1–3
Samson goes of his own accord into an alien containment in Gaza.
Whereas formerly the Philistine men worked to keep Samson out of
their women, now they knowingly let him into one suitable for their
purpose. They plan to hew and cut Samson fatally at daybreak, but
they do not cut him in time. At midnight, before being cut, he bursts
out of the containment, rips up its central symbol, the city gates of
Gaza (which are of course the once wild and living but now tame, ur-
banized, and inanimate products of the Philistines' previous cutting
and hewing), and then he carries them away to a distant hilltop like a
flood, a stormwind, or other such elemental outdoor power.

Thus the first Philistine attempt to implement their new policy of
containment is too crude. It needs refinement in both the containing
and the cutting; but the two central principles of the Philistine policy
and Samson's response to it—to pull their container down—will persist as the ideational framework in the second, longer story of the
second pair, the story of Delilah.

To tame and urbanize a bull, and to make it useful for cultural
work, one must not only pen but also cut it. If the cultural purpose of
the containment and the cutting is only to stop its rampant destructiveness, one may of course cut it to death, but that is very wasteful.
If, however, one cuts it only a little in just the right place and in the
right way, but not fatally, then the skillfully curtailed beast may well
be kept, harmlessly contained thereafter for fun and profit. So, too, a
vine in a vineyard, or a fruit tree planted in the containment of an orchard and pruned to bear; or a sheaf of grain, which is of no use until
it is reaped and tied, or threshed and hampered. Samson is like all

these things that are grown outdoors, needing to be cut, tied, and penned, but not to a lethal degree, since much benefit may yet be had from him by wise tricksters, both for their amusement (as a strong-man-clown on holidays) and for lightening the labor of their living as a beast of burden (turning the mill to grind the grain for the nourishment of Philistine bellies on workdays). Thus, in his maturity Samson becomes a ripe and harvested article, penned and trimmed for Philistine consumption. Their only mistake in an otherwise admirable cultural procedure is to overlook a necessary periodic renewal of the trimming. Not having been cut to death, but only pruned for the purpose of cultural exploitation, Samson still has in him a living residue of capacity for further growth, and if the growth proceeds too far unchecked, he has a potential also to run wild again and do more feral harm. Untended by a watchful Philistine eye and a timely intervening Philistine hand wielding the sharp, delimiting edge of a cutting instrument, Samson grows unkempt and untame again, and so brings down disaster on everyone in the great final quaking of the earth when Samson extirpates the Philistines of urban habits. Having once taken up the sharp blade of civilization, one may never put it down again; the urban Philistines perish in their thousands because they have not understood this, just as earlier the agrarian Philistines (who were less numerous but more widely dispersed than the urban ones) perished by the thousand because they did not understand that when beasts of burden die, one must not leave their carcasses lying about as carrion to attract and be used by dangerous feral predators such as dwell in caves in the wilderness.

Samson's deadly flaws are more complicated. He cannot cut, nor bear cutting, and Yahweh turns away from him when, inevitably, he comes within the influence of men who can and do. Pity poor Samson, taking the blame from Yahweh for a deficiency of character which no one but Yahweh himself has created in him. How like that dreadful god Yahweh it is always to be disappointed, blaming and abandoning his own imperfect creatures for failures inherent in Yahweh's own mistakes of creative design. But we must wait for Job to come to grips with that problem; Samson is too early for it, and too much by far a stock character of international folktale tradition.

Folktale heroes trying to find suitable spouses and productive marriages must, as I have detailed more fully elsewhere, accomplish four things and experience four (Bynum, 1981:142–63) different kinds of relationship with nubile women on the way to marital contentment (Bynum, 1978:265–70). Because he is generally well known—better on the whole than any other single character of oral narrative tradition—I use Homer's Odysseus for example.

A successful folktale husband must meet four tests to prove himself fit for marriage. He must demonstrate himself a master over wood, as Odysseus does in his naval carpentry (raft-building) on the island of Ogygia, (*Od.* 5:234–61) in his almost occult construction of the olivewood bedstead in his house on Ithaka (*Od.* 23:177–204) (the means of sustaining a genealogical lineage being once again firmly secluded indoors), and in his unique knowledge of the trees in Laertes' orchard (*Od.* 24:336–44). He must also be a master of water, as Odysseus was in prevailing over Poseidaon's angry seas (*Od.* 4:282–381). He must be a prodigious killer/provider of animal food, as Odysseus was both in his hunting (from the boar-hunt with Autolykos onward) (*Od.* 19:435–54; 10:156–77, *et passim*) and in cattle-lifting during his Wanderings (*Od.* 9:464–70, *et passim*), as well as in the multitudinous livestock which he owned on Ithaka (*Od.* 14:96–104). Finally, he must make a shrewd selection of just the right wife for himself from amongst a number of proffered opportunities, as Odysseus did in preferring his own Penelope to either Kalypso or Nausikaa (*Od.* 7:308–33).

Besides many true multiforms expressing this same consistent pattern of story in an almost infinite variety of motifs, oral traditions everywhere also entertain equal numbers of deliberate devagations from this pattern which are themselves standard patterns. That is to say, traditional storytellers intentionally replicate characters with common backgrounds and common courses of incident, but with deliberate deflections of the common pattern so as to produce markedly divergent destinies from closely similar beginnings. Samson is an excellent case in point. He masters wood magnificently in his portage of the gates of Gaza to the hill at Hebron. Water springs up for him on demand out of the dry rock in the hollow of Lehi. He is only too obviously a prodigious killer and provider of food, even out of a lion's carcass and even while chained in the Philistine prison. So he successfully meets three of the would-be husband's qualifying trials; but he fails the fourth one. Infatuated beast that he is, he cannot disabuse himself of the obsession with Delilah—he is really much more animalistically ruttish than civilizedly sexy—and he cannot exercise even ordinary common sense about selecting a bedmate; again he fails in a vital social and cultural skill.

The oral traditional story pattern underlying the Samson saga shrewdly integrates that error with another deliberate truncation of another traditional requirement too. Again like Homer's Odysseus, successful husbands customarily meet and deal in conventionally prescribed ways with four different kinds of nubile woman. Two of them are, like Odysseus' Circe and Kalypso, very interesting females (Bynum, 1978:265–70). A right-thinking man may well get into bed with them, but then he must leave them and move on. Samson correspondingly has his nameless whore in Gaza and his Delilah. There is also another woman, undeniably attractive and eligible, who must however imperatively be left untouched by a successful hero: Odysseus' Nausikaa and Samson's Timnite woman. From her, Odysseus (and a thousand others like him in as many other ethnic traditions) wisely passes on to his Penelope, a woman who will be steadfastly his right wife so long as he lives. But here again Samson's destiny falls short, not by accident but by traditional design. He does not leave Delilah when he obviously should, after she has so blatantly and dangerously tried to trick him, and he does not proceed from her to any other woman with whom he could abide permanently beyond the transiently interesting Delilah. Thus he has during his lifetime two whores and a marriageable woman (the Timnite) whom he ought to leave alone both for his own family's good and for the good of the Philistines; but he never has a wife at all.

Samson's very name, with its strange form and still undeciphered meaning, is another enduring obstacle to a ready understanding of him. It is, however, an intriguing coincidence, and possibly even a fact of some interpretative value, that in ancient Greek mythology, too, the entire category of wild "men" called Centaurs typically had personal names either as obscure and (for men) as unusual in form as "Samson" was in Hebrew, or else names that marked them as outdoor beings implicitly unfit for civilized life in houses.[2] Nestor in the first book of the *Iliad* seems to mean this same race of sub-human beings when he speaks of φηροὶ ὀρεσκῷοι (1:268), "wild (ones) who reside/are situated in the mountains." The meaning of the generic name "Centaur," which occurs in the *Odyssey* (21:295), is quite as uncertain as the meaning of "Samson," and so is the personal name of the first Centaur mentioned as such in the Greek tradition, Eurytion. This Eurytion also made trouble over a nubile woman whom he was too wild to wed (*Od.* 21:295–304), as did the Centaur Nessos (meaning?) again in the later narrative told by Apollodorus (*Bibliotheca* II, 151–52, 7, 5–6), and Homados ("din-maker") yet again in the tale retold in Diodorus Siculus (*Bibliotheca Historica* IV. 12.7), all imitating (or anticipating) Samson's misconduct over the woman at Timnah. The noisy Homados had a name only a little less specific as to the nature of his unfitness for indoor living than did that other Centaur Doupon ("thudder, he-of-the-reverberating-footfalls"), whose heavy-footedness brings to mind once more Samson's first movements in the camp of Dan between Zorah and Eshtaol (Judg 13:25). As though in confirmation of such a traditional linkage of meaning between these two Centaurs' names, Homer even made a regular line-ending formula, terminating with a three-syllable verb: ὅμαδος καὶ δοῦπος u-- (I 569, 556), ". . . din and thump (of battle)."

---

[2]For lists of Centaurs' names and a categorization of them as ὀνόματα ἐπώνομα, see Roscher (II.1, col. 1072–74).

Other Centaurs' significant names marked them too as unsuited for indoor habitation, and could never be mistaken for the personal names of real humans. So, for example, Petraios (Stone-, Boulderperson); Oreios (Mountainperson); Peukeidai (Pinesons); Arktos (Bear); Dryalos (Treeman). The most famous of all the Centaurs, Cheiron, dwelt in a cave on Mount Pelion in Thessaly all his life; and he undoubtedly would have had no difficulty duplicating Samson's capture of foxes by the hundreds, for his name says unambiguously that he is Seizer, Catcher, Taker-of-Game.

Those of the Thessalian tribe of Centaurs whom Peirithoos, Theseus, and the Lapiths did not slay in the famous War of the Lapiths and Centaurs were, with few exceptions, killed separately by Herakles (Apollod., *Bibliotheca* II, 83–86 [5,4]; D.S., IV.12.3–8). That there was a certain likeness between Samson and Herakles was recognized before the end of classical antiquity. What has not been recognized is that the Centaurs share in many details of that likeness quite as much as Herakles and Samson do; Herakles was thus indistinguishable in some respects from the very Centaurs whom he slew in enmity or by accident. Like Samson at Gaza, at Ashkelon, and at the Rock of Etam, and like the Centaurs at the wedding of Peirithoos, (Pseudo-Hesiod, *Aspis*, vv. 178–90) in the attack on Alkyone by Homados, (D.S., IV.12.7) or in the attack on Deianeira by Nessos,[3] Herakles also suffered episodes of unbridled excitement, frenzied energy, or plain madness, as in the burning of his children by Megara (Apollod., *Bibliotheca* II, 72 [4, 12]; D.S., IV.11.1–2; Hyginus, *Fabulae* 32), the killing of Oineus' wine steward (Apollod., *Bibliotheca* II, 150 [7, 62–63]), and the slaying of Oichalian Iphitos (*Od.* 21:22–30; Apollod., *Bibliotheca* II, 127–30 [6, 1–2]). Again like Samson and the Centaurs (Cheiron), Herakles was an extraordinary seizer or catcher-of-wild-beasts (the Nemean lion, Erymanthian boar, Cretan bull, Lernaean Hydra),[4] which he overcame either by bludgeoning them with his famous attribute, the club from Nemea (Apollod., *Bibliotheca* II, 71 [4, 11, 8]), or more often by grappling with his bare hands. Thus, like Samson and the Centaurs, Herakles, too, did not go about his tasks cutting or hewing; and in dispersing the Stymphalian birds he employed means that were the very essence of the Centaurs' names Homados and Doupon.[5] None of the three—Samson, Centaurs, or Herakles—ever

---

[3]The story of Nessos is in Apollod., *Bibliotheca*, II, 151–52 (7, 5–6).

[4]Apollod., *Bibliotheca*, II, 74–76 (5, 1) (the lion); II, 77–80 (5, 2) (the hydra); II, 83–87 (5, 4) (the boar); II, 94–95 (5, 7) (the bull); Diodorus Siculus, IV.11.3–12 (the lion, boar, and hydra); IV.13.4 (the bull).

[5]Apollod., *Bibliotheca*, II, 92–93 (5, 6); Apollonius Rhodius, *Argonautica* II, vv. 1052–57; Diodorus Siculus, IV.13.2; Pausanias, 8, 22, 4.

solved the problem of maintaining an agnatic lineage,[6] and all were ruined in the end by women's wiles worked upon them while they were enthralled with amorous infatuation. The irresistible allure of Hippodamia for the Centaurs at the wedding of Peirithoos (Ovid, *Metamorphoses* 12:210–41), of Alkyone for Homados (D.S. 4.33.1), of Hippolyte for Eurytion, or Delilah for Samson, and of Iole for Herakles[7] caused the deaths of all of them. Delilah's witchery with Samson's magic hair and Deianeira's with the potion of Nessos in Herakles' fatal shirt-of-fire (Hyginus, *Fabulae* 34) are all of a piece. So women's magic finally does to death both Samson and Herakles, whose very identities and physical might were intended from the beginning to serve as instruments in a sky god's plan for clearing the earth of alien persons and other obstacles to its colonization by a chosen people. Once they have accomplished their designated superhuman tasks, they are persons of such violent and overbearing natures that there can be no place either for them personally or for any descendants of theirs who might be like them in the peacefully domesticated world which they were sent by heaven to subdue. Correspondingly, the same mortal women who would help civilized men people the land fail in their attempts to cooperate with such rude, physically superhuman but culturally subhuman brutes in perpetuating their kind. Instead of the mutual, life-long help customarily tendered to each other by properly acculturated husbands and wives, we find accordingly a mutual destructiveness between the type of Samson and Herakles and their females. Each allies himself with one woman whom he cannot keep (Samson with the Timnite and Herakles with Megara of Thebes); each of these women then pass out of their hands into the keeping of other men, who however fail to protect them as good husbands should, so that both women are subsequently murdered.[8] Thereafter Samson and Herakles both ally themselves again with other women, who, however, now magically destroy *them*: Samson by Delilah and Herakles by Deianeira.

---

[6]The Heraclidae, though very numerous, share with their eponym a common unhappy destiny of dispossession *dem Haus aus*, demonstrating yet further the general principle that in the absence of an inheritable *oikos* lineage is irrelevant. Bastards, exiles, colonists, and adventurers whose whole lives passed in the service of others in lands not their own, the Sons of Herakles were just such descendants as Samson might have begotten on Delilah, or the whore of Gaza, or others of those women's kind; for the failure of the Old Testament narrator to disclose what illegitimate offspring the ruttish Samson begat does not mean that he got none in the original tradition.

[7]Hyginus, 35–36, states the tradition concisely.

[8]Pausanias, 10.29.7; Hyginus, 32; Diodorus Siculus, 4.31.1. Observe the juxtaposition of the would-be husband's chthonic sojourn with the destruction of the wife whom he cannot keep, as in the Samson saga.

Some cognoscenti have supposed that a number of earlier myths were subsumed and the names formerly associated with them were driven out of ancient Greek mythic tradition by the extraordinary popularity of the Herakles saga in the classical age. However that may be, the story of Orion,[9] whom Homer knew (*Od.* 5:121-24), also conforms in its surviving part to the present, intentionally defective narrative pattern of a would-be husband's failure. No differently than Samson or Herakles, Orion too was a strong man, and in his case not only his inception but indeed the whole of his unusually long, ten-month gestation had to be accomplished out-of-doors and *in* the ground (as though nativity for him were simultaneously both plant and animal). Like Manoah, Orion's nominal (i.e., his cultural or adoptive) father was also as childless as a dead stick, although here the reason seems to have been the man Hyrieus' (the name means "pisser") failure to understand the reproductive possibilities of his *membrum virile* beyond its more mundane (and more frequent) utility for micturition. One may reasonably wonder whether in the original oral traditional telling there wasn't something rather like that wrong with Manoah, too. The gods kindly demonstrated to Hyrieus how it was done, so that the latter was eventually able to beget other, more survivable children than Orion proved to be (Apollod., *Bibliotheca* III, 111 [10.1]). Yahweh seems not to have been so kind to Manoah; or if he was, no text reports it.

Like Samson and Herakles, Orion also lived long enough to bed a pair of transiently interesting women with whom he could not finally abide, and then foolishly forced his attentions on yet a third female whom he ought rather to have left alone. In Orion's story, these three were Side, Merope, and Artemis. Side was murdered (by Hera); Orion ruined Merope and her father, who subdued him by cutting him in a way it took him a long time and much trouble to mend; but then Artemis destroyed him as the result of his too familiar companionship with her, a companionship that should never have arisen in the first place. Like Samson, Herakles, and the Centaurs, Orion was thoroughly feral.

Folktale, epic, and balladry in ethnopoetic traditions everywhere in the world abound in such-like "wild men" tales, and a good book further explaining the Samson saga against the full panoply of that rich background is waiting to be written by any willing author. Indeed, the only peculiar thing about the Samson saga when it is viewed against that background is that there are so few (any?) multiforms or variants of it—no (other) Centaurs or Orion to accompany

---

[9]A general discussion of the mythic tradition relating to Orion is in Fontenrose. Except where noted, the account given in the present paper follows Palaephatus, LI (V).

the Herakles—in the attested Hebrew tradition. But there is no more space here to say all the other things that should be said about this same complex of traditional story as seen from the Tsimshian Indian point of view in their famous story of Asdiwal, (Boas:65–145) or in the Nyanga Mwindo (Biebuyck and Mateene; Biebuyck), or in the Finnish tale of Joukahainen's Singing Contest in the *Kalevala*, (Magoun, 1969:173–76; 1963:14–21; Juusi, Bosley, and Branch:102–9), or in the South Slavic Marko Kraljevic (Karadžić, II:39 and 40), or Hasan of Ribnik (Parry and Lord: 2, 18, 19), or in the medieval Greek *Digenes Akrites*, and so forth—all of which are massively pertinent.

I have often heard it said that the strange story of another notable hand-wrestler and outdoorsman in the Old English *Beowulf* can rightly be understood only by concentrated attention to the text itself and the nuances of its Anglo-Saxon language. Anglo-Saxonists particularly are wont to say that. Homerists generally insist that the *Iliad* and *Odyssey* will yield their secrets only to Homerists, and that nothing un-Hellenic is really relevant. Hispanicists tell me that the *Cid* is too exquisitely Spanish to be grasped by any means but those found in the medieval Spanish language and text itself. And, of course, the English Robin Hood ballads are *sui generis*; so, too, the stories in the Finnish traditional oral narrative poetry; etc., etc., etc.

My experience has been different. The Muslim oral traditional epos of the South Slavs has given me means for understanding the Finnish poetry in the *Kalevala* that seem not to have been available to any of the Finnish-speaking scholars. I came to terms with Beowulf in Central Africa; with the English Robin Hood in the Azeri tradition of Kurroglu; with the medieval Spanish Cid in Australian Blackfellow tales; with an important part of the *Odyssey* in the pre-Columbian cultures of the Pacific Northwest; with the Achaian siege of Ilios in Radloff's Kazakhstan; and with the story of Samson as I have just tried to understand it from the Tangu tradition in New Guinea. I think it is a great mistake to avoid "ethnopoetic analogies" in interpretative criticism of any text that has an ethnopoetic origin so conspicuously as the Samson saga does. Indeed, it is not even possible accurately to evaluate in what parts such a text has an ethnopoetic background in the first place, or to determine which specific ethnopoetic analogues can be of critical value, unless and until one knows the oral tradition as a whole quite well.

So I acquiesce ungrudgingly to a study of Samson without folklore, but to Samson without the oral narrative tradition never; and I am receptive to explanatory investigation of the Old Testament as a whole only with the oral tradition in all its multiplicity of ethnopoetic branches.

WORKS CONSULTED

Apollodorus (mythographus)
1894   *Bibliotheca.* Ed. R. Wagner. Pp. 1–169 in *Apollodori bibliotheca, Mythographi Graeci,* 1. Leipzig: Teubner.

Apollonius Rhodius
1961   *Argonautica.* Ed. H. Fraenkel. *Apollonii Rhodii Argonautica.* Oxford: Clarendon Press.

Biebuyck, Daniel
1978   *Hero and Chief: Epic Literature from the Banyanga (Zaire Republic).* Berkeley: University of California Press.

Biebuyck, Daniel and Kahombo C. Mateene, eds. and trans.
1969   *The Mwindo Epic from the Banyanga (Congo Republic).* Berkeley: University of California Press.

Boas, Franz, ed. and trans.
1912   *Tsimshian Texts.* New Series. Leiden: E. J. Brill for Publications of the American Ethnological Society.

Bynum, David E.
1978   *The Daemon in the Wood: A Study of Oral Narrative Patterns.* Cambridge, MA: Center for the Study of Oral Literature.
1981   "Myth and Ritual: Two Faces of Tradition." Pp. 142–63 in *Oral Traditional Literature.* Ed. John Miles Foley. Columbus: Slavica.

Diodorus Siculus
1888–   *Bibliotheca historica,* (Books 1–20). Ed. F. Vogel and K. T.
1906   Fischer (post I. Bekker & L. Dindorf, *Diodori bibliotheca historica*). 3rd ed. 5 vol. Leipzig: Teubner.

Euripides (tragicus)
1902   *Heraclidae.* Ed. G. Murray. *Euripidis fabulae,* vol. 1. Oxford: Clarendon Press.

Fontenrose, Joseph
1981   *Orion: The Myth of the Hunter and the Huntress.* University of California Publications: Classical Studies, vol. 23. Berkeley: University of California Press.

Herodotus (historicus)
'1932–   *Historiae.* Ed. Ph.-E. Legrand. *Hérodote. Histoires.* 9 vols.
1954   Paris: Les Belles Lettres.

Hesiod(us)
1970   *Scutum.* Ed. Friedrich Solmsen. *Hesiodi Theogonia Opera et Dies Scutum.* Oxford: Clarendon Press.

Homer(us)
1931   *Ilias.* Ed. Thomas W. Allen. *Homeri Ilias,* vols. 1–3. Oxford: Clarendon Press.
1984   *Odyssea.* Ed. P. Von der Muehll. *Homeri Odyssea.* Stuttgart: Teubner.

Hyginus
n.d.   *Fabulae.* Ed. Herbert J. Rose. *Hygini fabulae.* Leiden: A. W. Sijthoff.

Karadžić, Vuk Stefanović
1958   *Srpske narodne pjesme.* Ed. Radomir Aleksić, Nikola Banašević, Vojislav Đurić, and Vido Latković with notes and explanations by Svetozar Matić. Vol. 2. Belgrade: Prosveta.

Kuusi, Matti, Keith Bosley, and Michael Branch
1977   *Finnish Folk Poetry: Epic, an Anthology in Finnish and English.* Ed. and trans. Matti Kuusi, Keith Bosley, and Michael Branch. Helsinki: Finnish Literature Society.

Lactantius Placidus
1898   *Commentarios in Statii Thebaida et Commentarium in Achilleida.* Ed. Ricardus Jahnke. *P. Papinii Statii opera,* vol. 3. Leipzig: Teubner.

Magoun, Francis Peabody, Jr., trans.
1963   *The Kalevala.* Ed. Elias Lönnrot. Cambridge, MA: Harvard University Press.
1969   *The Old Kalevala and Certain Antecedents.* Ed. Elias Lönnrot. Cambridge, MA: Harvard University Press.

Mavrogordato, John, ed. and trans.
1956   *Digenes Akrites.* Oxford: Clarendon Press.

Nilsson, Martin P.
1961   *Greek Folk Religion* (= *Greek Popular Religion* [1940]). New York: Harper & Bros.
1967   *Geschichte der Griechischen Religion*, 3rd ed. *Handbuch der Altertumwissenschaft* 5/5. München: Beck.

(Publius) Ovid(ius Naso)
1982   *P. Ovidii Nasonis Metamorphoses*. Ed. William S. Anderson. 2nd ed. Leipzig: Teubner.

Palaephatus (mythographus)
1902   *De incredibilibus*. Ed. N. Festa. Pp. 1–72 in *Palaephati περὶ ἀπίστων* (*Mythographi Graeci* 3.2). Leipzig: Teubner.

Parry, Milman, and Albert B. Lord, eds. and trans.
1953   *Serbocroatian Heroic Songs*, vol. 2. Cambridge, MA, and Belgrade: Harvard University Press and Serbian Academy of Sciences.

Pausanias (periegetes)
1903   *Graeciae descriptio*. Ed. F. Spiro. *Pausaniae Graeciae descriptio*, 3 vols. Leipzig: Teubner.

Roscher, W. H.
1890–   "Kentauren." Cols. 1032–88 in *Ausführliches Lexikon der*
1894   *griechischen und römischen Mythologie*, vol. II.1. Ed. W. H. Roscher. Leipzig: Teubner.

Sophocles (tragicus)
1928   *Trachiniae*. Ed. A. C. Pearson. *Sophoclis fabulae*. Oxford: Clarendon Press.

Strabo
1852–   *Geographica*. Ed. Augustus Meineke. *Strabonis geographica*,
1853   3 vols. Leipzig: Teubner.

7. HUMOR AND THEOLOGY OR THE SUCCESSFUL FAILURE OF ISRAELITE INTELLIGENCE: A LITERARY-FOLKLORIC APPROACH TO JOSHUA 2

Yair Zakovitch

ABSTRACT

In this paper the author unveils the humor invested in the story of Rahab and the spies. The expressions of humor can be discovered by comparing the story to other instances of the same story type found in the Bible and determining its unique character *vis-à-vis* the other stories.

Our story is counted among those of both the "spy story" story-type (Numbers 13–14; Josh 7:2–5; Judg 1:22–26; 18:2–11; 2 Sam 17:17–22) and the story-type of "the woman who rescues a man" (1 Sam 19:9–17; 2 Sam 17:17–22, and cf. Judg 4:17–21; 16:1–3). These two story types, borrowed from the world of folklore, well served the author's purpose in formulating the story and its message, and their juxtaposition assured maximum effectiveness. The story-type of "the woman who rescues a man" is fundamentally a woman's story-type whereas the "spy story" type is entirely masculine. In our story dominance is given to the woman who makes the male spies appear to be worthless lackeys. The sexual element that was an essential part of the original base of the story-type of "the woman who rescues a man" was toned down in order to accommodate the story to the conservative nature of biblical narrative and to make even further fun of the men—soldiers who do not behave in a masculine manner. Putting the bungling spies in the shadow of a Canaanite harlot produces an important link in the cycle of stories which seek to teach the lesson that "vain is the help of man" (Ps 60:12)—military intelligence included and that "The Lord will fight for you, and you shall hold your peace" (Exod 14:14).

The Bible inspires a certain respect and seriousness in its readers, a sense that they must walk its paths with diffidence. This is because the Bible is not a book like any other but the "book of books," the Holy Scriptures of the nation of Israel. The Bible portrays the relationship between God and his people Israel, based on God's righteous rule over his world and his people, showing grace and mercy. The history of the nation of Israel is thus explained as deriving from the people's obedience to the divine commandments, or of their turning away from their God: great saving acts on the one hand, and unbearable punishments on the other. Ethical and didactic in character, biblical literature's purpose is to inspire every Israelite—by means of the story of God's action in history—to follow the Lord and enjoy his favor: "That they may set their hope in God, and not forget the works of God, but keep his commandments; and may not be like their fathers, a stubborn and rebellious generation, a generation that did not set its heart aright, and whose spirit was not faithful to God" (Ps 78:7-8).

We who take the way of a "close reading" of the biblical text certainly would not propound a frivolous approach to the Bible. On the contrary, we base our method on the assumption that one can reveal the meaning of the text only by paying full attention to every detail of its form and by persistently searching for the meaning of every word in its context (cf. M. Weiss; Zakovitch, 1982; 1985). Nevertheless, we must object to any approach that puts shutters on Holy Scripture or insists on a "dry-rot" type of seriousness. If we wish to discern the meaning of a biblical story, we must dispel all darkening clouds, shake the book free of all dusty religious notions, and be prepared to smile, snicker, or even laugh out loud; fire will not descend from the heavens, nor will bears come out of the woods to punish our presumed irreverence. In fact, the realization of the author's wry smile or wink in the composition of a literary unit may lead to a clearer understanding of the story's meaning and message. I shall here discuss the story of Joshua's spies in Jericho (Joshua 2) in order to demonstrate that a healthy sense of humor is often necessary for the full appreciation of a biblical narrative.

The story of the spies in Rahab's house is, at first glance, something of an embarrassment. Why should the "Book of the Wars of the Lord," the account of God's wondrous saving acts in settling the nation in its land, begin precisely at the house of a harlot? Why does the Jericho prostitute get such a prominent place in the story, on the very opening pages of the books of the Former Prophets? The problems aroused by such an apparently ignoble beginning, which takes place in the days of Joshua,[1] can be fully resolved and their rhetorical func-

---

[1] It seems that the story of Rahab and the spies was not approved of by one of the editors of the book of Joshua, who did not wish to include it in his book. Several proofs can be adduced for this.

The story disturbs the chronological continuity at the beginning of Joshua's command to cross over the Jordan in another three days: "Then Joshua commanded the officers of the people, saying, 'Pass through the camp and command the people, saying, "Prepare provisions for yourselves, for in another three days you will cross over this Jordan . . ." (1:10–11). An additional reference to the sphere of time is found at the beginning of chapter 3:1–2: "Then Joshua rose early in the morning; and they set out from Shittim and came to the Jordan . . . So it was, after three days, that the officers went through the camp." But the crossing does not take place on the same day; after the officers command the people, Joshua commands them: "And Joshua said to the people, 'Sanctify yourselves, for *tomorrow* the Lord will do wonders among you'" (v. 5). Apparently, the words "for in another three days" (1:11), and "after three days" (3:2) refer to a crossing on the third day, the day they arrived at the Jordan river (cf. such passages as Gen 40:13, 19–20; 42:14–18; Exod 19:15–16; Lev 13:4–5; Deut 15:1 [cf. v. 9; 31:10]; Josh 9:16–17; 1 Kgs 12:5–12; 22:1). Chap. 3:5 on the other hand, which presumes that an additional day has gone by, "for tomorrow . . . ," contradicts these verses. Moreover, v. 5 is a foreign element in the story of the crossing: the officers' commanding of the people (v. 4) does not assume an additional day and in v. 6 also there is no hint of this assumption. Verse 6 is the direct continuation of v. 4: after the officers give orders to the people, Joshua gives orders to the priests.

Apparently, v. 5 was added to chapter 3 in the wake of the secondary integration of chapter 2 between chapter 1, which presents the command to cross the Jordan, and its execution in chapter 3. The story of sending the spies takes place after the order to cross the Jordan in another three days (1:11). Joshua sends spies from Shittim (2:1), and they apparently return there before crossing the Jordan (3:1). But the spies' mission goes on beyond the third day mentioned in 1:11 and 3:2: the first day of the spy mission, at the earliest the day of the order of crossing, the spies end up at Rahab's house where they lie down for the night (2:1–2); after the search of her house Rahab suggests they hide in the mountains "three days" (4:16), and her suggestion is taken: "Then they departed and went to the mountain, and stayed there three days until the pursuers returned" (v. 22). Even if, on the third day of their hiding, they come down from the mountain and return to Joshua's camp, this would be the fourth day of their mission, while they should have crossed the Jordan on the third day. Accordingly, the editor who included the story of Rahab in his book, added chap. 3:5, which postpones the crossing an additional day. (For the chronology, see Zakovitch, 1979).

The story of Rahab contradicts the story of the tumbling of the walls: It is said of Rahab: "for her house was on the city wall; she dwelt on the wall" (v. 15), which contradicts the account of the sparing of her house with the tumbling down of the wall in chapter 6 (for this reason these words were omitted by the Septuagint, or by its *Vorlage*).

The editor who finally integrated chapter 2 in the book of Joshua, added in chapter 6 verses relating to the fulfillment of the oath to Rahab (vv. 17b, 22–23, 25). The continuity of chapter 6 is not disturbed in the least if these verses are excised. The fact that chapter 2 is a secondary element in the book of Joshua is, however, no claim as to the lateness of the chapter—just the opposite: it seems that the story was found offensive, and whoever rejected it composed in its stead a more honorable tradition (chapter 6) concerning the manner of conquest of the first city in the land of Canaan. It is extremely difficult to get rid of a tradition, however, and particularly impossible to ignore it, and a later editor who was familiar with and appreciated this story, reinserted it into the book. He then tried, as well as he could, to smooth out the seams between the story and its literary context both by the addition of 3:5 and by adding the verses concerning Rahab in chapter 6. For the problem of the relation of chapter 2 to chapter 6 see recently Soggin (38–39).

tion appreciated, if we are prepared to decipher the story equipped
with a sense of humor. I shall not suggest a "close reading" of the
story itself but will deliberately limit myself to those features that
give evidence of a certain narrative jocularity. One thing, however,
should be remembered: the instances of humor in the Bible are extremely subtle and even covert—the biblical narrative is no Marx
Brothers-style slapstick comedy. At times one can discern a degree of
whimsicality only by means of a parallel, comparing a particular
story to other expressions of the same story-type, the abstract pattern
we reconstruct from several stories similar in content and whose
plots can be divided into parallel stages.

Such story-types came into being in the traditions of oral literature, which preceded written biblical literature. Religious and ideological considerations brought about extensive changes as the
original story-types of the oral traditions were adapted to their
written form in the Bible. The oral traditions were not committed to
writing in order to entertain readers, nor to preserve them for
posterity in a period of crisis and save them from oblivion as the
Scandinavian school of biblical research (e.g., Nielsen) has claimed.
They were written down in order to ensure a character worthy from
an ideo-religious point of view, to seat God "on a high and lofty
throne," to cast the heroes of folk traditions in an honorable mold,
and to purge the traditions of all that conflicts with the sublime
conceptions of the ideological and religious framework of the Holy
Scriptures. These changes, undergone by the folk story-types in the
process of their incorporation into biblical literature, do not make the
work of reconstructing the original traditions and types an easy task,
and I am aware that the ground I venture to walk on here is quite
slippery.

One way for reconstructing traditions involves comparing a single story to its fellows of the same story-type. In so doing, we become
aware of the story's deviations and uniqueness over against its partners, and it is precisely in these deviations, which can at times testify
to the parodic use of the story-type, that expressions of humor are
likely to be found. In the hypothetical (for the time being) biblical
"index of story-types" the story of Rahab and the spies will be found
under the rubric of spy stories (cf. Malamat, 1970; 1979), along with
the story of Moses' dispatching of the spies (Numbers 13–14 and its
echo in Deut 1:22–40); Joshua's sending of spies to Ai (Josh 7:2–5); the
Josephite's sending of spies to reconnoiter Bethel (Judg 1:22–26); the
Danites' spy-mission to Laish, their new territory (Judg 18:2–11); and
the case of David, who sends his two spies, Jonathan and Ahimaaz, to
Absalom's camp (2 Sam. 17:17–22) (cf. further Num 21:32; 1 Sam 26:4;
2 Sam 15:10). The theological or theocentric character of biblical literature brought about changes in the literary type of spy stories, which

originally surely emphasized the spies' courage—the heroics of skilled Israelite intelligence agents, who, upon encountering difficulties in their mission, prove their resourcefulness and manage to extricate themselves from any danger. In the Bible, however, as we shall see further on, the spies' own resourcefulness and success in their mission is no guarantee of success in battle.

An additional story-type to which our story belongs is that of "The Woman Who Rescues a Man." Of the biblical spy stories, that of Jonathan and Ahimaaz, who are saved thanks to the wisdom of the woman from Bahurim, also belongs to this pattern, as does the story of Michal who helps David her husband escape from King Saul, her father (1 Sam 19:9–17). This story-type, as we shall see below, includes two additional stories, the story of Sisera who expects Yael to act according to the dictates of the pattern and rescue him from the advancing Israelites (Judg 4:17–21), and the story of Samson's visit to the harlot of Gaza—a story very similar to ours (Judg 16:1–3).

An examination of this story-type demands that particular attention be paid to the fact that this is fundamentally a woman's story-type. At this juncture, then, we cannot refrain from saying a few words about what usually happens to heroines in the transition from oral literature to the written literature of the Bible. The Bible is "The Book of the Wars of the Lord," in which the central role is given to men: the patriarchs, the judges, the priests, the kings, and the prophets. The female characters stand in the shadow of men, even though there are exceptions: Deborah and Jael (Judges 4–5), Delilah (Judges 16), the wise woman of Tekoah (2 Samuel 14), the wise woman from Abel Beth-maacah (2 Samuel 20), Bathsheba with Solomon (1 Kings 1), the wicked Jezebel (1 Kings 21), the Shunammite (2 Kings 4), Ruth and Naomi, Queen Esther, and others.

In the folk tales re-worked and written down at the hands of the Brothers Grimm and Walt Disney, heroines are not only "passive and pretty, but also unusually patient, obedient, industrious, and quiet," (Stone:44). "The only test of most heroines requires nothing beyond what they are born with: a beautiful face, or a pleasing temperament. At least that is what we learn from the translation of the Grimm tales and especially from Walt Disney" (Stone:45). The more original versions of the women stories, however, reveal that this literary genre knew of more active women: "In none of these tales do we find the stereotyped conflict between the passive, beautiful woman and the aggressive, ugly one. Most of the active heroines are not even described in terms of their natural attributes—and Mally Whuppee is presented as less attractive than her stepsister. Like heroes, they are judged by their actions" (Stone:46).

The Bible does contain, as mentioned, a few women-stories. But since the Bible is a book with a male orientation, only when a female-story fits the Bible's overall agenda was it committed to writing in its original oral form. In the stories of Deborah-Jael, for example, the heroes are women who disgrace the foreign enemy Sisera, and the heroine Esther succeeds in changing the dim-witted king Ahasuerus' mind at the banquet, since this king is interested only in wine and women.

The customary passivity of female protagonists is, furthermore, usually accompanied by the expurgation of sexual motifs in the written and re-worked versions of the folk stories: "Overt sexual references if they ever find their way into original collections, rarely appear in children's books"(Stone:46). The classic versions of the stories of Rapunzel, Cinderella, and the like are rather less innocent than the revamped versions intended for children. An original, sexual version of "Sleeping Beauty" is adduced by Lüthi (30) that demonstrates the considerable gulf between the oral folk story and its written adaptation.

The biblical story, for its part, was not entirely purged of erotic elements, as a few of these stories were deliberately preserved in the Bible, always for ulterior motives. The book of Genesis tells of Reuben and Bilhah, his father's mistress, since it must explain why Reuben lost his birthright (Gen 35:22; 49:3–4); the story of the rape of Dinah was retained in order to portray Simeon's and Levi's revenge, in consequence of which cruel behavior they lost their birthrights (chap. 34; 49:5–7). An additional rape story, of Tamar by her brother Amnon (2 Samuel 13), explains why Solomon was made king instead of his older brothers. The terrible story of Lot's daughters, who sleep with their drunken father (Gen 19:30–38), is permeated with derision toward the two sister nations Ammon and Moab which, according to the story, are the offspring of Lot's two daughters. All other sexual elements which survive in written biblical narrative can be explained in a similar way, though we have no space here to do so.

We shall thus pay special attention to the balance of power between the sexes: the man's wisdom and initiative as opposed to the woman's, his actions as opposed to hers, as well as clues which might point to the sexual character of the story-type should something of these elements remain in our story. I stress again that the examination of the narrative types will not be done systematically; I will discuss only those details which might help in uncovering the author's wry humor.

The opening of our story may already hint that something is about to go awry as the initiative to dispatch the spies is not God's but Joshua's: "Now Joshua the son of Nun sent out two men as spies . . ." (v. 1). According to Num 13:1, in the story of Moses' sending out spies, it is God who instructs Moses to deploy men to spy out the land. But the second edition of this story in the book of Deuteronomy replaces the divine initiative with human initiative: a mission which ended so disgracefully—the spies' evil report of the land—could not possibly have been initiated by God. The characterization of our spies, who are not even mentioned by name but simply as "two men" (and in chapter 6:23 they are even called "young lads!"), further heightens the prevailing sense of disgrace. True, an aristocratic birth is no guarantee, in our day, of success in spy missions. But it seems that at the base of the biblical stories lies the notion that spies worthy of their name must come from good families, like Moses' spies: "every one a leader among them" (Num 13:2), "all of them men who were heads of the children of Israel" (v. 3); like the Danite spies: "five men of their family from their territory, men of valor" (Judg 18:2) (cf. Ehrlich:234; Silver; Talmon:50–52); and even David is careful to select his spies from priestly families—the sons of Zadok and Abiathar (2 Sam 15:35–36). Joshua does not select the well-born or even soldiers as his spies; he may simply have grabbed the first two lads who happened to be near his tent when he went out to dispatch spies—sheer irresponsibility!

Does Joshua's sloppiness end with the selection of the spies? Let us look closely at how he briefs them before going out on their mission. Contrast Moses, who deals at length with questions of geography and strategies: "So Moses sent them to spy out the land of Canaan, and said to them, 'Go up this way into the South, and go up to the mountains, and see what the land is like: whether the people who dwell in it are strong or weak, few or many; whether the land they dwell in is good or bad; whether the cities they inhabit are like camps or strongholds; whether the land is rich or poor; and whether there are forests there or not . . .'" (Num 13:17–19, and cf. also the abridged version in Deut 1:22). Joshua, whose opening words are similar to those of Moses, dispatches the spies without any briefing at all: "Go, view the land, especially Jericho" (v. 1). Such a beginning— inexperienced spies taken from the ranks of the common people, sent forth on their mission with no real instructions—promises the reader an unconventional story at least, and in our case, a story full of humor.

Our two spies waste no time: "So they went, and came to the house of a harlot named Rahab, and lodged there" (v. 1). Josephus had difficulties accepting the fact that instead of applying themselves to the mission at hand the two spies head straight for the house of a harlot. He thus fills in a supposed gap in the biblical story:

> For, undetected at the first, they had surveyed their entire city unmolested, noting where the ramparts were strong and where they offered a less secure protection to the inhabitants, and which of the gates through weakness would facilitate entrance for the army. Those who met them had disregarded their inspection, attributing to a curiosity natural to

strangers this busy study of every detail in the city, and in no wise to
any hostile intent. But when, at fall of even, they retired to an inn hard
by the ramparts, to which they had proceeded for supper, word was
brought to the king as he supped that certain persons had come from
the camp of the Hebrews to spy upon the city and were now in Rahab's
inn . . . (*Antiquities*, Book v, chap. i, sec. 2).

Josephus' spies exhibit exemplary behavior, and his account is
humorless to the same degree. One could conceivably justify our
spies' action—perhaps they chose to come to the harlot's house precisely because in such a place soldiers let loose both their swords and
their tongues. But this is not the case. Our spies do not come to this
house for the sake of the people, but for their own sake: "and they
lodged there."

In order to understand the motives of the spies' action it is
worthwhile first to point out what a harlot is and whether those who
come to her house do so only to enjoy her physical charms—as in
Samson's visit to the harlot of Gaza: "Then Samson went to Gaza and
saw a harlot there, and went in to her" (Judg 16:1)—or whether the
services a harlot might offer are not necessarily limited to the sexual
realm. Targum Jonathan to the Prophets translates the Hebrew word
for harlot as "inn-keeper," but this does not mean that her services do
not include those in the sexual realm as well, since this is how
"harlot" is translated in many additional verses (such as Ezek 23:44).
Kimhi appropriately remarks: "a harlot, literally, or a food-seller, as
translated by Jonathan 'inn-keeper' . . . The correct understanding is
that of Jonathan—a prostitute—since there is no difference between a
harlot and an inn-keeper: both give themselves to any and everyone."
Abarbanel explains the connection between a harlot and an inn-
keeper thus: ". . . And I think that Jonathan ben Uziel also would not
contradict the explanation of the commentators, since every woman
inn-keeper, due to the number of men who have dealings with her in
her house . . . will necessarily be a harlot, because one of them will
seduce her . . . as well as due to the fact that most women who practice this trade were formerly harlots." Could it be, then, that our spies
came in order to lie with the harlot, or were they simply looking for a
nice hotel? In either case the spies give the impression of being far
removed from the world of espionage. After the wanderings in the
wilderness the spies seek the pleasures of civilization and the delights
of the big city, whether this means well-cooked food and a soft, clean
bed at an inn, or the favors of a woman better kept than the daughters
of the wilderness—thanks both to her profession and to the fact that
big-city life pampers the body more than the scorching desert sun.
The story does not provide us a clear answer as to why the spies
came to Rahab's house, but it is clear that nothing happened between
them. In a similar story, Samson does not hesitate to make use of the

harlot: "Then Samson went to Gaza and saw a harlot there, and went in to her" (Judg 16:1), Joshua's two spies do not go in to the woman but to her house. Note that it is precisely the use of the ambiguous word ש.כ.ב, "to lie down," that indicates that they did not lie with her, since it is clearly stated "and they lodged *there*," which should be compared to additional passages in which a place-description and the root ש.כ.ב, "to lie down," is found, with no hint whatsoever of any sexual activity (Gen 28:11; 1 Sam 3:9). The spies' coming to the house of the harlot, and not to the harlot herself, and the use of the ambiguous verb ש.כ.ב are of importance for the continuation of the plot. Nevertheless, the ne'er-do-well character of the spies is already apparent: if they have already neglected their spy mission "to spy out the land," or "the nakedness of the land" (Gen 42:9,12), and come to the house of a harlot, we would expect that they take full advantage of the opportunity their visit provides, that is, to see Rahab's nakedness. But the two simply head straight to bed, and even their sleep is hardly undisturbed, as will be seen further on in our reading.

In other stories of the pattern of the Woman Who Rescues a Man from Danger, the men come to the house of the woman in order that she rescue them, such as in Sisera's coming to Yael's tent (Judg 4:17–18). In this story there remains only a faint echo of the sexual component: it appears that in the oral tradition Yael allows, and even encourages, Sisera to come to her, and precisely at the moment when he expects a bounty of pleasure, he meets his end. A clearer echo of this tradition can be seen in the poetic formulation of the same tradition: "between her legs he sank, he fell, he lay down,/Between her legs he sank, he fell;/Where he sank, there he fell dead" (Judg 5:27). The expression "between her legs" reappears in the Bible only once more, where its meaning is clear: "her placenta which comes out from between her legs" (Deut 28:57) (cf. further, Zakovitch, 1981). In the story of David's spies the two also come to the house of the woman from Bahurim only in order to hide. In this story there is no longer any trace of sexuality: the two do not even enter the house but go down (by themselves) into the well in the courtyard, and the woman only covers them up. Moreover, the narrator hints at the woman's decency by mentioning that she is married: ". . . and they came to a man's house in Bahurim" (v. 18), and the man—the woman rescuer's husband—is not mentioned again! It is worthwhile noting that a modern expression of the narrative type of the rescuing woman—the beginning of Günther Grass' *The Tin Drum*—can serve to provide clear evidence of the organic relevance of the sexual element! Only our spies, then, come to a house where one might enjoy oneself, but know no pleasure. They lie down to sleep but they can't even manage to doze off since Rahab was forced to hurry and rescue them. The need to rescue them is thus the direct result of their coming to Rahab's house, and not the reason for their going there. Such a state of affairs may indeed raise a smile on our lips.

The utter failure the spies brought upon themselves is clear from the next passage: "And it was told the king of Jericho, saying, 'Behold, men have come here tonight from the children of Israel to search out the country'" (v. 2). The spies, then, arrived at Jericho at night—that is, toward evening (and see below, v. 3)—and on that same night their identity, as well as their whereabouts, is made known to the king. True, the news of Samson's presence in Gaza quickly takes wing; compare the similar formulation: "When the Gazites were told,[2] 'Samson has come here'"(v. 2). But Samson did not arrive in Gaza "stealthily," in order to spy, and it would not make much difference if he were noticed or not. Such a hero as Samson need not worry for his own skin, as the continuation of the story bears out. Not so the two spies, the knowledge of whose arrival at Rahab's house signals the utter failure of their mission. It is true that another pair of spies were also seen by the enemy in the course of their mission—Jonathan and Ahimaaz, David's spies—but this took place during the execution of the mission itself: "But a lad saw them, and told Absalom" (2 Sam 17:18)—part of the risk of every secret agent—and not during a quest for bodily pleasures of one sort or another.

In the king's speaking to Rahab through his emissaries, there is an apparent harshness of style and duplicity: "Bring out the men who have come to you, who have entered your house . . ." (v. 3). And to be sure, among the ancient translations there is one that latched on to the first words: "who have come to you" (Peshitta), and one that forgoes the first words and renders the last: "who have entered your house" (Septuagint). But the redundancy is only apparent: the king simply points out the two possibilities at hand, whether they came for sex "who have come to you," or in order to sleep "who have entered your house." In Abarbanel's words: "that the king's emissaries said to her 'bring out the men who came, whether they came to sleep with you, or whether they came for food and lodging. For whatever reason they came, bring them out.' This is what 'who came to you' means—to sleep with her, and 'who came to your house' means to ask for lodging. And the words 'for they have come to search out all the country' come to say: 'do not think that they came to sleep with you or to ask for lodging, as they said, for then you would consider how you could hand them over to us . . . But bring out the men, for they have come in fact to spy out the entire

---

[2]Only in Targum Jonathan: אתחוה, and in the Septuagint according to the Alexandrian text ἀπηγγέλη, and in the Vatican text ἀνηγγέλη. The word can apparently be explained as haplography under the influence of the neighboring לאמר.

land. So do not have compassion on them, for they seek your life, and that of all the people of the city.'"

The two possibilities raised by the king of Jericho will play an important role in the immediate continuation of the story, in Rahab's answer (v. 4), which will choose from among them that which serves her purpose. Abarbanel noted another important detail: the king of Jericho judges the spies according to their mission and not according to their coming to the harlot's house, which reveals a total abandoning of their duty. Even though they do not behave as spies and show themselves unworthy of the name, the king seeks to accuse them of espionage. All this serves to certify them as first-class bunglers.

Rahab's response is double-ended, both in deed and in speech: "Then the woman took the two men and hid them."[3] Further on we will discuss the relation between "hid them" in this verse, and the account of Rahab's covering the spies with flax on the roof in verse 6. We indicate here that their concealment apparently preceded the words of the king's messengers to Rahab: Rahab was aware of the danger—one way or another—before she was asked to hand over the spies. In Kimhi's words: "She had already taken them and hidden them before the king's messengers entered her house, when she sensed that the king was aware of the matter." A similar action sequence is found in the story of the rescue of David's spies. Before the arrival of the king's messengers at the house of the woman from Bahurim, "a lad saw them, and told Absalom. But both of them went away quickly and came to a man's house in Bahurim, who had a well in his court; and they went down into it. Then the woman took and spread a covering over the well's mouth, and spread ground grain on it; and the thing was not known. And when Absalom's servants came to the woman at the house . . ." (2 Sam 17:18–20).

Hiding the spies before the arrival of the king's messengers may be intended to hint at Rahab's wisdom: perhaps behind the vague words "And it was told the king of Jericho" lies Rahab? Could it have been Rahab herself who informed the king in order to make the spies feel obligated to her, and to make them swear to spare her when Jericho is conquered? This hypothesis, which at first glance seems rather far-fetched, not only solves the problem of Rahab's motivation—what led her to hurry and hide the spies—but also adds to the humor of the story. Very early on she appreciates the golden opportunity that has fallen to her, and all the characters—from the spies to the king— are pawns in this harlot's hands. She does, to be sure, take a great risk, but the potential reward—sparing her and her family's lives—

---

justifies it. According to this understanding of Rahab's motivations, it is not compassion she shows toward the spies but cruelty: just when they ask to lie down to sleep, Rahab places them in danger. And should someone question why the narrator would want to hide from the readers the fact that Rahab was the source who "graciously offered" the information to the king, the answer is that when we do not know everything, we gain the impression that it was Rahab's good-heartedness that led her to rescue the two bunglers. Only when she asks that her deed be repaid do we begin to doubt her good-heartedness and honesty.[4] The narrator's avoidance of saying that the spies were hidden before the arrival of the king's police is also intended to enhance the reader's suspense. The reader knows that the spies lay down (to sleep) before the king's men arrive, but until one hears of their hiding, one has no idea whether they will be captured or not.

The words "Then the woman took the two men and hid them" compel us to consider the relationship between the actions of the male spies and the actions of the female harlot, Rahab. It is Rahab who initiates and acts, while the two secret agents are simply objects to be manipulated by her, for better or for worse. This is in complete contradiction to the behavior of men in parallel stories of this type. Samson has need of the harlot only when he goes in unto her; the harlot is a sex object for Samson and she plays no part in rescuing him. In the spy-story of Jonathan and Ahimaaz in Bahurim, the spies are also not without initiative, like our two lads. Ahimaaz and Jonathan find themselves a place to take shelter from Absalom: "And they came to a man's house in Bahurim, who had a well in his court; and they went down into it" (2 Sam 17:18). Moreover, the words "and hid them" bring about a clear association to a sub-type of the "woman who rescues a man" story—the "woman who hides a child" (e.g., Exod 2:2–3; 2 Kgs 6:29; 11:1–3). Here, the child is necessarily passive, as in the story of the hiding of the infant Moses by his mother: "she hid him three months" (Exod 2:2). Note the use of the same verb, צ.פ.ן.

Rahab again reveals great wisdom in her words to the king's messengers: "Yes, the men came to me." Thus, of the two possibilities indicated by the king, Rahab chooses the first, and for good reason: if

---

[4]If we are correct in asserting that Rahab was the one who informed the king of the spies' coming to her, then our chapter is quite similar to the story of the Gibeonites (chapter 9). In chapter 9 the Gibeonites, like Rahab, are fearful of the Israelites and their God (vv. 9–10; cf. 2:9–10) and, by a ploy, get the Israelites to swear that no harm will befall them (v. 15). Note that just as Joshua erred in sending out spies at all—an action which shows that his faith in God is less than absolute—so the Israelites err in not inquiring of the Lord in the Gibeonite affair, but trust them: "Then the men of Israel took some of their provisions; but they did not ask counsel of the Lord" (v. 14).

the men had come to her in order to lie with her, it would be reasonable to assume that they had finished their business and gone on their way, just as Samson does when he leaves the city at midnight (Judg 16:3). If, on the other hand, they had come only in order to seek a place of lodging, they would surely still be in her house. In Abarbanel's words: ". . . [Rahab says] 'It is true that the men came here but not in order to ask for lodgings but to lie with me.' And this is true— 'the men did come to me,' and she said this in order that they would think that they had already left, for after laying with her they would have gone." Note that Rahab's cleverness again puts the spies in a ridiculous light. First the king relates to them as real spies; now Rahab relates to them as real men. And just as they were unworthy of the first, so are they unworthy of the second! Rahab's answer to the king also concerns what she was not asked: "but I did not know where they were from." Again, in Abarbanel's words: "[Inquiring into a client's past] is not compatible with the habits of harlotry"—a harlot does not demand a passport or an identity card from those who come to enjoy her services.

In v. 5, in her desire to create an impression of loyal patriotism, Rahab hurries, apparently in order to send the pursuers on the trail of the two spies: "And it happened as the gate was being shut, when it was dark, that the men went out." Unlike Samson, who does not consider such trivial matters as the closing of the gate and, accordingly, is forced to take the gate with him when he leaves, the spies, according to Rahab, apparently hasten to leave the city before the gate is closed. While the woman of Bahurim appears to send the pursuers in the direction of Jonathan's and Ahimaaz's flight—"They have gone over the water brook" (2 Sam 17:20)—Rahab practically does one thing, and its exact opposite. On the one hand she says: "Where the men went I do not know" (the second half of her former words: "but I did not know where they were from"), and on the other, she seems to encourage the pursuers to go and catch them, by expressing her assurance that they will indeed catch them if they do not tarry (and thus spare her from both danger and embarrassment): "Pursue them quickly, for you may overtake them." While Rahab works her charms on the pursuers, the spies sit in their hiding-place, thoroughly grateful to their rescuer.

Verse 6 returns us to them: "But she had brought them up to the roof and hidden them with the stalks of flax, which she had laid in order on the roof." This verse seems simply to be an expansion of what is stated in v. 4: "and she hid them," with the narrator's words here in the past perfect tense. In Kimhi's words: "It was already stated above 'and she hid them,' and now it is said 'and she had hidden them,' in order to explain how she concealed them." Before, the narrator did not want to unduly disturb the action of the royal guards' search and, accordingly, sufficed himself with a brief remark that reveals a little and conceals twice as much. The simple use of the words "and she hid them," above, also leaves us in suspense as to where the spies were hidden at the last moment and whether their hiding was sufficiently secure in order to throw the guards off their trail. Now that the pursuers have already gone on their way, and while they are yet "pounding the pavement" in vain pursuit of our spies, the time is ripe to reveal where the spies were left—far from the harlot's bed, on the roof. Moreover, we are now able to enjoy bemusedly, without any suspense, the picture of the two would-be spies lying together, covered with the stalks of flax (cf. Feliks:279). Here, again, all the action is attributed to Rahab, and the spies are but pawns in her hands. This contrasts with David's spies, who choose their own place of hiding while the woman helps them only when she spreads "a covering over the well's mouth, and spread ground grain on it" (2 Sam 17:19). Even the deceived Sisera is more active than the spies in the course of his being hidden: he tells Yael what to do and asks her to stand at the opening of the tent, putting his pursuers off the trail should they inquire of him (Judg 4:20).

In v. 7 we leave the pursued on Rahab's roof and have a look at the pursuers. Rahab, the only woman in the story and one whose experience with men is far from negligible, succeeds, then, to fool everyone with no difficulty. The pursuers act according to her advice and go out on the chase: "So the men pursued them." And note that here Rahab plays the role of the simple-minded harlot, not knowing who the Israelites are, or where they are at that moment. The pursuers, on the other hand, understand that they must search for the spies on the way to the fords of the Jordan, which lead eastward, where the Israelites are encamped. In the continuation of the story she will send the escapees, who will be of the utmost importance as the guarantee that her life will be spared, in the opposite direction (v. 16). The pursuers do not forget to return to close the city-gate after they leave: "And after the pursuers had gone out, they shut the gate." This act also might bring a smile to our faces: by closing the gates, they intend to protect the city from the danger without while, in fact, they secure the safety of the spies within .

Whereas in v. 2 it is said of the spies that "they lodged there," v. 8 says: "Before they lay down . . ." By the recurrence of the verb .ש.כ.ב we see that the two spies, seeking a restful night in Jericho, only meet with frustration. Before they are even able to lie down, they are hastened to the roof to hide. And if they thought to catch some sleep under the stalks of flax, then "she came up to them on the roof" and prevents even this. Moreover, the verb .ל.ו.ן, "and lodged" (v. 2), was the last verb that attributed any action to the spies themselves. From there until v. 8, up to the words "Before they lay down," they are entirely passive. From here on we cannot expect any significant action on their part.

Now in vv. 9–13, the spies will be forced to listen to Rahab's long speech, a speech that in all its seriousness underscores an intentionally ironic gap between the Canaanite's fear of the Israelites, on the one hand, and, on the other, the spies themselves, hardly representatives of these fear-inspiring people. The two frightened spies, whose lives were saved a moment before by this prostitute, now hear from her: "I knew that the Lord has given you the land, that the terror of you has fallen on us, and that all the inhabitants of the land are faint-hearted because of you." Rahab, who had previously played the unknowing fool ("but I did not know where they were from . . . where the men went I do not know" [vv. 4–5]), is now clearly aware of that which is worthwhile for her to know: "I knew that the Lord has given you the land . . ." She speaks here in the past tense, as if the matter were already accomplished (cf. Deut 3:18; 12:1; and below, v. 24), whereas the next two parts of the verse are in the present tense and reflect the result of Rahab's recognition of God's powers. Her fear is not inspired by the bungling spies but, rather, exists despite them. Even the pathetic state of the spies cannot detract from her belief in God's ability to accomplish his plan, nor from her fear of the Israelites, his people. The expressions of Rahab's Godly fear recall the Song of the Sea (cf. already *Mekhita de-Rabbi Shimon bar Yohai,* "Bešallaḥ,"9), and refer to it in chiastic order, as is common in internal biblical quotations (cf. R. Weiss; Zeidel):

Exod 15:15–16	Josh 2:9

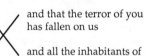

| All the inhabitants of Canaan will melt away | and that the terror of you has fallen on us |
| Terror and dread will fall on them | and all the inhabitants of Canaan have melted away |

While in Exodus the fear is of the Lord alone, Rahab's words express a fear of the Israelites as well. Nevertheless, we should not allow Rahab's words to mislead us for an instant. Her fear of the Israelites is the direct result of fear of God, as is clear from the next verse: "For we have heard how the Lord dried up the water of the Red Sea for you when you came out of Egypt" (v. 10; cf. Joshua's words at 4:23). Alongside the miraculous event of the crossing of the Red Sea, Rahab mentions, to be sure, an event in the mortal realm—the Israelites' victories: "And what you did to the two kings of the Amorites who were on the other side of the Jordan, Sihon and Og, whom you utterly destroyed" (v. 10). But here, too, it is not the heroics of our spies or even the military prowess of the Israelites that is a factor, but the power of the Lord: "And as soon as we heard these things"—repeats the beginning of the previous verse—"our hearts melted"—God, who dried up the Reed Sea, melted their hearts—"neither did there remain any more courage in anyone because of you (cf. Josh 5:1), for the Lord your God, He is God in heaven above and on earth beneath" (v. 11; cf. Deut 4:39). Rahab's words reveal that she, a small-time prostitute from Jericho, knows better than Joshua how great and powerful is Yahweh, the God of Israel. If Joshua had trusted in God's power as much as Rahab, he would not have needed to send out his bungling spies! Rahab's speech-making creates quite a striking picture. She speaks with confidence and ease, proclaiming her fear of the Israelites, yet all the while, in fact, the fate of the Israelites rests in her hands.

Rahab concludes by mentioning God's name because now she wants the spies to swear to her future safety: "Now therefore, I beg you, swear to me by the Lord, since I have shown you kindness, that you also will show kindness to my father's house" (v. 12). Rahab was and remains a harlot with a calculating mind, and her story is the only one from the type of the "woman rescuer" in which the heroine does what she does for gain's sake. Now it is clear to us why she saw fit to save the spies—and maybe even to put them in danger in the first place—and to betray her own countrymen. By cold calculation she realized that her people were already doomed and that by giving shelter to the spies she would save her own and her family's lives. She smoothly represents the matter as "a life for a life": "since I have shown you kindness, that you also will show kindness to my father's house,"—though, in fact, there is no real equality: she is not content that the "favor" be shown only to her, but asks that it also be applied to her entire family. The small-time harlot does indeed know how to calculate; one by one she enumerates all of her relatives: "and spare my father, my mother, my brothers, my sisters, and all that they have, and deliver our lives from death" (v. 13).

Now, at last, the spies open their mouths for the first time in the entire story (v. 14); but, as expected, their words reveal neither initiative nor originality. The passive spies agree to Rahab's request that they swear by God, and their speech is taken entirely from her own words. She concludes with the words "and deliver our lives from death," and they open with the words "our lives for yours."[5] In the continuation of their words, too, the spies borrow her words. She said, "I knew that the Lord has given you the land" (v. 9), and they say, "And it shall be, when the Lord has given us the land." Rahab

---

[5]For a characteristic formulation of the notion of *lex talionis* cf. Exod 21:23; Lev 24:18; Deut 19:21; and cf. further 1 Kgs 20:39, 42.

said, "you also will show kindness" (v. 12), and the spies say, "we
will deal kindly and truly with you."

After the spies give their word to Rahab, she again takes up the
reins: "Then she let them down by a rope through the window, for
her house was on the city wall; she dwelt on the wall" (v. 15).[6] Nothing can stop Rahab from fulfilling her plan to save herself and her
family; even the locked gate will not prevent her from sending the
spies away safely. Samson overcame the closed gate in his own way:
his great physical strength enabled him simply to take it with him
(Judg 16:3). Rahab uses her wits. This manner of escape again emphasizes the passivity of the spies. Like marionettes they are dependent
on Rahab's graces, their lives hanging in the balance every moment.
Of course, the spies promise to spare Rahab; but that time is yet to
come. In the meantime they are saved by her resourcefulness. Michal,
Saul's daughter, rescued David in the same way: "So Michal let
David down through a window" (1 Sam 19:12).[7] There, however, the
picture is balanced further on in the text when David becomes the
subject: "And he went and fled and escaped," a series of three verbs
emphasizing David's own initiative. Also, in the story of David's
spies the woman does not expect to benefit from her actions. When
the danger is past, the two come up out of the well on their own and
proceed on their way: "Now it came to pass, after they had departed,
that they came up out of the well and went . . ." (2 Sam 17:21).[8]

However, in our story the spies are so valuable to Rahab that she
leaves no detail to chance or to their initiative and supplies them with
specific instructions: "And she said to them, 'Get to the mountain,
lest the pursuers meet you. Hide there three days, until the pursuers
have returned. Afterward you may go your way'" (v. 16). Rahab
understands human nature better than the Israelite secret service
men. If they valued their lives they would do wisely to go in the
opposite direction. They should not hurry to return to the east bank
of the Jordan but go up to the mountain and wait three days until
their pursuers give up the search. Like our spies, Samson also goes
up to the mountain when he leaves Gaza; but this he does on his own
initiative, and not out of fear of his pursuers. As opposed to our

---

[6]The words "for her house was on the city wall; she dwelt on the wall" were
omitted from the text reflected in the LXX in order not to contradict chapter 6; cf.
above, n. 1.

[7]In the LXX of Josh 2:15 the rope is not mentioned, and it is possible that it was
omitted to assimilate it to the story of David and Michal. For the phenomenon of
literary assimilation, cf. Zakovitch, 1985b.

[8]Cf. the influence of this story-type on the story of Paul's escape from Damascus (Acts 9:23–25), and especially: "But his disciples took him by night and let
him down through the wall, lowering him in a basket" (v. 25). Cf. further 2 Cor
11:32–33.

heroes, Samson climbs the mountain only in order to aggravate the failure of his enemies and to taunt them: "And he took hold of the doors of the gate of the city and the two gateposts, pulled them up, bar and all, put them on his shoulders, and carried them to the top of the hill that faces Hebron" (Judg 16:3). Verse 22 shows to what extent the spies take pains to heed the harlot's instructions to the letter: "Then they departed and went to the mountain, and stayed there three days until the pursuers went back."

The continuation of the story presents a new puzzle. After the spies have been lowered and stand outside the wall in the dark, their dangerous predicament demands absolute silence. Yet it is then that they choose to speak with Rahab. On this problem Abarbanel comments: "Why did they not say all this while they were on the roof, when she adjured them, but after she let them down through the window with a rope they exchange words with her and make conditions, while the place and the time were not so appropriate for conversation." Josephus, also sensing this problem, solves it off-handedly in his paraphrase of the passage. He places the entire (abbreviated) conversation prior to the lowering of the spies: "So having made this compact, they departed, letting themselves down the wall by a rope" (*Antiquities*, Book v, i.2). Note that Josephus represents the spies in a more honorable light and attributes action to them! But Josephus' solution conflicts with the biblical story,[9] in which the spies later direct Rahab to: "Bind this line of scarlet cord in the window through which you let us down" (v. 18). Abarbanel solves the difficulty in a different way: "Any vow or oath a man makes while under bondage or duress will not be fulfilled, and for this reason, after they left her house and were already outside the city, they said to her 'do not think that what we vowed to you when we were hidden on the roof is valid. It is not, for we are absolved from our oath since we were coerced there. But now, while we can freely choose, we will make the vow anew . . .'" This solution serves nicely to answer another, more serious question also noted by Abarbanel: "Why did they repeat here things that they already said on the roof?" It fails, however, to solve his initial question, concerning the dangerous timing of the spies' speech-making. And, indeed, it seems to me that vv. 17–21 are a secondary addition to the story, intended to integrate into the story the matter of the scarlet cord. The cord, tied in the window, is meant to insure that Rahab and her house will not be harmed, a sign similar to the mark of blood on the Israelites' doorposts in Egypt, the blood indicating that God is to pass over the Israelites' houses and prevent the destroying angel

---

[9]Accordingly, one should be restrained from being as overly-sophisticated as Martin (1969).

from harming them (Exod 12:21–22). Note that just as the Israelites are directed to remain inside their houses in Exod 12:22, so do the spies direct Rahab to remain indoors (v. 19; cf. Zakovitch, 1968:28–30). Rahab's immediate binding of the scarlet cord in the window, however, is rather surprising, since it might arouse the curiosity of the people of Jericho: "and they departed, and she bound the scarlet cord in the window" (v. 21). Again Abarbanel points to the difficulty in interpretation: "Why did Rahab tie the scarlet cord in the window immediately, for this was unnecessary until God would give them the land?" His clever answer: "She in her cunning did not wait to tie the scarlet cord at the time of battle, when it was needed, because then the people of the city would notice the scarlet cord and kill her." The Septuagint translator (or his Hebrew *Vorlage*) already sensed this difficulty, and omitted the concluding words of the addition. The possibility that these words are an addition on top of an addition, whose purpose is to connect together all the loose ends of the re-worked story, should not be ignored. A proof that vv. 17–21 is an addition can be found in v. 22, as it is the direct continuation of v. 16; in v. 16 the spies are commanded by Rahab to go to the mountain and hide there, and in v. 22 they do as she says.

In any case, since vv. 17–21 are a part of the final version of the story, we must examine the extent to which these verses fit the rather sorry image of Joshua's two agents. The fact that the spies suddenly open their mouths when they are out of Rahab's house, outside the wall, is certainly not out of character. It is fitting that these two secret agents, who are ignorant of the ABC's of spying and transgress the elementary rules of caution when they enter the city, would also fla-grantly disregard the same rules when they leave, shouting at the top of their lungs while being pursued. The capture of the spies is pre-vented only by the fact that their pursuers swallowed Rahab's bait and went enthusiastically in the direction of the fords of the Jordan. This line of the narrative, then, adds a further humorous element to the story. The sudden talkativeness of the spies also fits in well with the grin-raising picture: only now, when they are again under their own control and outside the city, do they summon the courage (rather unwisely) to make their voices heard. Perhaps the fact that they speak at such length in the dark, and raise their voices (if they did not do so Rahab could not have heard them) is meant to help them encourage themselves, to restore their self-confidence—like children who sing or whistle when they find themselves alone on a dark street.

The spies wish to leave Rahab with the impression that they are men of decisiveness, as if they are now setting the conditions. There is, in fact, no great news in the speech, but in their version the charac-ter of the situation undergoes a change; this time the words of the

spies have a more legalistic bearing than the oath they swore while
on the roof. They add conditions to the agreement: "So it shall be that
whoever goes outside the doors of your house into the street, his
blood shall be on his own head, and we will be guiltless. And whoever is with you in the house, his blood shall be on our head if a hand
is laid on him" (v. 19). Nevertheless, the confusing style of the spies'
speech should be noticed. The beginning of their speech, for example,
"We will be blameless of this oath of yours which you have made us
swear" (v. 17), is disconnected and incomprehensible until we reach
the end of the speech, the closing of the inclusio in v. 20: "And if you
tell this business of ours, then we will be free from your oath which
you made us swear" (note the repetition of what was already stated
at the beginning of v. 14).

Rahab, aware of the danger of loud chatter in the dark, keeps her
words to a minimum, disregarding the additional fact that their
words introduce nothing new and, therefore, do not require any detailed answer. Accordingly, Rahab gets rid of them curtly:
"According to your words, so be it" (v. 21; cf. Gen 44:10).

With v. 22 we are back to the original layer of the story, and the
spies now return to Joshua and give him their report: "and they told
him all that had befallen them" (v. 23). The narrator spares us the
retelling of their adventure—indeed, what could they possibly have
to report at all? That straightaway on their coming to Jericho they
went to the house of a prostitute? That before managing to do anything their presence in the city became known and that the harlot was
the one who hid them and saved them from their pursuers? That
right after their pursuers went off in the wrong direction the harlot
lowered them down with a rope through her window and told them
to hide out for three days on the mountain? Such a report would
amount only to a ludicrous account of the spies' failure. The narrator
understates the report, as if out of consideration toward the two
ne'er-do-wells, but also because at this precise moment their shame-
ful failure becomes a great success: "And they said to Joshua, 'Truly
the Lord has delivered all the land into our hands, for indeed all the
inhabitants of the country are fainthearted because of us'" (v. 24). The
spies were in one single house and met one single woman—Rahab—
but they are nevertheless capable of giving a general report. Note the
two-fold occurrence of the word "all" in this verse; the spies have
learned a lesson from Rahab. It was she who said to them "the Lord
has given you the land," and also "all the inhabitants of the land are
fainthearted because of you" (v. 9).

The spies are none other than a mouthpiece for Rahab, a Canaanite prostitute from whom Joshua learns his lesson: that God had
given the land into the hands of Israel. Joshua, who not only made a
superfluous action by sending the spies but even chose a pair of spies

unworthy of the mission, in the end gains an encouraging report. This report is even better than that of Moses' spies, who were properly briefed for their mission but nevertheless gave an evil report of the land and incited the people to rebellion (Num 13:26–33; cf. also Deut 1:28). It is precisely Joshua and Caleb's words in this story, not based on any military logic but on faith, that reflect the biblical belief: "If the Lord delights in us, then he will bring us into this land and give it to us. . . . Only do not rebel against the Lord, nor fear the people of the land, for they are our bread; their protection has departed from them, and the Lord is with us. Do not fear them" (14:8–9). To be sure, a good report from military intelligence is no guarantee of success in the Bible; Joshua's spies to Ai give a properly strategic report, according to their understanding (Josh 7:3), but they do not know that God's will, and his righteous judgment, do not necessarily align with military concerns (v. 4). Only when an optimistic report contains theological elements is the optimism justified, such as in the spy-story of the Danites: "Arise, let us go up against them, for we have seen the land, and indeed it is very good. . . . For God has given it into your hands. . ." (Judg 18:9–10).

Our biblical story, which is none other than a parody of spy stories, comes, then, to a happy ending. God, whose will in any event is to deliver his people, will indeed deliver them. Joshua has finally learned what he should have known from the start, though in an unpleasant way. Rahab and her family, whose lives have been spared, will serve as a universal reminder of this lesson.

James Bond, the archetype of the perfect secret agent in the last decade, is, of course, the absolute opposite of Joshua's two spies. Agent "007" is the symbol of the ultimate spy, whose every adventure— even the most difficult—ends in success. The urgency of his mission does not, as we know, deter him from relations with women; in many cases, it is the woman herself who brings him closer to his goal, even though she may originally have belonged to the enemy camp. No, Bond has no need—God forbid—for prostitutes. The greatest female patriots, not to mention the most beautiful, cannot resist his masculine charms. This is far from being the case with the Israelite secret agents. Our two spies, whose anonymity alone spares them from disgrace, do not even manage to succeed with a small-time harlot. It is precisely the ambivalent wording of the sexual element (hinted at here and there in narratives belonging to the story-type "woman who rescues a man") that presents the spies in such a ludicrous light. Their chain of errors—gross blunders that any novice spy would avoid—almost results in the complete failure of their mission; but it is turned into a stupendous success when, at last, they echo Rahab's words in Joshua's ears.

The author's use of humor well serves the story's theological intent while his manipulation of two well-known story-types, borrowed from the world of folklore, assures the story's success. The story-type of the "woman who rescues a man" is fundamentally a woman's story-type, whereas the "spy" story-type is a man's. In our story roles are exchanged and dominance is given to the woman who robs the male spies of their very identity. Even the sexual element, a fundamental part of the "woman who rescues a man" story-type, is toned down not only in order to fit the conservative character of the Bible but also in order to scorn these military men who do not live up to their more manly prototypes.

In spite of its comic-book characters—a clever, calculating Canaanite harlot and two bungling spies—this story was selected to stand at the beginning of the account of God's saving acts towards Israel, in order that every Israelite might know that there is no wisdom and no heroism apart from God alone. A Yiddish proverb says, "If God wills, even a broom can shoot"; if God wills, even two incompetent buffoons can provide the right message for a leader who sought to act according to military protocol, instead of realizing from the start that success will solely be the result of God's strength and mercy. Our story, then, is an important link in the series of stories which seek to show that "vain is the help of man" (Ps 60:13 = 108:13)—the intelligence branch included—and that "The Lord will fight for you, and you shall hold your peace" (Exod 14:14).

WORKS CONSULTED

Ehrlich, A. B.
　　1908　*Randglossen zur hebräischen Bibel* I. Leipzig: Hinrichs.

Feliks, Y.
　　1968　*Plant World of the Bible.* Ramat-Gan: Masada [Hebrew].

Grass, Günther
　　1962　*Die Blechtrommel.* Frankfurt am Main: Fischer.

Lüthi, M.
　　1976　*Once Upon a Time.* Trans. L. Chadcayne and P. Gottwald. Bloomington and London: F. Ungar.

Malamat, A.
　　1970　"The Danite Migration and the Pan-Israelite Exodus-Conquest: A Biblical Narrative Pattern." *Biblica* 51:1–16.

1979 "Conquest of Canaan: Israelite Conduct of War According to the Biblical Tradition." *Revue Internationale d'Historie Militaire* 42:25–52.

Martin, W. J.
1969 "'Dischronologized' Narrative in the Old Testament." *VTSupp* 17:179–86.

Naveh, J.
1982 *Early History of the Alphabet.* Jerusalem-Leiden: Magnes.

Nielsen, F.
1954 *Oral Tradition.* London: SCM.

Silver, D.
1962 "Some Thoughts on Language in the Light of the 'Plain Meaning' of the Bible Text" *Leshonnenu* 26:3–6 [Hebrew].

Soggin, A.
1972 *Joshua.* OTL. London: SCM .

Stone, Kay
1978 "Things Walt Disney Never Told Us." Pp.42–50 in *Women and Folklore.* Ed. C. R. Farrer. Austin: University of Texas Press.

Talmon, S.
1958 "Divergences in Calendar Reckoning in Ephraim and Judah." *VT* 8:48–74.

Weiss, Meir
1984 *The Bible from Within.* Jerusalem: Magnes.

Weiss, R.
1962 "On Chiasmus in the Bible." *Beth Mikra* 7:46–51 [Hebrew].

Zakovitch, Yair
1979 *The Pattern of the Numerical Sequence Three-Four in the Bible.* Jerusalem: Makor [Hebrew].

1981 "Siseras Tod." *ZAW* 93:364–74.

1982 *The Life of Samson.* Jerusalem: Magnes [Hebrew].

1985a *Every High Official Has a Higher One Set Over Him—A Literary Analysis of 2 Kings 5.* Tel-Aviv: Am-Oved [Hebrew].

1985b "Assimilation in Biblical Narratives." Pp. 175–96 in *Empirical Models for the Development of the Hebrew Bible.* Ed. J. H. Tigay. Philadelphia: University of Pennsylvania Press.

1986 "Rationalization of Miracle Motifs in Biblical Narrative." Pp. 27–34 in *Proceedings of the Ninth World Congress of Jewish Studies,* vol. 1. Jerusalem: Magnes [Hebrew].

Zeidel, M.
1957 "Parallels between the Book of Isaiah and the Book of Psalms." *Sinai* 19:149–76; 229–40; 272–80, 333–55 [Hebrew].

8. A RESPONSE TO ZAKOVITCH'S "SUCCESSFUL FAILURE OF ISRAELITE INTELLIGENCE"
Frank Moore Cross

Let me begin by applauding Professor Zakovitch's search for humor in the Hebrew Bible. I believe there is a rich vein to be mined. As some of you know, I am particularly fond of the Book of Jonah, a parody of the prophet, which is at once profound and hilarious. The narrative opens with God's command to Jonah to go to Nineveh. Told to go to Nineveh, the metropolis located as far east as known civilization reached, he set out for Tarshish, the farthest known outpost in the west. Farthest east/farthest west: already the broad humor of the book is signaled in the first verse. When he finally goes to Nineveh, after an excessively spectacular ride back to the mainland, he preached a sermon to the Assyrians, "Yet forty days and Nineveh will be overthrown." What is the upshot of Jonah's sermon? Jonah was one hundred percent successful. From the king down, all the Ninevites repented. Even the cattle wore sackcloth and fasted. All converted: the nation reputed to be the most evil and violent on the face of the earth. Wonderful. Conversion with one sermon. Marvelous. Who can read this with innocent credulity? How can the most pious reader miss the author's delight? Jonah succeeded in a fashion which brings even Moses' stock down. After all, Moses could not persuade Pharaoh with ten plagues.

While I have found great pleasure in reading Zakovitch's paper, I have taken my task to be adversarial. My praise will be brief. My critiqué will be less brief. As noted above, I have no objection to one's finding humor in biblical stories. On the contrary, I welcome the break with German scholarship. Further it seems a plausible enterprise to look for irony or burlesque in a tale of military intelligence (a term some have labeled an oxymoron). Yet I must confess that Zakovitch finds a bit more humor in the story of Rahab and the spies than I do. Our disagreements are based in large part on rather different presuppositions with which we approach the biblical account: in methods of textual criticism with which we establish the text, in the date of the sources of the Pentateuch and the Deuteronomist, and finally in what I must describe as the dismaying fashion in which Zakovitch treats the story, sometimes as originating in an oral tale intolerant of historical evaluation, sometimes as a sober report of events, open to historical reconstruction or speculation.[1]

Zakovitch assigns the story of Rahab to the genre (or story type) "spy stories." I suppose so. Or it may be described as an escape story, escape thanks to a woman of doubtful virtue, a stock theme of spy thrillers and westerns. But I believe he has overlooked an additional and indeed the salient element in the present form of the tale, a motif beloved in Israelite tales and which gives the story of Rahab its particularity. It is a tale which recounts how a foreigner gives a *credo*, acknowledging Israel's god as the true god. The story of Balaam comes to mind. Brought to curse Israel, Balaam blessed Israel and sang praises to Israel's god. There is the story of Naaman the Aramaean general who converted, and the Phoenician sailors on the Tarshish ship in Jonah who profess faith in Jonah's god. So too Darius the Mede in Daniel 6, and Nebuchadnezzar himself in Daniel 2, testify "of a truth it is that your God is the God of gods and the Lord of kings" (2:47). The story form is early and late, from the premonarchic oracles of Balaam to the court tales of the Book of Daniel. In my opinion it is in this stream that the tale of Rahab fits most comfortably. The climax of the story is Rahab's recitation of the *magnalia dei*. This motif, the foreigner's *credo*, is not a common one in the ancient Near East where the easy tolerance of a sophisticated polytheism held sway. But this type of story finds a natural matrix in Israel's religious culture with its sovereign, jealous god.

Turning to details in the text of Zakovitch's paper we note that he argues that Joshua chose "inexperienced spies taken from the ranks of the common people" and that Joshua "may simply have grabbed the first two lads who happened to be near his tent—sheer irresponsibility." What is his evidence? The text says that Joshua sent "two men, spies." Simply. Zakovitch arrives at his view by comparing the Priestly account of Moses' selection of spies with the Deuteronomist's account of Moses' sending out of spies. (How this applies to Joshua sending out spies is unclear, but never mind.) In the Priestly source, Moses at God's command chooses "princes," *nĕśîʾîm*, whose names are recorded. In the Deuteronomic source in Deuteronomy 1, spies, not named, are chosen by Moses with no mention of the divine command. Zakovitch argues that the Deuteronomistic account is a "second edition" of the Priestly account,

---

[1]My critique is based on Zakovitch's written version, which I received before the conference, and quotes that version. I note that the version presented orally exhibited some revisions of which I have not been able to take account.

omitting the divine command, and the names and aristocratic origin of the spies, in view of the "disgraceful" end of the mission. Therefore the Joshua account, omitting names and aristocratic genealogies, as well as divine direction, points to the "sloppiness" of Joshua's selection of spies. I find this argumentation unconvincing. First of all, the Deuteronomistic account of Moses selecting spies is not a "second edition." In my view, Deuteronomy 1, belonging to the Josianic edition of the Deuteronomistic history (Dtr1) is in fact earlier than the P account in Numbers 13. Certainly this is the consensus of scholarship. But even if we suppose that the P traditions are late Pre-Exilic, which in principle I think is possible, against most non-Israeli scholars, still the earliest account of the spies is certainly the JE story of the twelve spies, and this account, like that of Deuteronomy 1, singles out only Caleb for specific mention. In short, Zakovitch's "close reading" is in fact uncritical reading. He attempts to bolster his argument for Joshua's spies being "inexperienced spies taken from the ranks of the common people," "grabbed" by Joshua, by referring to Joshua 6 when the spies are called *nĕ'ārîm*, which he translates "young lads." But surely Zakovitch knows that men-at-arms may be called *ná'ar*, even noble young men at the head of an army, namely Absalom in revolt against his father David, not to mention Jonathan's armor bearer. And on seals *ná'ar* always refers to a high ranking official, which we generally translate as "steward" or "agent."

In short I find no basis in the text for supposing Joshua to be "sloppy," or the spies to be inexperienced simpletons. The storyteller is laconic. In one verse he relates Joshua's sending of spies, instructing them, their entrance into Jericho, and Rahab's house, and their lying down therein. Detail at this point of the story is not in the teller's interest. Rahab is the focus of the story. He brings us (and the spies) to her with minimal background, a familiar oral technique in traditional narrative in Israel. The mode of selection of the spies, the detail of instruction of the spies, the spies' journey to Jericho, their activities on the way, how they got into the city, what they saw in the city, how they learned the whereabouts of Rahab's house and found their way to it, and their motivation in seeking it out—none of this is told to us by the storyteller. Evidently it is irrelevant; and in the story proper, no one has a name, not the spies, not the king of Jericho, only Rahab the harlot.

In my view, therefore, Zakovitch's basic contention, that the spies are inexperienced youngsters drawn from the common folk, is baseless. Nothing is said of the spies' incompetence or naïveté, nothing is said of their lowly birth. The text says "men, spies." Zakovitch's exposition strikes me as midrash, not "close reading."

Is there humor in v. 1? Spies are sent on a mission in preparation for holy war, *ḥērem,* and end up in a harlot's house. One may argue that there is here a juxtaposition of incompatibles, an element of ironic incongruity which often is at the heart of humor. Escape of a chaste Western hero with the aid of a prostitute is a familiar modern folk motif—and amusing. I am not sure that in ancient Israelite society, as opposed to modern Jewish or Christian or Marxist society, the incongruity was as obvious. In any case, is it incongruous that spies end up in a brothel, or rather in a prostitute's house? What better place to hide in a strange and alien city? Where else is anonymity better protected, admission without question easier in a very small city? In any case, Gary Cooper, John Wayne, 007, and Clint Eastwood regularly have used houses of ill repute as safe houses. And they never play effeminate, stupid, blundering, or inexperienced men in their roles. Brothels belong to spies' turf, even spies on a holy mission. And yet it is an amusing, titillating motif, and perennially popular.

In v. 2 Zakovitch translates *way-yiškĕbû šāmmāh,* "and they lodged there," and states that the spies went straight to bed. (Whose bed, one may ask.) He, if I read him correctly, does not credit them with chaste intentions, but with ineptitude. But the expression means "and they lay there." It is ambiguous and I think designedly so. Here I am puzzled by Zakovitch's exposition. Early in the paper he notes that the root *škb,* "to lie down," is used in v. 2. But later he states that the verb *lwn* is used in v. 2, "to lodge." Not in the Massoretic Text. What is interesting, however, is that the *Vorlage* of the Old Greek had *way-yālînû,* "and they lodged" (*kai katelusai ekei*), in its text, an obvious substitute for *way-yiškĕbû,* "and they lay down," no doubt to dissolve the ambiguity. So Zakovitch is not without support. But surely the Greek reading is secondary.

Several other text-critical issues, ignored by Zakovitch, are crucial for understanding the text. One example will illustrate. In the Massoretic Text is the statement that the spies entered the city at night (v. 2); but the Old Greek omits "at night" in v. 2, and states rather that the spies came to Rahab "at night" (v. 3). Where does this "at night" belong, in v. 2 or v. 3? Zakovitch's exposition depends on the Massoretic reading being original. I think the Old Greek reading is clearly original. But his failure to discuss the textual problem is disingenuous. The Massoretic Text supports his argument; the Old Greek reading dissolves it.[2]

Zakovitch proposes a hypothesis that Rahab herself is the informer who tips off the king as to the spies' presence in her house. He

---

[2]Another example of failure to establish a critical text is found in v. 3: *hbʾym ʾlyk ʾšr bʾw lbytk.* The Old Greek reads *hbʾym lbytk,* the Syriac *hbʾym ʾlyk.* MT is a textbook case of conflation of variant readings. But Zakovitch reads into this passage the subtle exegesis devised by late Rabbinic ingenuity.

admits that his suggestion is implausible at first glance. I should add that it is gratuitous and implausible at close examination. It is illegitimate surely to engage in such speculations about a folktale. If we were dealing with a historical report, perhaps such a question could be raised. But we have a tale, originally a folktale. The text simply says that the king was told about the spies, by someone unspecified. There the matter must rest.

Let us turn to another passage in the paper: "By cold calculation she [Rahab] realized that her people were already doomed and that by giving shelter to the spies she will gain her own and her family's lives. She smoothly (sic!) represents the matter as 'a life for a life,' since I have shown you kindness (*ḥesed*) that you will also show kindness to my father's house, though in fact there is no real equality; she is not content that the 'favor' be shown only to her, but asks that it also be applied to her entire family. And the small-time harlot does indeed know how to calculate: one by one she enumerates all her relatives."

I do not like a number of his expressions here. "Cold calculation": where is this in the text? "Small-time harlot": how does Zakovitch know that Rahab is not a big-time harlot, a famous harlot?[3] "No real equality": apparently Zakovitch thinks it equitable for her one female life to be spared for two male lives. Not equitable in my arithmetic. But this is to miss the point. The background of their sworn oaths of fealty must be understood in the context of early Israelite society. Tribal society was structured by obligations of kinship, and what may be called fictive kinship or kinship-in-law, kinship extended by adoption, oath, and covenant (see Cross). Oaths of fealty binding two parties properly apply to the *bêt ʾāb*, the lineage, and Rahab makes it clear that her covenant with the spies is to follow this normal pattern. A parallel example laid out in the Bible may be found in the fealty oaths exchanged by David and Jonathan. Jonathan reminds David in 1 Sam 20:14–20: ". . . If I die, never break faith (*ḥesed*) with my house (lineage). And when Yahweh exterminates all the enemies of David from the face of the earth, the name (lineage) of Jonathan must never be allowed by the family of David to die out among you, or Yahweh will make you answer for it."[4] Rahab makes no unusual demand, no cold calculation. Her request fits the conventions of the time.

---

[3] I have little doubt that Rahab of Jericho was a famous courtesan of whom Israelite tradition preserves only a fragment, comparable to Balaam traditions in the Bible and in Transjordan (Deir ʿAllā).

[4] The text is that of the New American Bible, prepared by P. W. Skehan and the writer. It is based partly on the Old Greek, partly on conjecture. Cf. McCarter (337). David's endeavor to carry out his obligation to Jonathan is recorded in 2 Sam 9:1–7; 21:7.

I think Zakovitch does Rahab—as presented in the tale—grave injustice.[5] She is remembered as hiding the spies of Israel in a vulnerable moment, and as giving crucial intelligence at a critical time in Israelite history. She is recorded as being ingrafted in Israel along with her family "unto this day." Above all, if I read the tale rightly, she is remembered as a righteous gentile who recognized the God of Israel: "For the Lord your God, he is God in heaven above, and in earth beneath." That she saved her *bêt ʾāb*, her lineage, through entering covenant with the spies, and otherwise shows cleverness, should not be held against her, given her place in society. The suggestion of Zakovitch that she informed on the spies to the king I hold to be simple calumny. Rahab may not have been a harlot become saint, but she was a woman remembered for good in Israel, a credit to her profession![6]

WORKS CONSULTED

Cross, Frank M.
    forth-   "Kinship and Covenant." In *From Epic to Canon*.
    coming

McCarter, P. Kyle, Jr.
    1980   *1 Samuel*. AB. Garden City, NY: Doubleday.

---

[5]Zakovitch might have strengthened his case by arguing that Josh 2:9b–11 is a Deuteronomistic *credo*, secondarily intruded into an older tale, the Deuteronomistic addition altering an older story in which Rahab was treated less favorably. Literary critics have long recognized Deuteronomistic style and language in these verses. But Zakovitch engages in no literary criticism (at this point). He takes the text here as it is, without levels of tradition, and tries still to make his case.

[6]In later Jewish tradition Rahab receives much better treatment than at the hands of Zakovitch. Rabbinic tradition has her marrying Joshua and having as her progeny a string of prophets including Jeremiah (*b* Meg 14b). In a Jewish genealogy of David utilized by Matt (1:5,6), Rahab is named wife of Salmon and great grandmother of David (called to my attention by Brita and Krister Stendahl). The author of Hebrews lists her among the heroes of faith (11:31), and James declares that she was "justified by works" (2:25).

B. BIBLICAL PROVERBS AND RIDDLES

The essays on proverbs and riddles offer a range of approaches to questions of aesthetics and style, structure and genre, cultural and literary context. Cross-cultural interests in non-biblical proverbs and riddles and a methodology informed by semiotics inform a number of the papers.

The scholarly debate between Galit Hasan-Rokem and Roland Murphy mirrors contrasts between the essays on narrative by Zakovitch and Cross. In analyzing Gen 2:18 and 2:24, Hasan-Rokem emphasizes the importance of the sayings' literary context, suggesting that these sayings influence the meanings of surrounding narrative texts. As for Robert Alter, repetitions of key words are important markers and makers of meaning and message. Hasan-Rokem also discusses the close relationship between riddles and proverbs, genres on a sliding continuum of wisdom performance. Hasan-Rokem's approach, which is influenced by semiotics, socio-linguistics, and Rabbinic-style associative exegesis, allows her to understand Gen 2:18 and 2:24 in the context of essential human concerns with moral choice and mortality; her contextual literary analysis thus opens into a study of Israelite cosmology.

Professor Murphy is uncomfortable with the open sweep of Professor Hasan-Rokem's work. Most essentially, he doubts that the sayings at 2:18 and 2:24 are proverbs at all, the former for him being a saying employed as a "motivation clause," the latter an etiology employed as a narrator's aside. He suggests that these sayings "sound" like proverbs because we as members of the on-going tradition have come to hear them or treat them as such. This most basic difference in opinion raises questions about the limitations of and effects of our response to texts as readers and interpreters, and about the very nature of tradition. What can we or do we bring to a text? What happens when a genre of literature that originates in an oral and immediate situation of performance becomes an integral part of a written narrative?

An awareness of the dynamics of performance situations is important to Camp and Fontaine's insightful and multivocalic reading of Samson's riddle in Judges 14. Like Hasan-Rokem, Camp and Fontaine explore the riddle in its literary context, employing a method that is influenced by structuralist semiotics. They also ask what can be learned if for the sake of study we treat the narrative scene of riddles as an actual performance situation. Edgar Slotkin reminds us of the universal connection between riddles and weddings (a point raised also by Hasan-Rokem in her study of proverbs and the first conjugal relationship) and of the sociological significance of these links. Slotkin makes the deceptively simple but critically important observation that riddles are rarely solvable unless one already knows the answer—and knowing the answer means that one shares a communication culture with the riddler. This suggestion may turn the lengthy scholarly debate about whether or not Samson's riddle was solvable into a red herring. More importantly, it shows how the riddle becomes another way by which the narrator of the Samson tale comments on the lack of communication and community between Samson and the Philistines.

9. AND GOD CREATED THE PROVERB . . . INTER-GENERIC AND INTER-TEXTUAL ASPECTS OF BIBLICAL PAREMIOLOGY—OR THE LONGEST WAY TO THE SHORTEST TEXT*

Galit Hasan-Rokem

ABSTRACT

The article analyzes Gen 2:18 and 2:24 as instances of proverbs in narrative. On the basis of former research on the poetics of proverb usage in folk narratives, the proverbs are shown to be inserted at the point when the most extreme experience of ambivalence appears in the text. The proverbs are discussed as hermeneutic keys for the narrative. The dialectic relations of the proverbs and other traditional materials such as myth, custom, and ritual in the wider cultural context, create a model for ethical decision in the specific framework of the biblical narrative of creation.

*To Freddie Rokem, for sharing so much temporary resolution of deep contradictions. Discourses such as this paper are often the result of numerous encounters and discussions. As one can guess, knowing the presently analyzed text, my discussions and encounters regarding it have been too numerous to report or even to remember. I shall therefore limit the expression of my gratitude to the following: Dimitry Segal for teaching me oppositions and distinctions; David Shulman for pointing out equilibrium and its limits; Tamar Alexander for the common search for the right words for the right things; Paul and Rita Mendes-Flohr for their wisdom of time and of space. Tilly Eshel for trust and trustworthiness. Also: Guy Stroumsa and a postgraduate class, which he, D. Shulman, and I taught and were taught by, together. My students Dina Stein, Daliya Moskovitch and Ronit Yehuda, as well as Judith and Morton Narrowe, for many rewarding discussions. I thank my colleagues in the "Enigma Group" at the Institute for Advanced Studies at the Hebrew University of Jerusalem (1988–89), who devoted a session to this paper and shared their insights with me. I am also especially indebted to the comments and criticism by Moshe Greenberg, Michael Fishbane, and Uriel Simon at the same session.

אַ משל איז, לחבדיל, תּורה
A proverb is, with all allowances made, God's word.
(Yiddish Proverb)

The presence of proverbs in biblical literature has been appreciated by generations of readers and scholars. The proverbs of the Bible are introduced either in specific paremiographic collections such as Proverbs or Ecclesiastes, or embedded in other literary genres, such as narrative, prophetic discourse, and poetry (for a careful critical discussion, see Fontaine:2–27).

The compilation of specific paremiographic collections displays a distinct self-consciousness on the part of the creative sub-culture which is known under the name of "Wisdom," which produced genres known as "Wisdom Literature" in the Bible and through several subsequent centuries (e.g., in Ben-Sira, Mishna *Abot*, Gospel of St. Thomas). Such collections highlight the explicit function of proverbs and communicate a professed generic consciousness.[1] Moreover, it is reasonable to assume that at least some biblical proverbs had their original context in a living folklore tradition.

For the sake of this discussion we shall use a definition of the proverb based on our former research. A proverb is a short text summarizing an idea formulated in such a way that it implies collective experience and wisdom, and is applicable to numerous situations. This concise definition should be amplified with additional descriptive characteristics such as the use of poetic language and a multiple distribution of the text in a given culture (Hasan-Rokem, 1982:11).

Thus biblical proverbs are found in multiple distribution and use poetic language, e.g., "The fathers have eaten sour grapes, and the children's teeth are set on edge" (Jer 32:29; Ezek 18:2). They are introduced by formulae which indicate explicitly proverbial use: "Hence the proverb, 'Is Saul also among the prophets'" (1 Sam 12:12); "One wrong begets another, as the old saying goes" (1 Sam 24:13). Parallels from extra-biblical corpora underscore the proverbiality of others: "Dealers in proverbs will say of you, 'like mother, like daughter'" (Ezek 16:44; repeated in the TB *Ketubot* 63a).

It has also been shown that proverbs are polysemic and thus open for changes in different contexts (Krikmann; Hasan-Rokem, 1982). Semantic variation may be observed even in one specific context depending on the general line of interpretation consulted or the choice of the point of view by the interpreter (Hasan-Rokem, 1982; Alexander and Hasan-Rokem, 1988).

---

[1]That Wisdom literature is dispersed in biblical books which are not specifically Wisdom literature is widely accepted in research (e.g., Talmon).

The context in which they are introduced, thus provides the proverbs with their meaning. Accordingly, in order to grasp the full meaning of a proverb it is necessary to explicate relevant meanings in its given context. Proverbs also creatively influence the surrounding text. They project into the text paradigmatic meaning that transcends the immediate context, both in content as well as aesthetically. They may very well, therefore, serve as a hermeneutic key to those texts in which they are embedded. In the present paper we shall discuss two proverbs used in the Book of Genesis: "It is not good for the man to be alone" (Gen 2:18) and "That is why man leaves his father and mother and is united to his wife and the two become one flesh" (Gen 2:24).

In the narrative sequence of Genesis 1–2, language is employed in an interesting double function. On the one hand, it serves as the language of creation in God's performative utterances (J. L. Austin:233–52), in which words are immediately transformed into action: "God said, let there be light, and there was light" (Gen 1:3). On the other hand, this effective "showing" (Booth) of the acts of creation in Genesis 1 is followed by the "telling" version of Genesis 2: "When the Lord God made earth and heaven . . ." The presentation of Genesis 1 is superseded by the perspectivally and chronologically distanced account of Genesis 2, in which the act of creation is filtered through the knowledge about later events: "There was [yet] neither shrub nor plant . . ." (Gen 2:5). Instead of the first direct presentation, the second one reflects a telescopic look.

It is this double function of language which leads us to argue that Genesis 1–11, in addition to being a story about the emergence of the world from the abyss of nothingness, more specifically also could be seen as the myth of the birth of language. The conclusion of the sequence in the story of the Tower of Babel reinforces this line of interpretation. We shall not be able to demonstrate here the implications of this thesis throughout eleven chapters. This thesis will, however, inform our analysis of the proverb in the more immediate context of Genesis 1–2. Let us add that the nexus in this myth between the creation of the world and the creation of language is not totally unexpected in a culture in which communication by speech and text is the sole most important incarnation of divine revelation.[2]

Myth is here understood as a narrative discourse in which the human experience of the world, limited by time, space and death, is given a comprehensive and sacred framework. The negative aspects of limitation, separation and loss, are brought out by the staging of a

---

[2]John 1:1, "In the beginning there was the word" or "When all the things began, the Word already was" is clearly based on tradition in which the role of language in creation has been underscored. Cf. Gabel & Wheeler (201).

dialogical communication between God and human in a distant, irretrievable past. The positive aspects of divine creation—its endowment with meaning and the assignment of a central position to human beings—are given by the very interplay of the two modes of language, divine and human. Myth may therefore be characterized as a narrative in which human limitation and power originate in a primeval concrete, dialogical communication with God.

In the aforementioned proverbs—"It is not good . . ." (Gen 2:18) and "That is why . . ." (Gen 2:24)—the narrative context is one in which the language used in relating the emergence of language is self-referential.

The discourse of Genesis 1 shows God in his creative capacity (Jason). The creation by word, "God said, Let there be light" (Gen 1:3), is followed by an instant report of the perception of the effect, "And there was light." In the Hebrew *yĕhî ʾôr wayhî ʾôr* the *waw* consecutive serves as a minimal dividing line in the chiasm between the word of creation (in future tense) and its effect in the world (in past tense).

This binary structure reveals, however, the fundamental duality of the world in which God and human coexist, by embodying the duality of act and perception. Subsequently action and effect are followed by evaluations, subjective in form—"And God saw that the light was good" (Gen 1:4)—in which the opposition is temporarily balanced.

Due to the authority of God underlying the evaluations and the character of the phenomena evaluated, these statements gain the status of a general appreciation of the world. A harmonious interplay initially prevailed between the components of the world. The harmony is expressed in generative relations, as those between earth and the growth which it produces (Gen 1:11), water and the creatures with which it teems (v. 20), and in the hierarchical relations as man who is created "to rule the fish in the sea . . ." (v. 26). We need not elaborate here on how these generative and hierarchical relations themselves gain tense momentum and later unfold in crises and catastrophes.

The hierarchical and generative interrelationships in creation that prevail in Genesis 1, however, give way to new kinds of relationship, namely, transformative ones. This parallels the change of the language of creation from Genesis 1 to Genesis 2. The word for earth *ʾădāmâ*, is first mentioned in the verse most closely preceding the creation of Adam, *wĕʾet kol remeś hāʾădāmâ* (all the reptiles of the earth; Gen 1:25). But it is only in Genesis 2 that the use of one creation—earth-*ʾădāmâ*—as raw material for another creation—Adam—is introduced. The verbs ע.ש.ה. and ב.ר.א. of the creation *ex nihilo* are replaced by the verb י.צ.ר., consistently with the spelling out of the metaphor of the supreme potter. Thus the introduction of the verb ב.נ.ה., used for the creation of woman, follows that same logic. (For the use of the same verb root for creation of human beings and buildings in Akkadian, see Cassuto:88.) Man was created from clay, so are bricks; woman was created from man, as walls are built from bricks.

Proper naming, which is also introduced in Genesis 2, is transformative as well. It imparts the meaning of becoming an individual within a genus, which presupposes the appearance of more than one of a kind. A proper name is first applied to the specifically located "garden in Eden away to the east" (Gen 2:8), thereupon to the four rivers that issued from it. The principle of naming thus occurs in the text first in the anonymous voice of the later narrator. Man first uses it for the animals, apparently classifying rather than really naming, and later for his partner, twice. (For a narratological interpretation of the naming of the woman, see Rosenberg.) It is also in the context of the creation of woman that Adam is turned from a generic term to a proper name, by introducing the generic alternative איש.

The evaluation "good" (Gen 1:4 ff.) and the blessing "be fruitful" (Gen 1:28) are converted, we might even say contorted, to a prescriptive statement in which promise, prohibition, and threat interact to form the message: "You may eat from every tree in the garden, but not from the tree of knowledge of good and evil; for on the day that you eat it, you will certainly die" (Gen 2:16–17). Language is zoomed into human perspective, and chronology evolves as the language of explanation and motivation. Moral choice supersedes the simple functional relations of generation and hierarchy from Genesis 1.

In my research I have observed that proverbs are mostly, one could almost venture to say, always, used in contexts or co-texts charged with tension and unresolved contradiction. The binary structure of proverbs on one hand lays bare the opposition in the context. On the other hand it creates equilibrium, at least on the verbal and conceptual level, by employing devices of balance such as rhythm, rhyme, and the logical structure of the conditional sentence.

In the present case the harmonious creation of Genesis 1 (in my mind not really disturbed even by the creation of the great sea-monsters—Gen 1:21—quite the contrary) is shaken by the tone and the message of Genesis 2:16–17, and especially by the final threat "You will certainly die." This sentence (*double-entendre*) has an expressedly ambivalent relationship to "be fruitful and increase" (Gen 1:28). At face-value it negates and contradicts the preceding blessing, but reading backwards, it also necessarily presupposes the existence of that blessing. It is therefore in the context of this tense ambivalence that the following should be read: "Then the Lord God said, 'It is not good for the man to be alone. I will provide a partner for him'" (Gen 2:18). This introduces a new form and mode of language usage into the text. In the context of the myth of the creation of language, God has created a proverb—the proverb. As the creation of man is seen in terms of the creation of the genus, the creation of a proverb, in this context, creates the genre. Like the creation of the first human being, full-fledged in all capacities (notwithstanding a different opinion in Midrash *Genesis Rabba* 24:2), the first proverb also carries all the characteristics and potentials of the genre, linguistic, structural, contextual, and functional, as outlined in the above mentioned definition.[3]

That "It is not good for man to be alone" is a proverb today is not difficult to prove. Its usages in Hebrew (as well as other languages, e.g., August Strindberg's relatively unknown play "The Black Glove"), range from the verbal art of folk narrative to poetic devices in journalism, and lyrics in popular music. It is paralleled by texts from classical sources (e.g., the Aramaic או חברותא או מיתותא ("Company or death"), TB *Ta'anit* 23a) ascribed to Job or Honi the Circle-Maker; or in oral tradition, as the Yiddish אליין זאל זיין א שטיין ("Alone should [only] be a stone"). It is also echoed by antonyms such as the Swedish "Ensam är stark" ("Alone is strong"). The point I want to stress is that already in its original context it is used as a proverb, with all the characteristics of that specific poetical and rhetorical strategy when applied to a narrative.

The binary opposition which appears to be the core of the central message of the proverb is that between loneliness and companionship. The unsuccessful experiment to find a partner among the animals, however, narrows the problematic. It is not good for man to be alone, is here referring to human companionship, specifically of the opposite sex.

Let us turn back to the moment of crisis, so to speak, that elicited the use of the proverb. The most concrete verbal expression of the crisis is ". . . you will certainly die:" The linguistic form מות תמות,the so-called infinitive-absolute, imparts a special emphasis. And as the analysis of the language of Genesis 1 showed, God's words in the future tense are heavily charged with performative energy. God's word turns into action. The threat has created the verbal form, indeed the linguistic determination, that sentences man to his imminent death.

The movement from the threat to the proverb is therefore an example of one opposition being transformed into another, in the way which Claude Lévi-Strauss has shown to be the basic operation of the language of myths. And as Lévi-Strauss points out, the contradiction that is the source of all myths is that all that is born must die (Lévi-Strauss, 1969).

---

[3]The Midrash text in *Gen Rab* 22:17 describes the birth of a proverb in the context of the murder of Abel by Cain. "Since then it is said: Do not bestow good on the evil [one] and evil will not reach you."

In order to clarify further how temporary equilibrium is created by the proverb, let us briefly analyze its text and structure. The poetic language is literal and direct, without any figurative language, metaphor etc. in the proverb itself. Assonance may be discerned: *lōʾ ṭôb hĕyôt hāʾādām lĕbaddô*. Except for the word *ʾādām*, which is given, in all the others the stressed vowel is an *o*. The paronomasia of the first and the last part of the proverb *lōʾ ṭôb/lĕbaddô* creates a slightly chiastic effect, stressing Adam's central position in the proverb. The formula *lōʾ ṭôb* echoes clearly the co-text. (For the formulaic function of *ṭôb* in proverbs of Eccl 7, see Gordis:66 with 367, n. 14.) The word *ṭôb* has multiple relations with the context. It is a negative of the evaluation of creation in Genesis 1:*kî ṭôb* (Gen 1:7 and passim). It therefore not only echoes the total evaluation of all creation—*ṭôb mĕʾōd*, "very good" (Gen 1:31)—which has been understood to evaluate specifically the creation of the first human couple (Cassuto:83), but the whole series of evaluations in Genesis 1. It also refers directly to the language of the preceding threat—עץ הדעת טוב ורע "The tree of the knowledge of good and evil." From both these former uses of *ṭôb* follows the fact that the *lōʾ ṭôb* of the proverb cannot be a human category by the terms of the narrative. It is exactly the distinction between good and evil from which God has prevented man from having access. God's demand of man is therefore absolute, unmotivated obedience. But the proverb also dialectically serves the need for a logical motivation in human categories for the act of creating woman.

The midrash text in *Gen Rab* 8:9 shows that the Palestinian Amoraim also recognized the possibility that man's being alone may have been *"not good"* for God rather than for man:

> Rabbi Hoshaya said . . . when God had created first man, the serving angels mistook him [for God] and wanted to utter "Qadosh" [Holy] in front of him. What did the Holy One Blessed be He do? He "put the man into a trance" and everybody could see that he was human, as it is written "Have no more to do with man, for what is he worth? He is no more than the breath in his nostrils" (Isa 2:22).

By using the word-motif *ṭôb* (cf. Buber's analysis of the biblical "Leitwort") the proverb mediates the transition from the transcendent, primordial God (*kî ṭôb*) to the immanent God of moral order (*daʿat ṭôb wārāʿ*). It is God who tries to postpone the man's knowledge of good and evil, but it is also He who imposes on the man conditions in which this knowledge is necessary for him. Such contradictory conditions in a narrative are a suitable background for the insertion of a proverb in folk narrative texts or in social interaction.

The story of the creation of woman is prepared and motivated by the use of a proverb. It is also concluded with the use of a proverb.

The second proverb describes the social consequences of the event, in the verse following the naming of woman by man (ʾîš-ʾiššâ) and the realization that they are of the same bones and flesh: "That is why a man leaves his father and his mother and is united to his wife, and the two become one flesh" (Gen 2:24). This verse, of course, follows the former one, "Now this at last bone of my bones," etc. (Gen 2:23) and is motivated by it. Whereas v. 23 is the first statement directly made by Adam, the status of v. 24 is ambiguous. It could represent the words of Adam, although it is hard to assume that he could have possessed the information contained in it. It seems more logical to interpret it as the words of a narrator (or God, or even the first spoken reaction of the woman).

The two proverbs framing the creation of woman in 2:18 ("It is not good . . .") and 2:24 ("Therefore shall a man . . .") are in a complex relationship. "Alone" of the first proverb is an almost clinically precise description of Adam's situation. More lonely than he, no man has ever been, and will never be. All the other uses of the proverb will in some sense be figurative or removed in intensity and degree, compared to this original instance in which Adam is really the only, lonely, human being in the whole world. The other proverb, "That is why man leaves . . . ," on the contrary, refers to a situation in which Adam could never have been. He is in folklore frequently referred to as the one who had no father and no mother: *"Zwei Kinder ohne Vater und Mutter"* (Adam und Eva) (Röhrich:168). From a structural semantic point of view, the second proverb is yet another transformational phase of the opposition of the myth. The opposition between life and death, which was temporarily resolved in the uniting of the sexes, emerges anew, transformed into an opposition between generations, between breeder and offspring. The chain of archetypal human conditions leads from "be fruitful" (Gen 1:28) through "It is not good" (2:18), to "that is why man leaves . . ." (2:24) and finally, the concluding proverb in the series, a proverb which we shall discuss elsewhere at length, "Dust you are, to dust you shall return" (3:20). (Rosenberg [14] makes the interesting observation that as the first mentioning of death was followed by the creation of woman, and her naming, this second one is followed by a renaming, a symbolical rebirth of the woman.)

The proverb in Gen 2:24 may also be read as a reply or a comment on Gen 2:18. They create one coherent argument: "It is not good for man to be alone" (2:18)—"That is why a man leaves his father and mother and is united to his wife, and the two become one flesh" (2:24). In this seemingly paradoxical statement the opposition between the sexes is resolved or mediated and gives way for the op-

position between parents and children, which in modern terms may
be termed an oedipal conflict.[4]
The conflation of these two texts allows us to recognize an enigmatic formula: one becomes two become one. Or in outspoken riddle
language: what is it that is first one, then two, and then one again
(and actually then separate two again in 2:25 "And they were both
. . ." [cf. also Alter:31], and on the intergeneric relations of proverbs
and riddles Hasan-Rokem, 1974; Pagis:38, 60).
The presence of an enigma in the context of myth is not surprising. Myth is in and of itself the ultimate literary expression of the
enigma of existence, creation, and life and death. This may well be
the reason for the fact that Adam and Eve are often the subject of
riddles in European folk tradition. Among the riddles are some simple and short ones, such as the above-mentioned *"Zwei Kinder ohne
Vater und Mutter* [Adam and Eve]" and *"Wer ist gestorben und nicht ge-
boren* [Adam]" (Röhrich:168). Some are more complex in both form
and content, such as the following:

Ich bin gestorben und nicht geboren	I have died and was not born.
Ich heiratete meinen Vater	I married my father
als ich einen Tag alt war.	when I was one day old.
Und eine Mutter habe icht nicht [Eva]	And I had no mother [Eve].
(Röhrich:168).	

Even without quoting the last text, the association to the riddle of
the Sphinx in the Oedipus myth comes to mind. Besides the numero-
logical transformations in both riddles, the connection between riddle
and myth is also a balancing act on the dangerous borderline between
legitimate eroticism and dangerous incest.[5] We may also compare the
following passage from the Rig-Veda: "One-foot surpasses two-foot;
and two-foot leaves three-foot behind. Four-foot comes at the call of
two-foot, watching over his head and serving him" (Rig-Veda 10,
117–9) [1-sun; 2-human; 3-old man with cane; 4-dog (O'Flaherty:69–
70)].
The relationship of the proverbs in Genesis 2 to the riddle form,
may have yet another implication or key. In his book on proverbs in
ancient Israel, Thompson (132) suggests that the basic parallel form of
the biblical adage and *māšāl* may be understood as derived from an
ancient custom of riddle games. Riddling constitutes a section of

---

[4]Popular proverbs do refer to similar experiences; e.g., the Judeo-Kurdish:
"Mother is bother, sister is trouble, [but to] a wife [one says]: Come [I will carry
you] on [my] back, I will hold you to the end of (all) the world" (Sabar:222, no.
36).

[5]The enigmatic nature of sexuality is expressed in another example of the biblical proverb tradition: "Three things there are which are too wonderful for me . . .
and the way of a man with a girl" (Prov 30:19).

wedding rituals in several cultures (Noy; Pagis:62, 66). It appears explicitly in the only biblical wedding described in detail, i.e., Samson's (Zakovitch:103–17) and by implication in another famous relationship, i.e., Solomon's with the Queen of Sheba (Noy; Zakovitch:103). The creation of woman in Genesis 2 has an archetypal bearing upon the tying of marriage bonds in later Hebrew culture. From ancient times down to our own era, the Jewish marriage ceremony has included a blessing in which the bridal couple is compared to the first couple in the Garden of Eden.

Though I do not feel obliged or qualified to express an opinion on the exact method applied in the composition of the text of Genesis 1–2, my reading is based on a view, confirmed by biblical scholars too numerous to mention here, that it is an amalgamation of several layers, units, genres. Chapter 2, especially, reveals a consistent use of folk literary materials (Cassuto:55), proverbs, as we have shown, not the least. If Adam and Eve's nuptial alliance may be seen as the first, mythical wedding ceremony, the possibility of the incorporation of traditional text elements from ancient wedding customs, such as riddles, should not be dismissed.[6]

That the ambiguous nature of the marital status could be expressed in proverb form is known elsewhere in ancient West Asian literature (Kramer:156; esp. Lambert). That the text of Genesis 2 was initially associated with a different *Sitz im Leben* from the creation story, has already been assumed by Westermann (1974) in his monumental compendium of exegetical traditions and analytical study. Westermann even assumed that such a functional context may have been rooted in a rite of passage. But whereas he curiously enough offers only birth and puberty-rites (Westermann:267) as such possible contexts of use, it seems to us that both with regard to the specific context of the tale and the possible interpretation of the two verses as a riddling frame for the creation of woman, the most suitable such context would be a wedding.

In conclusion, we may reformulate the above discussion of the thesis, that there is a nuanced dialectic between a proverb and its context. In the Genesis narrative proverbs are employed to refer to concrete human experience as it has taken form in the folkloristic framework of custom and verbal tradition. The philosophical issues raised in the narrative resonate through the proverbs. Thus the proverb is inserted at the point when the most extreme experience of

---

[6]I have here concentrated on questions of meaning and composition, rather than the possible generative relationship between proverb and tale, i.e. which one preceded the other. It might therefore be interesting to refer to such findings as the following: ". . . proverbs represent the beginning of tribal wisdom and . . . they were current before myths and tales originated" (M. Austin, as summarized in Mieder).

ambivalence appears in the text. The proverb constitutes a model for ethical decision and illustrates the human effort to accommodate two seemingly clashing principles, morality and success. They provide counsel about the possibility to be both good and wise at the same time, which is a central vision of all biblical wisdom literature. In the specific context of the narrative plot of Genesis 2, the proverb, represents an adequate verbal strategy to cope with the intense ambivalence engendered by the threat of mortality.

This analysis also provides a perspective on the dialectical emergence of language within the context of the creation story. Thus it is implied that the Creator creates language and by virtue of language also creates the world. Whence follows the creation of linguistic and literary forms, such as the proverb: And God created the proverb.

WORKS CONSULTED

Alexander, Tamar, and Galit Hasan-Rokem
  1988   "Games of Identity—The Proverb Repertoire of a Sephardic Woman." *Proverbium* 5:1–14.

Alter, Robert
  1981   *The Art of Biblical Narrative.* New York: Basic Books.

Austin, J. L.
  1970   *Philosophical Papers.* Oxford: Clarendon.

Austin, Mary
  1933   "Sayings." *Virginia Quarterly Review* 9:574–77.

Booth, Wayne C.
  1961   *The Rhetoric of Fiction.* Chicago: University of Chicago Press.

Buber, Mordechai Martin
  1964   *The Way of the Bible.* Jerusalem: The Bialik Institute [Hebrew].

Cassuto, Moshe David
  1965   *Genesis.* Jerusalem: Magnes [Hebrew].

Dundes, Alan
1983   "Couvade in Genesis." *Folklore Research Center Studies* 7:35–53.

Fontaine, Carol R.
1982   *Traditional Sayings in the Old Testament.* Sheffield: JSOT.

Gabel, John B., and Charles B. Wheeler
1986   *The Bible as Literature—Introduction.* New York and Oxford: Oxford University Press.

Gordis, Robert
1955   *Koheleth—the Man and his World.* New York: Jewish Theological Seminary of America.

Gordon, E. I.
1960   "A New Look at the Wisdom of Sumer and Akkad." *BiOr* 17:122–52.

Gunkel, Hermann
1910   *Genesis.* Göttingen Handkommentar zum Alten Testament. Göttingen: Vandenhoek and Ruprecht.

Hasan-Rokem, Galit
1974   "Riddle and Proverb: The Relationships Exemplified by an Aramaic Proverb." *Proverbium* 15:936–40.

1982   *Proverbs in Israeli Folk Narratives: A Structural Semantic Analysis.* Folklore Fellows Communications, No. 232. Helsinki: Finnish Academy of Sciences.

Jakobsen, Thorkild
1976   *The Treasures of Darkness—A History of Mesopotamian Religion.* New Haven and London: Yale University Press.

Jason, Heda
1977   *Ethnopoetry: Form, Content, Function.* Bonn: Linguistica Biblica.

Kogut, Simcha
1982   "'Lĕzōʾt yiqqārēʾ ʾiššâ . . .' (Gen 2:23— A Folk Etymology." *Tarbiz* 51:293–98 [Hebrew].

Kramer, Samuel Noah
1956   *From the Tablets of Sumer.* Indiana Hills, CO: Falcon Wings.

Krikmann, Arvo
1974   *On Denotative Indefiniteness of Proverbs.* Tallinn: Estonian Academy of Sciences.

Lambert, W. G.
1963   "Celibacy in the World's Oldest Proverbs." *BASOR* 169:63–64.

Lévi-Strauss, Claude
1969   *The Raw and the Cooked. Introduction to a Science of Mythology,* Vol. 1. New York and Evanston: Harper & Row.

Marcus, Ralph
1943   "The Tree of Life in Proverbs." *JBL* 62:117–20.

Mieder, Wolfgang
1982   *International Proverb Scholarship. An Annotated Bibliography.* New York and London: Garland.

Murphy, Roland E.
1969   "Form Criticism and Wisdom Literature." *CBQ* 31:475–83.

Noy, Dov
1963   "Riddles at the Wedding Party." *Maḥanayim* 83:64–71 [Hebrew].

O'Flaherty, Wendy Doniger
1981   *The Rig-Veda.* London: Penguin.

Pagis, Dan
1986   *A Secret Sealed: Hebrew Baroque Emblem Riddles from Italy and Holland.* Jerusalem: Magnes.

Rosenberg, Joel W.
1981   "The Garden Story Forward and Backward: The Non-narrative Dimension of Genesis 2–3." *Prooftexts* 1:1–27.

Röhrich, Lutz
1968   *Adam und Eva: Das erste Menschenpaar in Volkskunst und Volksdichtung.* Stuttgart: Müller und Schindler.

Sabar, Yona
  1978   "Multilingual Proverbs in the Neo-Aramaic Speech of the
          Jews. Proverbs of Zakho, Iraqi Kurdistan." *International
          Journal of Middle East Studies* 9:215–35.

Scott, R. B. Y.
  1965   *Proverbs, Ecclesiastes.* AB 18. Garden City, NY: Doubleday.

Segal, M. Z.
  1930   "On the Poetic Form of Meshalim Literature." *Tarbiz* 1:1–
          19.

Talmon, Shemaryahu
  1963   "'Wisdom' in the Book of Esther." *VT* 13:419–55.

Thompson, John M.
  1974   *The Form and Function of Proverbs in Ancient Israel.* The
          Hague: Mouton.

Wallace, Howard
  1985   *The Eden Narrative.* Atlanta, GA: Scholars.

Westermann, Claus
  1974   *Genesis,* part 1. Neukirchen-Vluyn: Neukirchener.

Zakovitch, Yair
  1982   *The Life of Samson—A Critical-Literary Analysis.* Jerusalem:
          Magnes [Hebrew].

10. PROVERBS IN GENESIS 2?

Roland Murphy

I want to express my appreciation for the stimulating paper of Professor Hasan-Rokem. It made me look at the first chapters of Genesis in a new way. The title caught me up: "And God Created the Proverb." I was immediately reminded of Archer Taylor's well-known comment: "The definition of a proverb is too difficult to repay the undertaking: and should we fortunately combine in a single definition all the essential elements and give each the proper emphasis, we should not even then have a touch-stone. An incommunicable quality tells us this sentence is proverbial and that one is not" (Taylor:3). We hardly know what a proverb is, according to Mr. Taylor, and now we are confronted with a claim that God created the proverb—whatever it is! But at least we have been provided with Hasan-Rokem's reasonable descriptive definition: "a short text summarizing an idea formulated in such a way that it implies collective experience and wisdom, and is applicable to numerous situations." She also allows for its poetic language, and multiple distribution of the text in a given culture (which means, I presume, that the saying had to gain some currency among the people from whom it originated).

She rightly calls attention to the context of a proverb, which affects its meaning—what the paremiologists call "proverb performance." I felt somewhat uneasy when she went on to say that there is also a reverse interaction: proverbs influence the surrounding narrative, projecting into the text a "paradigmatic meaning." They are even possibly a "hermeneutic key" for the texts in which they are found. These two concerns will govern most of the observations which I wish to make.

The two proverbs submitted for discussion bracket a fairly clear sense unit in Genesis 2: "It is not good for man (*hā'ādām*) to be alone" (2:18); and "That is why a man (*hā'îš*) leaves his father and mother and clings to his wife (*hā'iššâ*) and they become one flesh" (2:24). Within these two verses the Lord reconsiders his experiment with animals, and woman is created. Now, do these verses provide a hermeneutical key? What is their relationship with the narrative? I will propose an analysis of Genesis 2 upon which we might all agree in a general way, and this will put us in a better position to understand the "proverbs."

Beginning at Gen 2:4 we leave the majestic Priestly presentation of the days of creation and enter into a highly imaginative presentation of the creation of *hā'ādām*, the origin of the woman, and the eventual encounter with the serpent and the ensuing fate (chap. 3). The creation of the *'ādām* comes quickly to the point, and then God places the man in the Eden garden for his nourishment. (We shall skip here the details about the four rivers, and also the trees and the prohibition of 2:16–17, which really prepare for the denouement of chap. 3). This is the context for vv. 18–24, which are the topic of our paper: God has put a single man in the garden, to till it and thus nourish himself. Then follows the divine decision: "it is not good for man to be alone." Hasan-Rokem points out well the proverbial qualities of the saying (*lō' ṭôb*, alliteration, etc.). But she glides over the following words in the verse: "I will make a helper . . ." It is rather abrupt to single out of the divine decision a proverb which motivates the decision itself. This is possible, but not compelling. The danger is that the saying has become a proverb after its initial appearance in the Bible, which is the source of so many later proverbs in western culture. Indeed, one can find Gen 2:18 quoted as a source for current proverbs (at least in Germany) in the *Geflügelte Worte* of G. Buchmann (I,14). Of itself, the "saying" is merely a motivation clause that leads the divinity to further action.

The further action, of course, is the creation (*yṣr;* cf. v. 7) from the same earth (*hā'ădāmâ*) that the man (*hā'ādām*) came from. Interesting: no fish will be among the animals that God now brings to man. As Westermann (228) notes, the implication is that it is the man who is to decide what kind of "help" they provide, i.e., how he would name them (there *is* a difference between man and animals). In the Priestly narrative there is a clearer statement of human superiority: "rule the fish of the sea, the birds of the sky," etc. (Gen 1:28).

In Genesis 2 a certain cooperation is solicited from "man" to determine his relationship to animals. In short, they are not compatible, in that no *'ēzer* is found among the animals. "Man" can name them, but the Divinity does not find among them a real helper for the *'ādām* (Gen 2:20). Hence the Lord God takes action, and by means of the *tardēmâ* he "builds" the man's rib into a woman and presents her before the man. The man's cry of jubilation is ecstatic in feeling and in words:

This one at last is bone of my bones and flesh of my flesh;
This one shall be called woman, because from man was taken this one!

What a statement! First the jubilant cry of the man who is surprised by the presence of one like himself, and second, the play on the words *ʾîš/ʾiššâ*, which continues the theme of "naming" of v. 20. This is the climax of the naming process, and the man has found his true *ʿēzer*. Human solitude has been replaced by human community.

At this point the narrative about the creation of man/woman ends with the saying that has been proposed as a proverb. Two things should be distinguished: an etiological explanation, and a proverbial saying. Verse 24 is clearly an etiological saying: "That is why (*ʿal kēn*) a man leaves his father and mother and clings to his wife and they become one flesh." The initial phrase (*ʿal kēn*) betrays the etiological formula that is found elsewhere: "He (Isaac) named it (a well) Shiba; therefore (*ʿal kēn*) the name of the city is Beer-sheba to this day" (Gen 26:33). Or again, the limp of Jacob/Israel: "That is why (*ʿal kēn*) the children of Israel to this day do not eat the thigh muscle on the socket of the hip . . ." (Gen 32:33). These are etiological explanations. But an etiological explanation can also include a saying, as in the case of Nimrod the hunter, "That is why (*ʿal kēn*) it is said, a mighty hunter before God" (Gen 10:9). It is significant that in only one of these etiological explanations is reference made to a "saying," and hence to a dictum that must have achieved some currency as a proverb among the people. Here one might distinguish between statements that deserve to be proverbs, and those which are explicitly given a proverbial tag. As already indicated, Gen 2:18, "It is not good for a man . . . ," has in fact become a proverb for later communities that have found the Bible a treasure trove for apt comments on situations. In other words, Gen 2:18 has become a proverb, but there is no sign in the Bible itself that it was understood as such.

What about Gen 2:24? First of all, it strikes the reader as a comment of someone who is standing outside the text and making an observation about vv. 18–23. This comment expands the initial datum about the creation of man and woman as an harmonious whole by introducing a new element: marriage. W. H. Schmidt, quoted by Westermann (233), aptly remarks: "It is not possible for the couple which has just discovered that they belong together to leave father and mother." As in v. 23, where *ʾîš* was used for the word play with *ʾiššâ*, so *ʾîš* is used in v. 24, only loosely connected with the foregoing since it refers to (marital?) unity between the man and the woman. Hasan-Rokem has cleverly pointed out the full implication of the text as it stands: "an enigmatic formula: one becomes two become one." The comment of Alter (31–32), who recognizes here the possibility of "a proverbial statement adopted verbatim by the writer," is worth quoting:

The explanatory verse 24, which begins with "thus" (*ʿal kēn*), a fixed formula for introducing etiological assertions, might well have been part of a proverbial statement adopted verbatim by the writer, but even if this hypothesis is granted, what is remarkable is the artistry with which he weaves the etiological utterance into the texture of his own prose. The splendid image of desire fulfilled and, by extension, of the conjugal state—"they become one flesh"—is both a vivid glimpse of the act itself and a bold hyperbole . . . After being invoked as the timeless model of conjugal oneness, they are immediately seen as two . . . naked (*ʿarumim*), unashamed, they are about to be exposed to the most cunning (*ʿarum*) of the beasts of the field, who will give them shame.

A separate question raised in our speaker's address is the relationship of the proverb to the riddle form (*ḥîdâ*). Naturally she points to the well-known riddles of Samson and their use in connection with the wedding ceremony described in Judges 14. All this can be granted, but I suppose the issue here is whether or not the lines in Gen 2:18, 24 are riddling. It is not enough to describe the passage as "the first, mythical wedding ceremony" as a justification for riddling. It is not a marriage ceremony, and I do not think it is an error on Westermann's part to have omitted mentioning marriage ceremony as a possible life-setting for Gen 2:24, where the biblical setting is the creation of humanity. True, Westermann (196) mentions only the birth of a child or puberty rites, and he dismisses even these as "only conjectures."

The claim has also been made that the proverbs "serve as a hermeneutic key to those texts in which they are imbedded." Let us experiment with this. Does the proverb in Gen 2:18a ("not good . . .") add anything essential to the narrative? I think not. The narrative clearly contains the unsuccessful experiment, and also a twofold statement about a fitting helper. The man is not "alone"—he seems to be having a busy time with the cattle and beasts, etc. The real key to the experiment is the man's joyful declaration in v. 23, when he recognizes "bone of my bones" as (implicitly) the fitting helper. As for Gen 2:24, the other "proverb," it clearly goes beyond the intent of the narrative (which is creation of the man/woman/community), and it adds another dimension (but not the "key"): the power of love between a man and a woman, which brings them into a particular unity.

Another question comes to mind: is Gen 2:24 to be read as a "reply or a comment" on Gen 1:18? Hasan-Rokem comments, "In this seemingly paradoxical statement the opposition between the sexes is resolved or mediated and gives way for the opposition between parents and children . . ." If I understand the relationship between the two verses correctly, the paradox is that on the one hand "two become one flesh." Therefore we are back to the "aloneness" of the man, if two are one. On the other hand, this is not really a comment on v. 18, which dealt with the inadequacy of the aloneness of the first man.

In Gen 2:16–17, the verses immediately before the first "proverb" about the man being alone, we have the divine command about abstaining from eating of the tree under pain of death. Our speaker considers this moment of crisis to have "elicited the use of the proverb," or: "the moment of threat to the proverb is therefore an example of one opposition being transformed into another." This I failed to see, but perhaps it can be clarified. It may be that I am laboring too much under the impression that 2:16–17 are really verses that are a preparation for the events of the chapter 3, and thus have nothing intrinsically to do with the man being alone.

WORKS CONSULTED

Alter, Robert
 1981   *The Art of Biblical Narrative.* New York: Basic Books.

Buchmann, George
 1967   *Geflügelte Worte.* 3 vols. München: Deutsche Taschenbuch.

Taylor, Archer
 1962   *The Proverb and an Index to the Proverb.* Copenhagen and Hatboro, PA: Rosenkilde & Baggers.

Westermann, Claus
 1984   *Genesis 1–11. A Commentary.* Minneapolis: Augsburg.

11. THE WORDS OF THE WISE AND THEIR RIDDLES

Claudia V. Camp and
Carole R. Fontaine

ABSTRACT

This article is a study of Samson's riddle in Judges 14 using the tools of folkloristic performance analysis. We examine the story from three perspectives: the interaction situation, the riddle situation, and the context situation, with attention given to the differences in point of view between the narrator and the characters. We conclude that this riddle is a carefully crafted traditional form. It is expertly used as a piece of crafty diplomacy by Samson, who is, nonetheless, thwarted in his attempt at Philistine marriage, for Yahweh uses Samson's wit to achieve the overriding divine goal of "an occasion against the Philistines."

Introduction

For those interested in the study of the rhetorical use of wisdom forms, few methods of analysis are as helpful and welcome as those found in the literature on folklore performance in social contexts (Seitel, Dundes, Kirshenblatt-Gimblett). The genre to be discussed here, the riddle (Heb. חִידָה) was apparently a favorite with the sages of Israel, given the appearance of numerous "degenerated riddles" in the book of Proverbs (Crenshaw, 1974:242; cf. Prov 5:1–6,15–23; 6:16–19,23–24;16:15; 20:27; 23:27,29–35; 25:2–3; 27:20; 30:15–33). However, as with the sayings preserved in that book, we have no contexts of use reported for the riddling forms found in Proverbs. Unfortunately, those wishing to investigate "riddle performance" in ancient Israel do not find themselves overburdened with textual examples, for the only complete riddle text used in a social context is found in Judges 14 at the beginning of the cycle of stories about the adult Samson. In 1 Kings 10, we read that the Queen of Sheba came on a state visit to "test" Solomon with חִידוֹת, but no actual riddle text appears. Josephus tells us that Hiram and Solomon engaged in a riddling contest

(*Antiquities*, Book VIII, 5.3), but, again, no riddles appear in this notice. Taking these three incidents together, we may say that riddling in Israel, at least as reported, seems to be associated with diplomatic contexts where the representatives of two groups clash or take counsel together. Hence, the form is rightly placed within wisdom's stockpile of linguistic tools. Beyond this limited observation, if we want to ask what motivates a riddler to select that form for use in a social interaction rather than a proverb or example story (or, for that matter, straightforward speech), we must turn to a close consideration of the dynamics present in Judges 14.

The story of the riddle contest between Samson and the Philistines presents the reader with twists and surprises on several levels. Indeed, the number of anomalous elements in the narrative has led one scholar to characterize the entire story as belonging to the genre of "riddle" (Greenstein:239). While there is more than a little bit of truth to such a characterization, we shall argue that an analysis that is attentive to different levels of reading of the story can ultimately make more sense of its parts and, thus, of their relationship to each other in the whole. The reason for this is, in part, because the different levels of the story require different methods of analysis. This paper will draw on methods of disciplines ranging from linguistics to folklore to the "closer-to-home" biblical studies approach of literary criticism.

What are the "levels" we refer to? First is that of the riddle itself. Previous scholarly debate has centered on several questions, the most important one being whether or not this is a "true" riddle.[1] Samson's challenge to the Philistines is, after all, based on a unique individual experience. Since most definitions of "riddle" assume that the answer must be available within the cultural or contextual situation of the riddlees, many scholars have classified this as what folklorists call a "neck riddle," i.e., one told by a narrative character in a life-or-death

---

[1]Bal (45), Soggin (243), and Moore (335) call it, respectively, "not logical," "unfair," and "bad." Crenshaw (113–14) considers it "unanswerable," but still a real riddle. Gray (330), Nel (540), and Margalith (228) all believe it is answerable, but they adduce quite different explanations of the answer. See Nel (536–39) for a complete review of literature on this text.

A second problem with respect to the riddle is whether the fact that Samson's "question" is framed as a declarative statement and the Philistines' "answer" as a question has any bearing on its status as a real riddle. Comparative folklore studies resolve this problem easily, for there is ample evidence for statement-like "questions" whose function as riddle challenges are understood from the context of use (Pepicello and Green:85). E. ten Raa, in fact, uses the the terminology "challenge" and "reply" to avoid confusion because this "reversal" of the "normal" pattern is so common in the culture he studied (392). Cf. Maranda's "riddle image" and "riddle answer" and Harries' "precedent" and "sequent."

situation to save the riddler's neck (Soggin:243; Crenshaw, 1978:113; Pepicello and Green:87). Such riddles are released from the constraints of answerability but are therefore also excluded from analysis alongside riddles told in actual social interactions (Pepicello and Green:87–88). It will be part of our intention to show that, even though Samson's riddle is based on his individual experience, he nonetheless expertly crafts it in such a way that the answer is indeed available to the Philistines.[2] It is a true riddle and can be analyzed as such using the methods of linguistics and folklore.

The second and third levels of reading are two that are virtually always confused by commentators. Although this is understandable, since they are tightly interwoven, a distinction can be very fruitfully made for purposes of analysis. The second level is what we might call "the interaction situation" (cf. Seitel; Fontaine:57–63, 75–76), i.e., "the actual event" of the use of verbal art, including "such considerations as the social occasion . . . , age and sex of the hearer and proverb user, social status, kinship categories, and so on" (Fontaine:58). Riddle per-

---

[2]Included in Professor Slotkin's insightful critique of our work is a question about whether the "answerability" of the riddle, in the sense of whether or not the Philistines can "deduce" an answer, is an entirely relevant category of analysis. Although we hesitate to take advantage of the "last word" that this printed page might seem to offer, this question is such a fundamental one to this project (and in a more general theoretical sense) that at least one more "word" seems appropriate. It is certainly true, as Slotkin suggests, that riddle answers are often not "rational" in a modern Western sense and, indeed, that in many cultures the answers are given based on memory of tradition rather than on deduction by participants in a given contest. On the other hand, anthropologists and folklorists also attest to cultures where making up and figuring out riddles on the spur of the moment is the norm (Maranda:56–57). Cross-culturally, there is great variety in the "cognitive requirements" for the solutions of riddles, particularly with respect to "their reliance upon memory . . . or their dependence on logic or intuition . . ." (Burns:158). Even students of riddles in cultures which rely on memory, or where solutions can be arbitrary or multiple, point to the connection of riddles with a culture's world view and the necessity for riddlees finally to "see the point" of the solution even if they do not "deduce" it (Ben-Amos; Glazier and Glazier:209–13; Lieber). Thus, the question of how the Philistines' answer relates to Samson's challenge is an important one for understanding the interaction.

Burns' article focuses on the existence of culturally conditioned rules of performance for the riddle genre in order to compare this "genre of traditional behavior" cross-culturally. It is precisely part of the effort of our paper to learn what we can of Israel's riddling rules. While Slotkin may be correct that we have pressed too hard on the point of the Philistines' ability to "deduce" the answer, we would hold that the text allows at least for the possibility of this rule of Israelite performance. Although we have not substantially revised this paper since its oral presentation, we gratefully acknowledge his critique, which has allowed us to sharpen at points the aspect of our discussion concerned with riddle performance.

formance, especially at the more complex level of the riddle contest, has culturally variable, but nonetheless discernible, rules that structure the interaction and distinguish it from regular conversation (Burns). To analyze the story on this level, we suspend our scholarly disbelief and accept the description of the event for what it purports to be, i.e., a real historical occurrence and, more to the point, a real occasion of riddle performance. This heuristic assumption of verisimilitude allows the use of folklorist methods to analyze the performance. Because scholars have consistently confused this level of reading—the riddle performance level—with the third level—that of the narrator—these methods have never been applied to Samson's riddle. While we acknowledge the problems involved in a naive historical reading of biblical texts, we shall argue that this particular text is well-suited to a heuristically historical reading for the purpose of performance analysis.

The third level of reading is that of the narrator. Obviously, this level cannot be completely extricated from the first two, since the narrator has final responsibility for all three. However, a literary reading of the text adds further dimensions to our awareness both of its artistry and of its purpose and goals. Given limitations of space, this third level will be the least thoroughly developed part of our presentation.

Our line of argument is based on Peter Seitel's model for analyzing proverb performance (see Diagram 1; cf. Fontaine), modified where appropriate to riddle performance (Diagram 2), that is to say, the purposeful transmission of a riddle in a social interaction (cf. Fontaine:72). The first section will consider the "interaction situation," or the various socially significant aspects of the relationship of the parties involved the interchange. The second section will address the "riddle situation," i.e, the relationship between the riddle's question and answer in grammatical and structural terms. The third section will deal with the "context situation," explicating the relationship understood by the riddler, Samson, between the referents of the riddle and the situation to which it applies. Seitel's model is designed to deal with the first of our two "levels of reading" mentioned above. Analysis of the third level, that of the narrator, will be woven in where appropriate.

I. The Interaction Situation

What were the power relationships between Samson and the Philistines before and after the riddle match, and what did each seek to gain by entering into it? Understanding the interaction situation and its significance requires a brief review of this section of the Samson story, with some effort made to sort out the perspective offered to

DIAGRAMS OF PROVERB AND RIDDLE PERFORMANCE

1. PROVERB PERFORMANCE:

II. PROVERB SITUATION

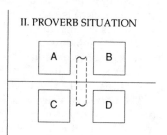

I. INTERACTION SITUATION
~ = status relationships; setting

III. CONTEXT SITUATION
----= relationship between II. and III.

X says to Y (~ , under the following conditions), "As A in this proverb
is related to (~) B, so C in this context is related to (~) D."
~ = relationship between topic and comment

2. RIDDLE PERFORMANCE

II. RIDDLE SITUATION

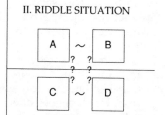

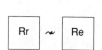

I. INTERACTION SITUATION
~ = status relationships; setting

III. CONTEXT SITUATION
? = guess how II. is related to III.

The Riddler (Rr) says to the Riddlee (Re) under the following circumstances (~),
"Guess (???) how A related to (~) B in this riddle is to be correlated to
C's relationship to (~) D in an unspecified context."

the reader by the narrator and that assumed of Samson himself.

The scene opens with Samson's having "gone down"—a four-times repeated verb in the story (vv. 1,5,7,10)—to the Philistine territory of Timnah, seen a Philistine woman, and decided on her for a wife. His parents plead with him to marry a woman from among his own kin, but he refuses. The narrator then informs us (v. 4) that the Philistines are rulers (מֹשְׁלִים) over Israel and that the woman (elliptically referred to by the pronominal it/her) is "from Yahweh" because "*he* (הוּא) is seeking an occasion against the Philistines." Samson and his parents then go down to Timnah. On the way, somehow inexplicably separated from them, he encounters a lion. The Spirit of Yahweh "rushes upon him" and he kills the lion, tearing it apart "as one tears a kid." Later on, he returns to the lion's carcass and finds a hive of bees and honey in it.

The narrative voice and Samson's own thoughts intersect at this point in a delightful pun. Most translations read that Samson "scraped out" the honey from the lion. The verb here, רדה, is an unusual one. The construction looks at first very much like a form of the verb ירד, go down, which we have already encountered three times. Once past that first, clearly deliberate source of confusion, we realize that only here of the 25 other occurrences of רדה does it seem to mean "scrape out." Elsewhere it means "to rule." This more common meaning of a relatively uncommon verb resonates with another Hebrew word meaning "to rule," משל, which was used in v. 4 in reference to the Philistine domination. But משל has a second meaning, namely, "to be like or similar," and is used nominally to mean "proverb" or "wise saying." Thus, implicitly, the narrator informs us, when Samson "scrapes out" the honey, he is also put in mind of a מָשָׁל of which we take the חִידָה to constitute a generic subset (cf. Prov 1:1–6; Ps 49:4).

Samson takes some honey as a gift to his parents without revealing anything about its source, presumably because both Israelite law in general and his Nazirite vow in particular forbid him contact with a corpse. He then goes down again to Timnah to hold his wedding feast. The Philistines, seeing him and perhaps also fearing him (the forms of the Hebrew verbs "see" and "fear" are suggestively similar), provide him with a retinue of thirty men. He then proposes his riddle, suggesting a wager of thirty of one sort of garment and thirty of another, and the Philistines accept. The riddle is as follows:

> Out of the eater came something to eat;
> out of the strong came something sweet.

The Philistines have the seven days of the wedding party to answer,[3] but after three days, they are angry and suspicious they've been had. They then threaten his bride (Bal calls her Kallah, "bride," since the narrator provides us no name) with the burning of her and her father's house if she does not entice her husband into giving her the answer. With much weeping, she overcomes Samson's resistance, and on the seventh day, the Philistines present him with his answer:

> What is sweeter than honey?
> What is stronger than a lion?

The Spirit of Yahweh then rushes on Samson again, causing him to go to another Philistine city, Ashkelon, where he kills thirty men for their garments. He gives these to the members of his entourage to pay his wager. He then returns to his home in anger, and Kallah is given to one of the Philistine men for a wife. We will not detail the rest of the story at this point, but suffice it to say that there are no less than three more violent encounters between Samson and the Philistines spiralling out of the cycle of vengeance begun here. One of the tragic ironies of the situation is that Kallah and her household are finally burned to death by her own countrymen, in spite of her compliance in the matter of the riddle.

Samson, then, is presented from the beginning of the narrative as a man of supreme and fearless self-confidence. He deals peremptorily with his parents, he decides on a wife without asking agreement from anyone involved, he tears apart a lion as one would tear a kid. In the latter process, moreover, he is already conceiving the riddle he will use to upset his future in-laws. Above all, he has experienced the onrushing power of the Spirit of Yahweh, though he seems to interpret it as confirmation of his right to claim the honey from a forbidden vessel, and does not know its larger purpose in Yahweh's seeking of an occasion against the Philistines. We must imagine, then, that when he enters Philistine territory unaccompanied by any sort of bodyguard, it is because he feels he can meet any challenge on his own. The Philistines' action in supplying Samson with a retinue of thirty men[4] is a subtle one. It is an act of respect to the bridegroom, but it is

---

[3]In his cross-cultural comparative study of riddles, Burns (159) notes that the existence and length of a period of contemplation is one of the variable rules of riddle contests. Seven days is relatively long, and may be the result of narrative hyperbole to emphasize the difficulty and/or significance of the riddle. The fact that there is such a period, however, sets this riddle event within the discernible bounds of cross-cultural riddle performance.

[4]The usual translation describing these men as "companions" is probably misleading. The usual Hebrew word for "friend, companion" (רֵעַ) is bypassed here in favor of מֵרֵעַ. The latter word is used only four other times in the Hebrew Bible,

also doubtless a sign of their fear of him and an effort to ward off any pre-emptive strike from him.

It is difficult to decide whether Samson feels threatened by this move or sees it merely as a challenge to be met. He is at a disadvantage in being on Philistine turf, and outnumbered, but he is in the household of his wife-to-be and assumes the Spirit of Yahweh is on his side. What purpose does the riddle serve him at precisely this moment? Burns' comparative study of riddling performance outlines six broad categories of riddle occasions: (1) as part of rituals of initiation and death; (2) in courtship and marriage festival contexts; (3) as interchanges between teacher and student(s); (4) as a form of greeting exchanges upon meeting; (5) embedded in other expressive genres (narrative and song, most particularly); and (6) "leisure-time" riddling (143–45). The Judges 14 narrative subtly interweaves several of these contexts for riddling. Samson has just passed through what we might term a rite of passage in his rending the lion in the wilderness between settlements; his upcoming wedding initiates him into full manhood in the ancient world. The riddling takes place within the context of his wedding feast and is embedded within the larger legendary cycle of Samson's doings. He has just met the retinue of Philistine companions, and the narrative suggests that the riddling occupies something of a "leisure-time" activity during the seven days of the wedding feast. Let us analyze more closely the dynamics of riddle performance as they apply to the "occasion" here described between Samson and the Philistines.

In their most helpful book, *The Language of Riddles*, Pepicello and Green argue that the goal of the riddle is to "create fictitious problems, competitive events that intensify social disparity" (124).

> Rather than working with the audience to restore proper (i.e., socially functional) perception of a situation, the riddler foists confusion on his [sic] audience by a variety of means. Despite the resolution of the conflict with the supplying of of the answer, riddles seek to generate tension as consciously as proverbs try to ameliorate it (125).

Riddlers are allowed to be rude; their judgment, however seemingly capricious, is accepted as final. Their goal is to present an unanswerable question and

> in riddling any textual or contextual clues that might be forthcoming in ordinary talk are submerged in and obscured as far as is allowable

---

two of which clearly indicate this person's role to be one of a political and/or military advisor (Gen 26:26; 2 Sam 3:8). Although the other two occurrences are ambiguous, they also could easily be construed in the same manner (Prov 19:7; 12:26). Cf. Boling (231) and the references to David's "thirty" in 2 Sam 23:13; 2 Chron 11:15.

within the prevailing performance tradition. In essence, riddling thrives on rending the social and communicative bonds between participants (125).

Riddles, moreover, function in such a way as to "allow reversal of normal power structures, so that in a riddling session it is the riddler who is in authority, whatever his [sic] status outside of a session *vis à vis* other members of that session" (128). Thus, by propounding the riddle at this moment, Samson assumes control of a situation whose advantage in that rather carefully balanced setting he may have felt tilting away.

However, this taking of control is done in the ludic, or playful, way characteristic of riddling (Pepicello and Green:134). The ludic quality of his action is set forth by Samson's opening sally: "Let me riddle you a riddle" (v. 12) he says, thereby signaling a conventional opening to a riddling act and the narrator's interest in the performance dimensions of the genre. Such a statement is referred to as a "metamessage" whose purpose "is to transform serious behavior into ludic action," much like the rules of boxing assure us that the fighters are not "really" fighting [?!] (Pepicello and Green:8, citing Bateson). It is just such a statement that signals a switch to "performance"—with its recognizable, though culturally variable rules—from mere behavior (Pepicello and Green:11; Harries:380; Burns:147, 156–57). Samson's ludic understanding of his riddling gesture is reinforced by the sort of wager he offers: an exchange of garments between the loser and the winner. He does not, contrary to the comments of some scholars, set up the conflict for a life-or-death, all-or-nothing outcome. Nor does he even put the wager in terms of who will get the woman he has in mind to marry, another high-stakes alternative that would have been open to him.[5] His wager is, rather, in line with the typical rules of cross-cultural riddle performance, which often feature some sort of reward-punishment or payment-deference component (Burns:158–59).

Whatever plans he may have originally had for his riddle, Samson's use of it at this moment is remarkably astute. He not only takes control of a situation that may have been slipping away from him, but he switches the terms of the contest from a potentially physical one (himself vs. the thirty Philistines) to a verbal one. He engineers the situation into more of a game, and the willingness of the Philistines to enter into this specialized performance suggests that

---

[5]The bride as prize to the successful riddlee is a motif that occurs in folktales (Crenshaw, 1978:102). In this case, we might note that Kallah's willingness to get the answer for her kinsmen may suggest an undertone of such a wager. If she is being forced into marriage with him, perhaps she thinks she might be "won back" by her family.

they also saw it as a way of gaining prestige points, as it were, without risking excessive loss. If their confidence was enhanced by their deployment of the bodyguard, they must now be breathing a sigh of relief that Samson shows no desire for battle.

We must not minimize the seriousness of the situation, however; wars have begun over lesser matters! Indeed, when the Philistines begin to think they have been presented with a truly unanswerable riddle their umbrage quickly shows. Their angry accusation to Kallah that they have been brought to the party to be impoverished suggests that they believe Samson has transgressed the boundaries of riddle performance. Samson's outrage is also explicable in terms of this model. He believes—and, as we shall demonstrate in a moment, with much justification—that his riddle is answerable. Not only does he lose both his riddle and his woman, but, from his perspective, it is the Philistines who have "broken the rules" of the ludic performance context. He thus resorts to the physical violence that such verbal art performances are supposed to contain (cf. Hamnett:381).

It is worth noting, however, that cultures vary in their understanding of what constitutes a "win" in a riddle contest: "some contests are won by the person or side that has the greatest stock of riddles to propose; others are won by the side able to supply the most answers; still others are won by the person or side able to answer the most difficult riddles" (Burns:148). In this text, it is not altogether clear why Samson terminates the riddle match when he does, though the narrator's agenda of an "occasion against the Philistines" certainly offers us a clue. Here again, a distinction between a reading at the level of the described interaction and a reading at the level of the narrator is useful. At the level of the interaction, the over-riding impression given is that the performance goal in this case falls into the last of Burns' categories, a "win" based on degree of difficulty: the Philistines answer a tough one and Samson acknowledges (though angrily) their success. On the other hand, both the Philistine's answer and Samson's subsequent comment on their unfair tactics are suggestive of further riddling. (Cf. Burns [153] on the role of overall performance evaluation, as distinct from the mere designation of "winner" and "loser.") Whatever the rules of actual performance were, they have become obscured in the narrative. In any case, Samson's own intention—that is to say the goal of his riddle performance as described here—was that of a diplomatic response to a threatening situation which also allowed his own self-confidence and control to be demonstrated and his right to claim his bride established. Yahweh's intention, however, as revealed to the reader but not to Samson, was to use both bride and riddle as an "occasion" against the Philistines. The narrator's intention, we might suggest, was to play one off against the other.

II. The Riddle Situation

Pepicello and Green (10) argue that riddles exploit "conventional patterns" drawn from the two interrelated systems: the linguistic and the aesthetic. Their analysis of the riddle as language suggests that "there is a block element, or what appears to be unsolvable opposition, contained within the riddle," and that

> this block element is directly related to the notion of ambiguity in two senses. First, there is often linguistic ambiguity, i.e., ambiguity in the grammatical form of the riddle. Second, there is contextual ambiguity, i.e., ambiguity produced through a conscious manipulation of social decorum that results in disorientation or confusion of the riddlee, within the riddle act itself (21).

Following their argument, we shall first consider the strictly linguistic notion of ambiguity, ambiguity that "refers to the situation that obtains in language when two or more different underlying semantic structures may be represented by a single surface structure representation (21–22). Contextual ambiguity, which is closely tied to the use of metaphor in riddles, will be addressed in the next section.

One further point must be made here, however, in order to suggest the direction of our argument. With respect to the sorts of blocks that occur in riddles, Pepicello and Green argue that there is a continuum from those riddles that form their blocks exclusively by the use of metaphor (i.e., by aesthetic means) to those whose blocks are exclusively grammatical. Indeed, some riddles use a combination of the two varieties of block. Thus, one thing the riddlee must figure out is whether one or the other of the two kinds of block is used, or both. Samson's riddle uses both grammatical and metaphorical blocks. The existence of the metaphorical block is obvious, especially once the answer is known, but the exact nature of it is not at all obvious until and unless one figures out the grammatical problems we shall outline below. We hope to show that the difficulties of modern scholars in understanding the workings of this riddle have resulted from their exclusive focus on the metaphorical level and blindness to the grammatical. The Philistines may well have failed for the same reason.

Linguistic conventions and ambiguity

Linguistic ambiguity present in the surface structure of the riddle "may be the result of processes that occur at the phonological, morphological, or syntactic levels of grammar" (Pepicello and Green:22). Understanding the grammatical source of the ambiguity is crucial to analyzing riddle performance because "the riddler, in creating ambiguity in the form of the riddle, has a double advantage. First, only he [sic] knows *where* in the composition of the riddle an ambiguity exists.

Second, only he [*sic*] knows *at what linguistic level* this ambiguity exists" (27).

Following are three versions of Samson's riddle challenge and its answer, first in Hebrew; second a very literal English translation; and third, a translation in English that is more idiomatic and, hopefully, more artistic.

v. 14: *Samson's challenge*

מֵהָאֹכֵל יָצָא מַאֲכָל
וּמֵעַז יָצָא מָתוֹק

From the eater goes out something to eat
and from the strong goes out sweet.

From the eater comes something to eat
and from the strong comes something sweet.

v. 18: *The Philistines' reply*

מַה־מָּתוֹק מִדְּבַשׁ
וּמֶה עַז מֵאֲרִי

What sweet from honey
and what strong from lion?

What is sweeter than honey
and stronger than a lion?

There are two observations to be made here. One is obvious in the Hebrew, and that is the remarkable alliteration of the letter מ (noted but otherwise not commented on by Crenshaw:55, 111–12). What Pepicello and Green's study makes clear is that such a linguistic device is not only a matter of the speaker's art (though it is certainly that), but is also a matter of the speaker's communicative (or communication obstructing) strategy, i.e., it has something to do with the block contained in the riddle. This fact leads to the second observation, which is that the alliterated מ provides *both* a clue *and* a block. In Hebrew, the letter מ followed by a vowel that changes depending on the phonological context, is also a word that is usually translated into English by the preposition "from." In other words, the phoneme מ also functions as the lexeme *from*. Moreover, מ also functions as a Hebrew morpheme which generates the participle in certain forms of verbs. In Samson's riddle challenge, at least the first two of these functions occur.[6] Thus, as we have suggested, alliteration of מ both signals its importance and, at the same time, introduces ambiguity as to what exactly its importance is.

To complicate matters, there is yet a fourth usage of מ that does not appear in the riddle challenge. This is an idiomatic syntactical usage in the construction of the comparative. As we see in the awkwardly literal translation of the Philistines' answer, if one wants to say "stronger than" in Hebrew, one must say "strong from"; "sweeter than" is "sweet from." The use of the "pregnant *min*," as Gesenius calls it, *in the answer but not in the question*, is, then, the source of deliberate syntactic ambiguity in the riddle. Samson's two-fold use of מ יצא, "go out from," leads (or, rather, misleads) the hearer into thinking that מ is being used in its usual sense as the preposition "from." In order to arrive at the answer, the Philistines have to make the syntactical switch to the use of מ in constructing the comparative. As Pepicello and Green have demonstrated, such grammatical miscues are one of the standard ploys of riddles. The traditional methods of biblical scholarship have not heretofore permitted commentators to notice the significance of the riddle's grammar and thus have not permitted them to gain a full understanding of the suitability of the answer.

Attention to the function of מ in the riddle also allows us to distinguish, on the one hand, the block preventing the *reader* from solving the riddle from, on the other hand, that confronting the Philistines. Again, differentiating between the level of the described interaction and the level of the narrator is useful. Because readers are informed by the narrator about Samson's adventure with the lion, our attention is drawn back to that event: getting "hooked" by the idea of honey scraped "out from" the lion prevents our thinking about the relationship of strength/sweetness and lion/honey in any other way. The Philistines, on the other hand, as we shall suggest in the next section, are distracted by the apparent sexual imagery of the riddle challenge in the context of the wedding feast. It is not the fact they don't know about Samson's experience that thwarts them, but rather their fixation on the connotations of something sweet to eat coming "out from" a strong eater. Samson (and implicitly the narrator) holds the advantage in both directions because only he can see all the connections. His experience with the lion as he prepares for his wedding has reminded him of his culture's traditional associations with lions and honey—*perhaps even in the specific proverbial form with its significant use of מ recorded in v. 18* (see further below)—and

---

[6]The word for "food" or "something to eat" (מַאֲכָל) is not a participle strictly speaking, but is a noun formed in a manner closely related to the formation of participles (*GKC*:236–37, 140).

allowed him to create the riddle challenge that will, in different ways, stump both contextual listeners and textual readers.

The use of parallelism

At a sort of crossroads between conventions that may be considered "linguistic strictly speaking" (i.e., grammatical) and those we may consider aesthetic lies the formulation of Samson's riddle in the typical style of Hebrew poetry, namely, two-line parallelism. We consider this a crossroads because parallelism is most usually grammatically based and yet it also affords the poet an opportunity for artistic creativity in her or his choice of the lexical and semantic content in each stich. Given that we have only one riddle in a performance context preserved in the Hebrew Bible, it is interesting to contemplate whether it was typical for riddles to be put forth in such poetic form. Moreover, given the Philistines' equally poetic response, we might ask whether the artistic conventions of this society demanded that a riddle so riddled receive an answer in kind.[7] Though lack of data prevents speculation on social conventions in the days of Samson, we have clear evidence for such literary preferences among the Israelite sages who produced the repetitively bilinear book of Proverbs and from whom one was to learn not only the use of the מָשָׁל ("proverb"), but also the use of riddles. The introduction to the book of Proverbs, from which we have taken the title for this paper, claims that the book will teach its reader to

> understand a proverb and a figure,
> the words of the wise and their riddles (1:6).

We might suggest, then, at least from the point of view of the narrator of the story and his or her audience, there was indeed a conventional compulsion upon the Philistines to respond to Samson's riddle in proper form.

The use of parallelism in the question provides an additional block to the answer, moreover, insofar it leaves unclear whether the answer will be in one or two parts. The usual poetic effect of the kind of synonymous parallelism found in Samson's riddle is to create a sense of a two-fold perspective on a single subject (Nel:542–43). The eater is to be identified with the strong, and the thing to be eaten is identified with the sweet. Thus, the implied question behind this question-which-isn't-a-question might be something like "under what circumstances does something sweet to eat come forth from a

---

[7]Clifford Geertz (1493–97) provides a fascinating description of argumentative poetry "battles" in Morocco. These are often "fought" by poets hired by feuding villagers to settle social conflicts, and style as well as content is crucial to victory.

strong eater?" The singular answer suggested by the wedding context (more on context in a moment) would presumably have something to do with love or, more likely, sex. Given that the answer desired by Samson—lion and honey—is apparently not singular (though cf. the discussion of Nel below), we might then see the use of parallelism as a further artistic-grammatical block available to the riddler competent in Hebrew language and poetic form.

Such a reading can be supported from the structural analysis of proverbs and riddles done by Alan Dundes. Dundes (108) describes both these forms as being composed of at least "one descriptive element, that is to say, one unit composed of one topic and one comment." The intent of a proverb proper is to make the topic explicit so that the proverb can function to provide order by means of its socially validated comment on that topic. The riddle, however, intends to obfuscate and call received orders into question. Its topic is therefore purposefully concealed. The creation of a bilinear riddle question further enhances this confusing concealment by suggesting the possibility of two topics instead of just one, and thus raising the further question of their relationship to each other as well as to the situation at hand.

It is quite possible that the Philistines realized that the parallel form of the question could lead to either a single or double-fold answer. If their efforts at answering were directed by the sexual innuendo that inheres in the marriage banquet setting, the possible permutations of an answer are many indeed. Although this discussion actually carries us over into our ensuing consideration of the context situation, we can hardly resist a moment's mulling of some of these possibilities (see Diagram 3). For example, if the "strong eater" is thought to be the bridegroom, then the "something sweet" he brings forth could either be vomit (from becoming drunk at the feast [מִשְׁתֶּה = "drinking celebration"]) or semen (in his ejaculation following an act of cunnilingus, or sexual "eating"). On the other hand, if the "strong eater" is the woman[8] (imaged either in an act of fellatio or a Freudian sort of fear of the "devouring" involved in the act of intercourse), then the "something sweet" to eat which she brings forth could be either her lubricating fluids which the man will "eat" during cunnilingus or the milk her breasts will provide at the final culmination of the sexual act. Moreover, if the riddle is thought to have a different subject for each half of the parallel structure, the answer might refer to the woman as "eater" who produces either her sexual lubrication or her breastmilk "to eat," while the man is the "strong one" who pro-

---

[8]Although a modern reader might be surprised to find an ancient patriarchalist describing a woman as "strong," Israel's sages revered the "woman of worth," who is said to "gird her loins with strength (בְּעוֹז) and make strong (תְּאַמֵּץ) her arms" (Prov 31:17).

duces his "sweet" semen; or, the man could be the "eater" who produces semen "to eat," while the woman is the strong one who produces her "sweet" lubrication or milk. No wonder the the Philistines
are confused![9]

III. The Context Situation

Our concern in the context situation is to analyze the relationship
of the elements of the riddle to the entire situation as seen by the riddler (see Diagram 3), with particular attention to how the metaphors
of the riddle inform and are informed by this context. This section of
the discussion is considerably more complicated and subtle when applied to riddles than it was when Seitel and Fontaine applied it to
proverbs. Context is a virtual prerequisite for deciding which of the
several available meanings of a metaphor are to be emphasized, and
how literally or figuratively its terms are to be taken. "Proverbs function to reduce confusion through the artful relocation of a social
problem" (Pepicello and Green:124). Thus, it is in the interests of the
proverb user that the relationship of the proverb's metaphors to the
social situation be relatively clear. Riddles, however, with their intention to disrupt, suspend the normal conversational context, and thus
use their homeless metaphors to confuse rather than to clarify.

Metaphor and metonymy

The metaphorical blocks are tricky indeed especially insofar as
they overlap with and reinforce the grammatical ones. To explicate
this situation fully we must turn to the semiotic analysis of Pepicello
and Green. While every ambiguity involves a confusion in the relationship of sign to referent, or signans to signatum,

> there is a basic difference in the nature of this relationship in metaphori-
> cal ambiguity as opposed to grammatical ambiguity. Specifically,
> metaphor functions in a paradigmatic mode, grammatical ambiguity
> functions in a syntagmatic mode. That is, metaphor functions according
> to systematized similarity that is focused upon by means of comparison,
> but grammatical ambiguity functions by contiguity, i.e., by its context.

---

[9]It may be that Samson's riddle functions similarly, in this aspect, to some
riddles observed by folklorists in other cultures, namely, by allowing the *consid-*
eration of taboo thoughts while preventing their actual expression by means of an
acceptably framed solution (cf. Glazier and Glazier:213–16). Such a tactic may
also, as Müller (467) suggests, be designed to embarrass the riddlees. Such conclusions depend, however, on the assumption that that these sexual fantasies
were thought by the ancient Israelites, as they apparently are by some modern
Westerners, to "border on pornography" (so Soggin:244).

Diagram 3. RIDDLE PERFORMANCE IN JUDGES 14

I. INTERACTION SITUATION

Rr: Samson the Danite

Re: Philistine retinue

~ = negative:
- Samson outnumbered 30:1
- in Philistine territory

positive:
- "Spirit of the Lord" on Rr's side
- in wife-to-be's *bêt 'ab*
- has honey—scraped out mashal

setting:
- feast: scene of redistribution
  of power, status, goods
- subtype: wedding feast

II. RIDDLE SITUATION

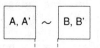

(A,B) Out of the eater came something to eat
(A',B') Out of the strong came something sweet

~ = ➛ , positive causation

? ?
? ?
? ?

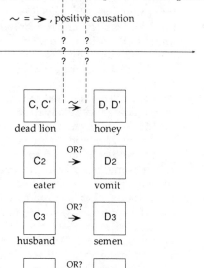

| C, C' | ≳ | D, D' |
| dead lion | | honey |

| C2 | OR? ➛ | D2 |
| eater | | vomit |

| C3 | OR? ➛ | D3 |
| husband | | semen |

| C4 | OR? ➛ | D4 |
| mother | | milk |

| C5 | OR? ➛ | D5 |
| Philistia | | Israel |

ETC ...

III. CONTEXT SITUATION
~ = ➛, positive causation

> Thus, metaphorical riddles are solvable by resource to the appropriate
> paradigm, although riddles based on grammatical structure must be
> linguistically contextualized (i.e., placed in a discourse) to be solvable
> (118–19).

Some riddles, however, function by means of a combination of
paradigmatic and syntagmatic strategies. Imagery may be used, for
example, but the imagery may be metonymous rather than
metaphorical in the strict sense, and metonymy, like a grammatical
form, requires context for clarity. The presence of metonymy, the
naming of attributes or parts of something to refer to the whole, is
evident in Samson's riddle's use of the terms "the eater" and "the
strong." Out of any sort of context, there are any number of things
that eat and are strong. Thus, the riddlee must resort to "shared cultural knowledge and/or immediate linguistic context (the riddle
unit)" in the attempt to solve the riddle (119). Within the riddle unit
itself, the most obvious clue—though also an ambiguating one—is
the idea that something sweet to eat comes out of the strong eater. As
noted above, this clue from the linguistic context, in combination
with the cultural context of the wedding celebration, suggests an answer relating most likely to sex.

More subtly, the use of metonymy, with its requirement of contextual interpretation, may be seen to function as a real clue, signaling the riddlee to attend to the grammatical level block which must
be overcome to arrive at the answer. The riddle seems to say, "Look
out, even though I'm composed of images which lead you to focus on
me at the level of metaphor, you really should be more concerned
with the contiguous, syntagmatic mode of my grammar!" A subtle
clue indeed, since neither Philistines nor later commentators seem to
have picked up on it! And yet a very accurate one as well, since we
find out in the answer that the meanings of both the strong eater and
that which is sweet to eat are located very close to the "literal" end of
their respective scales of meaning rather than at the more extended,
metaphorical end suggested by the wedding context.

Metaphor in context . . . and out

The Philistines' failure to figure out that strong and sweet were to
receive interpretations other than sexual ones can also be explained
semiotically. As Pepicello and Green (119–20) point out, the relationship between sign and referent is a "sliding one" because signs may
be homonymous (i.e., having functions other than the one found in a
given context) and synonymous (i.e., the same content can be expressed by other signs). The relationship of sign to referent is, thus,
an "asymmetrical" one that shifts according to context. Riddles, they
argue, "manipulate the pivotal semiotic element, context, in creating

confusion" (120). The way in which riddles manipulate context is by suspending all normal context, forcing the riddlee to start from scratch, as it were, in trying "to place the sign . . . in a locus that permits a definition of the signans-signatum relationship, and thus a solution to the riddle" (120).

The Philistines' efforts to contextualize the metaphors and metonymies of the riddle were, naturally, directed by the most obvious context available to them. We have already suggested some reasons why they were stymied in their efforts to come up with a sufficiently stylish and appropriate answer. The problem that has so bothered scholars, however, and that has led to the denigration of this as a "bad riddle," is the question of whether or not it was possible at all for the Philistines to contextualize the riddle in such a way as to arrive at the answer required by Samson. While recent scholars have been more appreciative of the riddle than earlier ones, and have devised arguments suggesting possible lines of reasoning the Philistines might have taken (Nel, Margalith), their lack of this semiotic perspective prevents their fully explicating the context switches that are required to move from Samson's originating experience to his question and from there to the answer. If it is typical of riddles to produce ambiguity by suspending normal context, then we must give Samson even more credit for wit than we already have. For this riddle demonstrates a remarkable skill not only linguistically and artistically, but also in its use of contextual cues and miscues to lead the Philistines astray.

Nel has undoubtedly come the closest of any to the full picture. He argues that "strong" and "sweet" are the key concepts in the riddle and, as metaphors, "a competent riddle-solver . . . must have been in a position to scan through the paradigms of possibly correct equivalents to them" (542). Three pieces of "circumstantial evidence" facilitate the task of choosing among alternatives within the paradigms: the fact that "honey is the sweetness par excellence," that the lion is similarly associated with strength, and that in the wedding context "love enjoys a certain priority" (542). The emphasis on love is most significant, for Nel argues further that the riddle's answer in v. 18, itself in question form, was a "crystallized riddle," which existed as a popular proverb, and whose answer was love.

> The two comparisons, as formulated in the parallelism ("sweeter than honey and stronger than a lion"), obviously converge in their conceptual reference (i.e., love). . . . The intention of the saying is constituted in the extraordinary comparison of specific qualities. The comparison shows that only one reality is presupposed; one reality of enormous "strength" and simultaneously of incomparable "sweetness": that is, love. So the skillfully constructed riddle of Samson displays the two key-words, sweet and strong, for its unravelling. The expected

answer is the popular proverb (v. 18) in which these two key-words
play a central role (542–43).

Although, according to Nel (543), "we have no explicit indications"
that Samson's question in v. 14a necessarily has love as its content, it
points "semantically to a specific reality and is structurally composed
in such a way as to indicate and anticipate the popular proverb of v.
18." Based on this analysis, Nel (543) observes that the main issue in
understanding Samson's riddle lies in "our interpretation of the creative process underlying the riddle."

Nel makes two important contributions in his work. The first is
his treatment of the metaphorical associations of strength and sweetness with the idea of love in the text. The second is his awareness that
the text reveals a "creative process" of riddle-formation to which the
interpreter must attend. Both of these contributions can, however, be
refined with the theoretical framework of Pepicello and Green. Attention to context, and to the shifting contexts in the text, add nuance
and detail to our understanding of the creative process.

The first context is, in effect, a contextless context, occurring as it
does in a liminal zone, in between the Israelite territory of Zorah and
the Philistine territory of Timnah (see Nel:534–35, for the significance
of the movement between locations). It is here that Samson has his
unique, personal experience, unreported even to his parents, of tearing open the lion and finding the honey. The narrative non-context
also corresponds to the radical contiguity of the lion-honey connection. How, the reader is led to ask, without knowing about Samson's
experience, could anyone ever see such a connection? Samson, however, does see a connection; indeed, he may see more than one connection as he "scrapes out" the honey and implicitly makes his *māšāl*.
One connection is that of strength and sweetness with love, as Nel
has pointed out (cf. Crenshaw, 1978:117–18 for a variation on this argument). Even if we do not go so far as to say that the answer in v. 18
is a "crystallized riddle" or popular proverb, the valuing of love's
strength in Song 8:6 and the proverbial use of honey and lions as the
respective epitomes of sweetness and strength[10] suggest a complex of
culturally known associations that both sparked Samson's memory
and imagination and provided one route for the riddlees to the correct choices in the metaphorical paradigms.

Nel offers, however, no argument from metaphor for the question
part of the riddle. Focusing entirely on the idea of love drawn from
the riddle's answer, he misses the rather obvious sexual connotations
of sweetness and eating in Samson's question. These sexual meanings, which would have probably enjoyed an even higher connota-

---

[10]For honey, see Prov 16:24; 24:13; 25:16,27; cf. Song 4:11; 5:1. For lions, see
Prov 28:15; Lam 3:10; Amos 3:8; Num 24:9; Isa 38:13; and *passim*.

tional priority in the context of baudy wedding riddling than the idea of love, perform an important and apparently effective part of the metaphorical block to an answer that has to do with love. One may well wonder, in fact, whether Samson had love on his mind at all. He has violently torn open the lion and then scraped out the honey, as he no doubt anticipates tearing open his bride to claim her honey. Given the proverbial connections of the strength of lions and the sweetness of honey, combined with the critically important grammatical clue in the use of מ, the Philistines, with sufficient wit, could presumably have moved from the sexual connotations of these words suggested by the wedding context to the more literal answer without even worrying about love.

If we shift our focus for a moment from the interaction situation described in the narrative to the perspective of the narrator, however, we find that here love is indeed an important consideration. Whether Samson has intended it or not, the solution to the riddle within the narrative as a whole depends on it. As Crenshaw (1978:107-8) has pointed out, the verb "to open" (פתח) functions as a technical term meaning "to solve (a riddle)." A variant of פתח, פתה, describes what Samson's wife is called upon to do by her countrymen, as they complain about the riddle's insolubility. "Entice (open)[11] your husband," they say. When Samson refuses, she complains that he does not love her. If he has failed to see the import of love for his situation before, he must confront it now. Once betrayed, however, his original interpretation of the situation reasserts itself.

> If you had not plowed with my heifer,
> you would not have found out my riddle,

he cries. Sex is again for him the issue. Although he tore open the lion, his wife is the one who, paradoxically, "opens" him. This reversal of sexual roles in the context of love, with female opening male, is intolerable to Samson, and his response reasserts the right of the man to open ("plow") the woman, even if, as he sees it in this case, the wrong men have done the opening (cf. Bal:43).

---

[11]The word-play actually involves a triple entendre. The verb פתה can mean either "be open" (*qal*: Prov 20:19; *hiph.*, "make open": Gen 9:27) or "be simple" (Job 5:2; Hos 7:11). The intensive *piel* form of the second meaning is often, as in this case, translated "entice" or "seduce," but could be equally well-rendered as "make simple" or "make a fool of." Indeed, the feminine singular imperative form used in 14:15 , פַּתִּי, sounds very similar to the word for simpleton or fool, פֶּתִי.

Conclusions

By way of conclusion, we shall describe the relevance of the fore-going discussion to the "levels of reading" outlined at the outset of the paper. First, with respect to the riddle itself, we have suggested that, far from being a "bad riddle" or easily dismissable as a "neck riddle," Samson's riddle is a carefully crafted traditional form, utiliz-ing effectively several different "blocking" devices available to him from the linguistic and metaphorical resources of the culture. Although the idea for the riddle is certainly derived from his personal experience, he uses these resources to generalize from his experience in such a way as to make the riddle answerable, if exceedingly diffi-cult. Indeed, his expertise is so great that he is able to to combine the ambiguous meaning of the context itself (is a wedding about sex or love, sweetness or strength?) with the ambiguity of his grammar and metaphors.

This conclusion is important for understanding the dynamics of our "second level," that of the interaction described between Samson and the Philistines at the marriage feast, and its consequences. If Samson's riddle is an answerable one, then the course of events de-scribed here is quite explicable in terms of folkloristic performance studies. Samson, with the skill of a seasoned diplomat, uses verbal art *both* to ward off possible physical violence *and* at the same time to establish or re-establish his possibly shaky control of the situation. Neither his verbal challenge nor his anger at the way the Philistines discovered his answer were unreasonable, though his succeeding ac-tions in killing thirty Ashkelonites certainly were.

But this brings us to the third level of the story, that of the narra-tor, who has already warned us in v. 4 that all Samson's efforts at dominance by peaceful means are intended by Yahweh to come to naught. Just as Yahweh has set up the riddle through the on-rushing Spirit which empowered Samson to kill and tear apart the lion, so now this Spirit rushes in once more to send Samson against the Philistines of Ashkelon. The ironic understanding of the narrator is that the human skill and inspiration for non-violent manipulation of social conflict is given by God and, paradoxically, that the human skill and drive for outrageous violence also comes on the same divine breath.

If we care to ask who this narrator might be—one who delights in the construction of poetic riddles in bilinear parallelism, one who shows awareness of proverbial metaphors and cultural allusions, one who enjoys the sweetness of sex and also enjoins against the strange woman, one who knows and teaches language skills for diplomatic use, one who is capable of drawing lessons of general application from the particulars of personal experience, and, most of all, one who knows all too well the inexplicable power and will of the deity to redirect the desires and intentions of the human heart—it can only be a member of the Israelite wisdom tradition. As they used to say in Israel,

> No wisdom, no understanding, no counsel,
> can avail against Yahweh (Prov 21:30).

Given the caution of folklorists in using narrative sources as examples of verbal art performance (Pepicello and Green:87–88; cf. Fontaine:72–74), it is perhaps ironic that in this case an understanding of the narrative level helps to justify our use of folklore methods, for one demonstrable purpose of this sage's story is to teach the construction, use, and final limitations of riddle performance in Israel.[12]

WORKS CONSULTED

Bal, Mieke
    1987   *Lethal Love: Feminist Literary Readings of Biblical Love Stories*. Bloomington and Indianapolis: Indiana University Press.

Ben-Amos, Dan
    1976   "Solutions to Riddles." *JAF* 89:249–54.

Boling, Robert G.
    1975   *Judges*. AB 6a. Garden City, NY: Doubleday.

Burns, Thomas A.
    1976   "Riddling: Occasion to Act." *JAF* 89:139–65 .

Crenshaw, James L.
    1974   "Wisdom." Pp. 225–64 in *Old Testament Form Criticism*. Ed. John H. Hayes. San Antonio, TX: Trinity University Press.

    1978   *Samson: A Secret Betrayed, A Vow Ignored*. Atlanta: John Knox.

---

[12]The authors would like to thank Sharon Bentley, Gerry Brague, and Connie Schütz for their cheerful technical assistance in the preparation of this manuscript.

Dundes, Alan
  1975   "On the Structure of the Proverb." Pp. 103–18 in *Analytic Essays in Folklore*. Ed. Alan Dundes. Studies in Folklore, 2. The Hague: Mouton.

Fontaine, Carole R.
  1982   *Traditional Sayings in the Old Testament*. Bible and Literature Series, 5. Sheffield: Almond.

Geertz, Clifford
  1976   "Art as a Cultural System." *MLN* 91:1473–99.

Georges, Robert A. and Alan Dundes
  1963   "Toward a Structural Definition of the Riddle." *JAF* 76:111–18.

Glazier, Jack and Phyllis Gorfain Glazier
  1976   "Ambiguity and Exchange: The Double Dimension of Mbeere Riddles." *JAF* 89:189–238 .

Gray, John
  1967   *Joshua, Judges, Ruth*. New Century Bible. London: Nelson and Sons.

Greenstein, Edward L.
  1981   "The Riddle of Samson." *Prooftexts* 1:237–60.

Hamnett, Ian
  1967   "Ambiguity, Classification and Change: the Function of Riddles." *Man* 2:377–92.

Harries, Lyndon
  1971   "The Riddle in Africa." *JAF* 84:377–93.

Kirshenblatt-Gimblett, Barbara
  1973   "Toward a Theory of Proverb Meaning." *Proverbium* 22:821–27.

Lieber, Michael
  1976   "Riddles, Cultural Categories, and World View." *JAF* 89:255–65.

Maranda, Elli Köngäs
  1971   "Theory and Practice of Riddle Analysis." *JAF* 84:51–61.

Margalith, Othniel
    1986   "Samson's Riddle and Samson's Magic Locks." *V T*
             36:225–34.

Moore, George Foot
    1901   *A Critical and Exegetical Commentary on Judges.* ICC. New
             York: Charles Scribner's Sons.

Müller, Hans-Peter
    1970   "Der Begriff 'Rätsel' im Alten Testament." *VT* 20:465–89.

Nel, Philip
    1985   "The Riddle of Samson." *Biblica* 66:534–45.

Pepicello, W. J. and Thomas A. Green
    1984   *The Language of Riddles.* Columbus, OH: Ohio State Uni-
             versity Press.

Raa, Eric ten
    1966   "Procedure and Symbolism in Sandawe Riddles." *Man* 1:
             391–97.

Seitel, Peter
    1969   "Proverbs: A Social Use of Metaphor." *Genre* 2:143–61.
             (Repr. in *Folklore Genres*, pp. 125–43. Ed. Dan Ben-Amos.
             Austin: University of Texas, 1976.)

Soggin, J. Alberto
    1981   *Judges, A Commentary.* OTL. Trans. John Bowden.
             Philadelphia: Westminster.

Sutton-Smith, Brian
    1976   "A Developmental Structural Account of Riddles." Pp.
             111-19 in *Speech Play: Research and Resources for the Study of
             Linguistic Creativity.* Ed. Barbara Kirschenblatt-Gimblett.
             Philadelphia: University of Pennsylvania Press.

12. Response to Professors Fontaine and Camp

Edgar Slotkin

I am venturing to disagree with Professors Fontaine and Camp on a few issues although I think at the end we shall be in basic accord. Let me start by agreeing that riddles are contests having to do with power but suggesting that different kinds of riddles in different kinds of societies depend upon or invoke different powers. It may be that riddling in Israel "seems to be associated with diplomatic contexts," as Fontaine and Camp suggest, but Samson's riddle as in many other cultures is associated specifically with a rite of passage. Dov Noy has pointed out parallels with other riddling behavior at weddings,[1] and I would suggest that this particular wedding calls out for riddles. All marriages are perhaps "diplomatic contexts," but an exogamous marriage, running in so many ways against Israelite tradition and lacking the normal diplomacy of parental arrangement, is in itself an image of a riddle.

Riddling is a kind of game. Camp and Fontaine refer to the riddle's ludic function, but I would say that the riddle is by definition a game and from that kind of game emerges a range of functions: the ludic is central. Games, in so far as they are competitive, thrive, to re-quote Pepicello and Green, "on rending the social and communicative bonds between participants" (125). But to stop there is to miss the complete performative nature of games, including riddle contests, which has been invoked as a method of analysis. Games create what Huizinga has characterized as play-communities and, to quote him directly, "A play-community generally tends to become permanent even after the game is over" (12). Indeed, we would not find any game as an activity associated with rites of passage if it primarily promoted dissension since integration, incorporation, is the final desired outcome of such events. In the case of exogamous marriage,

---

[1] For references to the use of riddles in rites of passages, including marriages, see Burns (1976). This article offers correlations between the occasions for riddling and the kinds of riddles asked.

especially this marriage which runs counter to normal cultural expectations, the riddle is a perfect expressive device. There is a kind of paradox involved in marrying a "stranger" and "enemy." So Samson's riddle wager, while no doubt reflecting everything that Camp and Fontaine say about the situation, in particular is an "expressive model" which "restates the paradox," to paraphrase Sutton-Smith (1976:111) on riddle situations in general. This expressive function of the riddle as game should be meaningful to all participants in a riddle contest. It should promote bonding between the participants. That it doesn't in Samson's case reflects, I would suggest, both the inherently "wrong" nature of the marriage and the real "occasion against the Philistines" that Yahweh has in mind.

To continue for the moment discussing the riddle as if it were a genuine performance, I find the discussion in the literature of whether or not it is solvable not really to the point—or maybe just not very interesting. This may be because I am myself terrible at solving riddles. But looking at a great many riddles cross-culturally or simply at Archer Taylor's great English language collection, we find comparatively few riddles that are solvable on any rational ground. That is, few so-called "true" riddles admit to logical solutions where one and only one answer satisfies the descriptive grid imposed on the riddle topic (see further Ben-Amos). Some riddles are solvable in that they depend on general or sometimes even arcane cultural knowledge. From the Second Targum on Esther, for instance, one of the riddles attributed to the Queen of Sheba runs: "Three entered a cave and five came forth therewith" (Ginzberg, vol. 4:147). The answer, "Lot and his two daughters and their two children," obviously depends on specific knowledge rather than logical reasoning. (This riddle, by the way, has few blocks and no figurative language.) But most riddles depend for their solution on either inspired guessing or simply knowing the riddle—which is to say, knowing traditions. They are not, to use some other ideas of Sutton-Smith, "achieved power games" but "ascribed power games" (Sutton-Smith, 1972:299–309). Among the Venda, for instance, "Riddling emerges as a competitive game for young people, in which what matters is the number of riddles a contestant knows. It has no importance as an intellectual or cognitive exercise, and no weight is given to understanding the meaning of riddles. They are mere formulae, and to know as many as possible by heart is important because it enables a contestant to distinguish himself in a riddling contest" (Hamnett:380).

The Venda may be extreme in this regard, and Hamnett who is summarizing Blacking here, convincingly indicates that the Venda are more typical than Blacking maintains by showing some intellectual interest among them in riddle content. But I think we tend to be ethnocentric in supposing that riddles and riddle contests cross-culturally are supposed to involve principles of deduction rather than memorization or some other mental ability. Take the Nova Scotia form of a widespread English language riddle:

> A stick in his tail,
> A stone in his throat,
> Come a riddle, come a riddle,
> Come a tote, tote, tote (Taylor No. 637).

The Nova Scotian answer to this enigma is "A boy with a cherry in his mouth." I would suggest that there is no way reasonably to reach this solution. Indeed, most occasions for these descriptors, the stick in his tail and the stone in his throat, are satisfied by the answer "cherry" alone. Where the boy comes from in the Maritimes I cannot easily imagine, and I would suggest that Samson's riddle is not less solvable than this Nova Scotian riddle. But even assuming the answer to be simply "a cherry," there is no logical reason the answer couldn't be "plum" or even "tennis ball with a pebble inside impaled on a pike" except that most riddles have natural phenomena or household objects as their referents. So unless the riddle is a traditional riddle and the riddlee is in genuine touch with that tradition, most riddles are basically unsolvable through reasoning.

Another way of putting this observation is that most riddles are designed not to be solved. Samson's riddle seems no exception. As Fontaine and Camp point out, the basic descriptors appear to be traditional enough—metonymies of their referents. The collocation of the two and the manner in which that collocation is expressed become effective blocks. The riddle, therefore, is an effective one, harder than many, less hard than some, not subject to a logical solution or tribal lore but probably open to traditional metonymic associations with strength and sweetness. It does not seem to be an abnormal riddle, a point that Camp and Fontaine make and that I agree with, though for different reasons. Being a normal riddle does not mean being a very solvable riddle in most situations where riddling is an active pastime.

I suppose that the question of whether or not Samson's riddle is solvable has been raised by Biblical scholars in order to evaluate the Philistine's response to not being able to solve it. Personally, I feel that what the Philistines did was what I would do if I found myself over my head in a wager on a riddle contest in Nova Scotia. The Philistines play hardball. Since the riddle did not admit to a logical solution and did not seem to admit to a solution based on general knowledge but on very specific knowledge—the riddle, after all, has been presented to us in that way[2]—they went after the specific knowledge. But I rather think these observations are missing the point. I am struck that Camp and Fontaine cannot for long sustain the fiction of a genuine performance situation with regard to this riddle. I am impressed that one of their major points about the solvability of the riddle reinforces in my mind that the riddle and its solution only make sense on the level they call the narrator level, the only level, after all, to which we have access. I was much enlightened by their discussion of the semantic range of the bilabial nasal מ and how it serves as a block by reinforcing the poetic function of the riddle. And I was fascinated by their splendid point about how this nasal serves as a proclitic to express our preposition "from" as well as serving in its same function in different contexts as a marker of comparison. But I do not see how this "pregnant מ" could possibly point to a solution of the riddle—only to the particular solution the Philistines eventually propose. Assuming again for the moment that the riddle has a *Sitz im Leben* we can abstract, there is nothing about its content, its context or its expression that requires the use of comparatives in its solution.

I would agree that the form of the riddle, its alliteration and especially the nasal proclitic, are set up specifically for a Philistine answer that is not only very witty but meaningful to the Samson story in at least two ways.[3] To follow my argument depends upon seeing how strange the Philistine answer really is. Samson's riddle seems to call for the solution "honey extracted from the body of a lion." Both cola of the riddle explicitly posit a connection between the two terms "eater" and "strong" on the one hand, "something to eat" and "sweet" on the other. But apparently Samson doesn't expect that connection to be made in the answer since the Philistines do not state it and Samson accepts, rather grudgingly perhaps, their response. This is strange since everything leading up to the answer that the narrator has told us forces us to suppose that the connection between a lion and honey is going to be a required part of the riddle's solution. But it turns out to be only a blocking device, one more obfuscating than the basic antithesis of the bicolon; the answer is simply "lion" and "honey." However, even then the answer is strange because, first of all, as has been pointed out to us, it is in the form of a bicolon which poses two seemingly rhetorical questions; and these questions contain those comparisons which create the morphophonemic link to the original riddle. It is also worth noting, I think, that the solutions

---

[2]Given the odd nature of the Philistine's solution (see below), it is possible to say that we, as readers, are as much fooled by the riddle as they are *because* we are given the specific information which lies behind the riddle's genesis.

[3]Nel (1963) and to some extent Greenstein (1981) make some of these points though reach somewhat different conclusions.

are not in a parallel relation to the terms of the riddle but in a chiastic relationship. The "honey" comes before the "lion," as if the eater were honey and the food were the lion.

Camp and Fontaine point out, quite rightly, that riddles in themselves do not have to take the form of questions, that many riddles, especially verse riddles, are kinds of descriptive statements. But if Samson's riddle is a common type, the Philistines' answer in the form of a question, as Greenstein (242) and others maintain, is distinctly rare, certainly not required by the riddle itself. I rather agree with Nel (542), who sees the Philistines' response as if it were itself a "crystallized riddle" with an answer in turn that most scholars have taken as "love." If this is the case, then we should probably regard Samson's riddle as a construct designed specifically for the Philistine answer, which was a traditional enigma. But certainly not by a performing Samson whose performances are characterized by a failure to understand the power of love. The riddles are only comprehensible as a unit by seeing them as the work of the narrator. Moreover, by making the Philistine riddle the answer to Samson's riddle and embedding both in the context of the Samson legend, the narrator has enriched this piece of traditional riddling, if that is what it is, immeasurably. To begin with, while the traditional answer to the Philistine riddle may be "love," there is a level on which the answer is "Samson." It is Samson, after all, who proved himself stronger than a lion. Is Samson "sweeter than honey?" Well, the Philistines may be paying him a more or less ironic compliment here. We remember that the riddle is supposed to be a game played between relatives at a festive occasion. Just as Samson's riddle, as Camp and Fontaine point out, directs us to both sex and its real answer, so the Philistines' riddling answer directs us to both Samson and its real solution: love. A chiastic relationship would seem to pertain to false answers and real answers, too.

There are several significant points to make here, if I am on the right track. On the one hand, the expressive function of reversible values that I suggested before was inherent in the use of a riddle to mirror an exogamous marriage is reinforced by a set of reverses in the relationship between riddle and solution. Along with chiasmus, we most explicitly find that a riddle posed as a statement is answered by a solution posed as a riddle.

More important, I think, is the connection between the false solution to Samson's riddle—sex—and the true solution to the Philistine answer—love. Camp and Fontaine have done a great deal just now to uncover this basic connection, and I can only append here to their analysis. The Philistines' response is witty enough to supply both the real solution to Samson's riddle and the false one. Moreover, Samson appears, at least formally, to answer the Philistines' questioning solution since we final another bicolon attributed to him which serves as an end frame to the riddling contest. This play on words acknowledges the sexual nuances with which all the riddling has been toying. But it also reveals Samson's blind side, as it were, his inability to distinguish his attraction to the Philistine woman from her problematic loyalties. Certainly, the entire episode points to the central paradox of Samson's legendary biography. Stronger than a lion, he is not stronger than love at the level he recognizes it, and he is eventually mastered by it only to wreak his vengeance at another festive occasion with Philistines. In turn, this suggests that the major riddle is the relationship between physical vigor and emotional maturity. Values seem reversed throughout the Samson story, only righted through entire collapse: the collapse of Samson's repeated efforts to make cultural connections with Philistines, the collapse of the Philistines' building on them, on their false god and on Samson, too. Just as riddles tie riddler and riddlee together in a bond of dissociation, so Samson's entire career, or that which the narrator chooses to tell us of it, links Samson and the Philistines together to achieve Yahweh's "occasion."

WORKS CONSULTED

Ben-Amos, Dan
  1976   "Solution to Riddles." *JAF* 89:249–54.

Burns, Thomas A.
  1976   "Riddling: Occasion to Act." *JAF* 89:139–65.

Ginzberg, Louis
  1913   *The Legends of the Jews.* 7 vols. Philadelphia: The Jewish Publication Society.

Greenstein, Edward L.
  1981   "The Riddle of Samson." *Prooftexts* 1:237–60.

Hamnett, Ian
  1967   "Ambiguity, Classification and Change: The Function of Riddles." *Man* 2:379–92.

Huizinga, Johan
  1950   *Homo Ludens: A Study of the Play Element in Culture.* Boston: Beacon.

Nel, Philip
   1985   "The Riddle of Samson." *Biblica* 66:534–45.

Noy, Dov
   1963   "Riddles in the Wedding Meal." *Maḥanayim* 83:64–71.

Pepicello, W. J. and Thomas A. Green
   1984   *The Language of Riddles.* Columbus: Ohio State University Press.

Sutton-Smith, Brian
   1972   *The Folkgames of Children.* Austin: University of Texas Press.

   1976   "A Developmental Structural Account of Riddles." Pp. 111–19 in *Speech Play: Research and Resources for the Study of Linguistic Creativity.* Ed.Barbara Kirshenblatt-Gimblett. Philadelphia: University of Pennsylvania Press.

Taylor, Archer
   1951   *English Riddles from Oral Tradition.* New York: Octagon Books [reprint:1977].

C. BIBLICAL LAW

The section in biblical law pairs anthropologists Gillian Feeley-Harnik and John Middleton with biblical scholars Edward Greenstein and Robert R. Wilson. The papers and responses richly explore issues of cultural context, in particular, images of Israelite social structure and mores preserved in the literary traditions of the Bible.

Feeley-Harnik's paper is a sensitive literary study of the tale of Ruth drawing comparisons between the "Moses-Aaron-Egypt" complex and the "Naomi-Ruth-Moab-Israel" complex. Feeley-Harnik suggests that the literary and intertextual connections between the stories of King David's ancestors and the Moses-led Exodus solve a contradiction in Israel's view of itself, in its cultural patterns and social relations. How can Israel, whose king is eternal and divine, Lord of the covenant, have a hereditary human king? By echoing motifs and themes of the Exodus, the book of Ruth shows the Davidic covenant to be a mirror of rather than a challenge to the Mosaic covenant. Feeley-Harnik thus views Ruth as an important mediator in Israel's symbolic system helping to bridge the gap between the reality of social structure and an ancient cosmological ideal. Feeley-Harnik comments on the role of women in Ruth and Exodus and explores dichotomies of public/private, outside/inside in the process.

Edward Greenstein is supportive of Feeley-Harnik's work and draws out implications of a feminist perspective, emphasizing that the story and its heroine are nevertheless circumscribed by a strongly anthropocentric framework. Like Zakovitch and Hasan-Rokem, Greenstein enriches the study of Ruth with relevant Rabbinic material. His major criticism of Feeley-Harnik's work, one which she herself shares, concerns the difficulty of placing this sort of literary study in a historical and anthropological context. Traditional literature is, of course, best studied within its cultural setting as a living reflection of and affecter of that culture. This approach becomes difficult when biblical scholars cannot reach consensus on dating a work such as Ruth. On the other hand, Lévi-Straussian style, Feeley-Harnik has pointed to an on-going problem or hitch in Israelite worldview, treating the traditional literary patterns of the Hebrew Scripture as a mythic complex in which contradiction and tension is eased via a process of mediation.

Robert Wilson's essay is a prolegomenon to the study of Israelite ethics that begins to explore ways in which traditional norms or customs, laws, and prophecy may have influenced the making of actual moral decisions by Israelites of various periods and groups. Wilson's paper is particularly relevant in methodology and content to problems we face in exploring the Bible "as folklore," and to Greenstein's questions about traditional literature and historical setting. At the core, Wilson asks how information contained and preserved in traditional media relate to the lives of actual people. Did the various law codes now preserved in the Hebrew Scriptures, for example, reflect and affect social reality? Wilson's work addresses and introduces some of these complex issues in sociology and literature.

John Middleton continues Wilson's examination of issues in Israelite ethics employing a map whose compass reads inside/outside. Middleton examines closely forms of prophetic speech listed by Wilson, with norms and laws, as one of the influences upon Israelite ethical perceptions. A particularly insightful aspect of Middleton's paper explores the edges or the boundary between inside and outside associated with magic, witchcraft and "other expressions of an ambiguous morality." While Middleton's map is formulated in relation to questions about the sources of Israelite ethics, it is entirely relevant to other slices of Israelite tradition, for example, to an analysis of tales of Samson that have been the focus of four of the essays in this volume. Concepts of inside and outside contribute to a deeper understanding of the characterization of Samson and to the riddling scene that encompasses and reveals the hero's relationship to the world beyond his own immediate kin.

13. NAOMI AND RUTH: BUILDING UP THE HOUSE OF DAVID

Gillian Feeley-Harnik

> Give her of the fruit of her hands,
> and let her works praise her in the gates.
>
> Prov 31:31

ABSTRACT

This paper explores the ambiguity of monarchy in the Hebrew Bible by examining the transition from Judges to Kings depicted in the book of Ruth against the background of the transition from bondage as Pharaoh's slaves to freedom as the Lord's slaves in Exodus. As Exodus 1–2 explained the birth of the Israelites out of Egypt, so—it is argued here—Ruth explains the birth of Israelite monarchy out of Moab. The point of the parallel conveyed in Ruth is that King David's monarchy is not a faithless, lawless recreation of Egypt in Canaan.

Monarchy, slavery, and polygamy are regarded as "fully valid yet wrong" in Israelite law: valid in that God ordained them, recognizing that "the imagination of man's heart is evil from his youth" as stated in Gen 8:21, yet wrong in calling into question the covenant relationship between God and Israel (Daube, 1959:1).[1] Biblical opinion on monarchy ranges from condemnation (Judg 9:8–15) to grudging acquiescence (1 Sam 8:4–22) to affirmation (Deut 17:14–20). The inherent conflict in the law is embodied in the contrast between Egypt and Canaan. Even the affirmation includes a warning against recreating Egypt in Canaan: "Only he must not multiply

---

[1] I am grateful to Professor Susan Niditch for inviting me to participate in the conference on "The Hebrew Bible and Folklore" and to the members of the conference for their insightful comments, especially Professor Edward Greenstein, whose response to the paper is printed here.

horses for himself, or cause the people to return to Egypt in order to multiply horses, since the Lord has said to you, 'You shall never return that way again'" (Deut 17:16).

As a social anthropologist, I wonder how that contradiction was experienced in the cultural patterns and social relations of ancient Israel. The scene in 1 Sam 8:4–22, where the elders ask Samuel to appoint them "a king to govern us like all the nations," is central to understanding the institution of Israelite kingship (McCarter:152–62). I will focus on the underlying transition from judges to kings that they themselves evoke (1 Sam 8:5), as presented not in the books of Judges or Samuel, but in the book of Ruth.

The book of Ruth is framed by references to judges at the beginning and kings at the end. Otherwise its time is measured by events in the participants' lives—their journeys, marriages, deaths, labors, and births—suggesting that the storyteller means the transformation of judges into kings to be understood more socially and conceptually than historically.[2] Indeed, most scholars have tended to interpret the references to the Davidic monarchy as incidental to the main plot. Scholars arguing for a late, even post-exilic date for the book of Ruth have suggested that although it provides a genealogy for King David, the story was intended primarily to justify the entry of strangers into Judaism in the time of Ezra and Nehemiah when their entry was contested (May and Metzger:325). There is a "clear trend," if not unanimity, among recent scholars to date the book of Ruth to the period of the monarchy (see Niditch, 1985:451). Yet even while they acknowledge the importance of the story as, in Sasson's terms (251), "a folkloric vehicle for the glorification of David," they still tend to interpret it primarily in terms of interpersonal relations: a betrothal (Sasson; Campbell; Alter:58–59); "the recounting of the nuptials of the Lord and his people" (Green:66); a "struggle for survival in a patriarchal environment" (Trible, 1976:166). Yet Green (55) concludes: "Though the story is judged to be fairly simple, as biblical narratives go, there is still no clear consensus on the plot even after a number of

---

[2]Campbell (50, 57, 169, 170–73) argues that although the genealogy at 4:18–22 may be a later addition, the *inclusio* provided by 1:1 and 4:17b is not. Berlin (109–10) argues that the genealogy was also integral to the original text. Presumably because of its stated time, the book of Ruth is found after Judges in the Septuagint and most other non-Hebrew versions of the Bible. In Hebrew Bibles, it is found either before Psalms or as part of the Festival Scrolls, the former probably being its original place (Campbell:34). Sasson (11–12), in contrast to Campbell, argues that the place of Ruth in the canon was influenced neither by its content nor its "purpose (however formulated)." In keeping with the interpretation presented here, I suggest that the book of Ruth begins the book(s) of Samuel as Exodus 1 and 2 begin the account presented in Exodus.

articles—some recent—dealing with this topic." The importance of law in the narrative has led other scholars to claim that

> the major exegetical issue of the book of Ruth revolves around the connection of Ruth's marriage to Boaz and the redemption of Elimelech's field with, respectively, the pentateuchal laws on levirate marriage and redemption, and with each other" (Beattie:65; see also Rauber:36).

My purpose is not to contest these interpretations, but to explore more closely how the move from judges to kings—be it valid or wrong—is grounded in the relations of Naomi, Ruth, and Boaz. Their story might appear to set a circuitous route to kingship, but I will argue that Ruth is as central to the monarchy as the beginning chapters of Exodus are to the Exodus as a whole and for similar reasons. Exodus 1–2 explains the birth of the Israelites out of Egypt; Ruth explains the birth of Israelite monarchy out of Moab. The point of the parallel is precisely that the Davidic monarchy is not a lawless recreation of Pharaoh's rule.

Part 1: Out of Moab

> In the days when the judges ruled there was a famine in the land, and a certain man of Bethlehem in Judah went to sojourn in the country of Moab, he and his wife and his two sons (Ruth 1:1).

That, too, is why Abram (promised children, but still without them), Sarai his wife, and Lot his brother's son, went down to Egypt (Gen 12:10). When Abram and Lot separate immediately after their return from Egypt, Lot chooses the Jordan valley (Moab), "well watered everywhere . . . like the land of Egypt" (Gen 13:10), leaving the more drought- and famine-prone Canaan to Abram, soon covenanted, but still without descendants.

Jeremiah, who lived during the last years of the monarchy in Judah, warned that "All the men who set their faces to go to Egypt to live there shall die by the sword, by famine, and by pestilence; they shall have no remnant or survivor from the evil which I will bring upon them" (Jer 42:17). Elimelech dies. Naomi is left with her sons, Mahlon and Chilion, who marry Moabite women, Orpah and Ruth, live ten years without having children, and die, "so that the woman was bereft of her two sons and her husband" (1:5).

Naomi starts with her daughters-in-law "to return from the country of Moab," having heard there that "the Lord had visited his people and given them food" (1:6). So the Lord told Moses directly to "depart, go up hence, you and the people you have brought up out of the land of Egypt" to the land flowing with milk and honey, promised to Abraham's descendants (Exod 33:1–3). Naomi would "return to the land of Judah" alone; she tells her daughters-in-law to "return each of you to her mother's house" (1:7–8) since "even if I should have a husband this night and should bear sons, would you therefore wait till they were grown?" (1:12–13), stressing ties through women. They answer in kind: "No, we will return with *you* to *your* people," to which she again responds: "Turn back, my daughters, why will you go with *me?*" (1:10–11, my emphases). In contrast to Moses, Naomi urges people *not* to follow her. But perhaps it is relevant to Naomi's reluctance that Moses does keep asking God why people should follow him, given his "uncircumcised lips" (Exod 6:12). Naomi's fears that she cannot give birth to marriageable sons (1:11–13) may be analogous to Moses' fears that his mouth is incapable of uttering persuasive speech; Ruth may be Naomi's Aaron.

Orpah does go "back to her people and to her gods," but Ruth "clings" to Naomi, vowing to follow her to her very grave (1:14–18). In choosing to follow Naomi, Ruth seems to recognize "the covenant which the Lord commanded Moses to make with the people of Israel in the land of Moab," where Moses himself died (Deut 29:1; 34:5):

> I have set before you life and death, blessing and curse; therefore choose life, that you and your descendants may live, loving the Lord your God, obeying his voice, and cleaving to him; for that means life to you and length of days, that you may dwell in the land which the Lord swore to your fathers, to Abraham, to Isaac, and to Jacob, to give them (Deut 30:19–20).

No pillar of cloud (Deut 31:15) testifies to the Lord's presence in this latter-day journey from Moab to Judah. Yet Naomi sees her own suffering as a clear sign that the Lord alone creates fullness and emptiness (1:13,20–21), or, as witnessed in the Lord's song that Moses taught the Israelites in the land of Moab: "I kill and I make alive" (Deut 31:21; 32:39).[3]

It was on the plains of Moab that Moses counted the Israelites who survived the purges and plagues with which the Lord punished their acts of apostasy in Moab (Numbers 25, 26). At the end of these censuses enumerating the sons of the Israelites, the daughters of Zelophehad came forth to inquire why their father's name should be taken away "because he had no sons? Give to us a possession among our father's brethren" (Num 27:4). The Lord declared that "the daughters of Zelophehad are right" (Num 27:7), going on to pronounce other general laws concerning next of kin. The resourcefulness of Zelophehad's daughters in becoming their father's heirs—in the plains of Moab, where the living are counted after many fathers,

---

[3]In Midrashic commentary, Naomi had been "full with sons and daughters" or pregnant (*Ruth Rabbah* 3:7, Soncino trans.).

husbands, and sons have died—echoes the resourcefulness of Lot's daughters, bereft of husbands, in continuing his line by conceiving and giving birth to Moab and Ben-ammi (Gen 19:30–38). The "determined" choice of "Ruth the Moabitess" not "to return from following" Naomi, her people, and her God (1:16–18, 22; see Num 32:15) suggests that she will be similarly resourceful. Indeed, the storyteller concludes the first part by noting that Naomi and Ruth "came to Bethlehem at the beginning of barley harvest" (1:22).

The parallels between the journeys out of Egypt and out of Moab suggest another instance of women's determination in the face of men's deaths: the saving actions of Shiphrah and Puah, the two Hebrew midwives who are named as fearing God, thus disobeying the King of Egypt and "let[ting] the male children live" (Exod 1:18). Trible (1976:221) makes the striking comment about the Exodus story that

> women nurture the revolution. The Hebrew midwives disobey Pharaoh. His own daughter thwarts him, and her maidens assist . . . As the first to defy the oppressor, women *alone* [her emphasis] take the initiative which leads to deliverance (Exod 1:15–2:10).

I would go still further to suggest that Exodus represents the women as giving birth to the revolution in the person of Moses, and that the book of Ruth represents Naomi and Ruth as performing a similarly heroic act—restoring men's lives by giving birth to kingship in the person of David.

Part 2: The Well Scene—Betrothal and Conception

Naomi's "kinsman of her husband's"—Boaz—is immediately introduced as "a man of wealth," and "Ruth the Moabitess," as she states she will in the very next line, seems to go directly to where he will be found (2:1–2). In contrast to the wilderness, these are tilled fields; Ruth does not wander, her not-returning-from-following intensifies. The narrator emphasizes that she works hard, "without resting even for a moment" (2:7), as Boaz hears when he learns that Ruth is "the Moabite maiden, who came back with Naomi from the country of Moab" (2:6). Now Boaz urges Ruth to cleave to his field and his maidens and young men, and he offers her water:

> Do not go to glean in another field or leave this one, but keep close to my maidens. Let your eyes be upon the field which they are reaping, and go after them. Have I not charged the young men not to molest you? And when you are thirsty, go to the vessels and drink what the young men have drawn (2:8–9).

When Ruth is quick to point out her foreign origins, Boaz responds by spelling out the comparison to Abraham already implied at the beginning of the story:

> how you left your father and mother and your native land and came to
> a people that you did not know before (see Gen 12:1)—

perhaps evoking in "the God of Israel, under whose wings you have come to take refuge" (2:11–12) the "eagle that stirreth up her nest" in the same Lord's song that Moses taught the Israelites in Moab (Deut 32:11).

Like the eagle, Boaz feeds Ruth with "produce of the field" (2:14; cf. Deut 32:13) so plentiful that she has enough "left over after being satisfied" to give to Naomi with her barley when she returns to the city in the evening (2:18). Ruth identifies Boaz as the man "with whom she had worked," in a passage where "worked" is repeated three times (2:19). Naomi responds, "Blessed be he by the Lord, whose kindness has not forsaken the living or the dead!" identifying Boaz as "a relative of ours, one of our nearest kin" (2:20). The scene closes with Ruth the Moabitess "keeping close" to Boaz's people as well as to her mother-in-law until the harvest's end (2:23).

Alter (58) identifies the scene in which Boaz offers Ruth water as a variant of the well scene he sees as representing betrothal in the stories of Abraham's servant and Rebekah (Gen 24:10–61), Jacob and Rachel (Gen 29:1–20), and Moses and the seven daughters of the Midianite priest Reuel (Exod 2:15b–21). The difference in Ruth is simply that gender and geography are reversed.[4] I suggest that these are scenes not only of betrothal, but also of conception. The reversals reflect the fact that the woman, not the man, has initiated both. Alter (55) notes the premonition concerning conception in the story of Jacob who has to remove the huge stone from the well. The association with conception is more evident in scenes he does not consider, the betrothal having already occurred, as indeed it has for Ruth. For example, the annunciation of Ishmael's birth to Hagar takes place at "the spring of water in the wilderness . . . on the way to Shur" (Gen 16:7–11), and his rebirth from near death at "a well of water" in the wilderness of Beer-sheba (Gen 21:14, 19), wildernesses of inelection from which Ishmael never emerges.

---

[4]Perhaps with Greek models in mind, Alter interprets these type-scenes as narratives about male heroes, not narratives about generational continuity involving men and women alike. His analysis of the betrothal type-scene helps to illuminate New Testament episodes that he does not consider, for example, Jesus Christ's encounter with the woman at the well who proves to be a Samaritan with many men but no husband (John 4:1–42). But here, too, the scene seems to involve not only betrothal but conception, a union that will produce "eternal life."

Moses' rescue is another instance of birth from water (Exod 2:1–
10). Moses was already alive, but he might as well have been unborn
given Pharaoh's edict. Pharaoh's daughter gave him renewed life
when she "drew him out of the water" (Exod 2:10), and—owing to
the intervention of Moses' sister working together with his mother—
returned Moses to his mother to nurse. Pharaoh's daughter is said to
have commemorated her birth of Moses in naming him after the Hebrew verb "to draw out." Moses is also an Egyptian name derived
from the Egyptian word "to beget a child" (May and Metzger:68, n.
10).[5]

Part 3: Tokens of Fertility

In part three, the storyteller tells how Ruth conceived on her
wedding night. The account begins when Ruth follows Naomi's careful instructions by washing, anointing her body, and dressing in her
best clothes; it culminates in the famous scene on the threshing floor;
and it ends when Ruth returns to Naomi, bearing tokens of her fertility. Naomi gives Ruth very explicit words of instruction as an older
woman might instruct a younger one. She concludes that "he will tell
you what to do" (3:4). In fact, Ruth tells Boaz to "spread your skirt
over your maidservant, for you are next of kin" (3:9). Although most
scholars agree that Ruth is asking Boaz to marry her, they disagree
about whether the storyteller is also suggesting that they consum-
mated the future marriage. As Niditch (1979:148) points out, the situation is definitely unusual and whichever the case, "like Tamar,
Ruth risks an accusation of harlotry." Carmichael (87), who focuses
mainly on Boaz's "treading" as an image of sexual penetration, dis-
tinguishes Ruth from Tamar and especially Lot's daughters, suggesting that her actions, "if somewhat daring and sailing close to the
wind," cannot be confused with theirs; "after all, her Israelite mother-
in-law directed it initially." I suggest that Ruth's actions are no less

---

[5]According to Exod 2:5–6, Pharaoh's daughter sent her maid-servant to get the
basket of bulrushes, but she opened it herself. Some later narratives of Moses'
birth depicted Pharaoh's daughter herself as saving Moses, as illustrated, for example, in frescos on the walls of the synagogue at Dura-Europos painted ca. 3rd
century C.E. (Weitzmann:228, 230). Midrashic commentaries on Exodus and
Deuteronomy suggest "a trace of a Jewish legend of a conception without a human father," possibly the conception of Moses (Daube, 1956:5). Such a legend
might have given rise to the stories of the virgin Mary's birth of Jesus as recounted in Matthew and Luke (Daube, 1956:9), which in turn provided bases for
the birth-stories of Alexander and Krishna (Derrett:290–91). Judging by these
studies, stories emphasizing the importance of women in reproducing social institutions, through the birth of key figures in whom they are embodied, are likely
to have been even more elaborate and widespread than the canonized scriptures
indicate.

daring than Moses' actions in purging the murmurers in the desert according to God's command, though we never hear God's command directly (Exod 32:26–28). Ruth's daring is evident from the fact that Boaz, who blesses her for her action, must also urge her not to let herself be seen (3:10, 14), presumably until he can carry out his part of the covenant.

I think the storyteller has deliberately created a situation that can be seen in more than one way, which for that reason alone (though the text provides specific clues) draws attention to other cases that turn on resemblances, thus on participants' and listeners' different capacities to distinguish what is from what seems to be. Gen 19:30–38 portrays Lot's daughters not as hardened committers of incest, but as women who are impelled to "preserve offspring" in the face of men's deaths by means they must assume their father would not see as right, since each waits until "he [would] not know" to lie down with him (as Boaz seems to urge Ruth to do in 3:14).

Likewise, in the case of Tamar, who is also faced with men's deaths, the text simply says that "she put off her widow's garments and put on a veil, wrapping herself up" (Gen 38:14). She knows she is not a harlot, and we know she is not a harlot. Judah "thought her to be a harlot for she had covered her face" (Gen 38:15), and later Hirah the Adullamite refers to her, euphemistically perhaps, as a cult prostitute when asking her whereabouts from "the men at the place," who respond, "No cult prostitute has been here," which Hirah is made to repeat verbatim to Judah (Gen 38:21–22). We could even see Tamar's putting off her widow's garments and putting on a veil from her perspective as preparing for a wedding night that is finally to bear fruit (as in Gen 24:65 and perhaps 29:23; Song 6:7). Judah himself says that Tamar acted "more righteously" than he (Gen 38:26), and Boaz likewise blesses Ruth a second time (3:10).[6]

The storyteller connects Ruth to Lot's daughters by repeatedly referring to her own Moabite origins, by Naomi's instructions and Ruth's actions in going to Boaz when he has lain down after eating and drinking, and by Boaz's own blessing that she has not gone after young men, which suggests that he is much older than she, and reminds the listener of Ruth's choice to cleave ever more closely to his side (3:3, 7, 10). Connections to the story of Tamar and Judah are made through the repeated references to next of kin and explicitly in 4:12. After Boaz blesses Ruth, he emphasizes that

> I am a near kinsman, yet there is a kinsman nearer than I. Remain this night, and in the morning, if he will do the part of the next of kin for

---

[6]Niditch (1979:148–49) concludes that "Ruth's radical approach to her problem is viewed as positive by the author as was Tamar's," and notes that early rabbinic opinion concerning Tamar was also positive.

you, well; let him do it; but if he is not willing to do the part of the next of kin for you, then, as the Lord lives, I will do the part of the next of kin for you. Lie down until the morning (3:12–13).

The passage suggests, as the story of Tamar and Judah illustrates, that the firstborn is not always first to inherit. Election does not follow automatically from primogeniture. It is a matter of choice—God's choosing, people's choosing—the voluntary contractualism that is fundamental to the covenant that God made with the Israelites in the wilderness (see Hillers:80–81; Walzer:73–98). The storyteller introduces the nearer kinsman to reaffirm the point that Ruth's own strangeness makes concerning the strangeness of the Israelites themselves. This began with Abraham whom God commanded to "go from your country and your kindred and your father's house to the land that I will show you" (Gen 12:1), and continued with Moses who names his firstborn son Gershom because "I have been a sojourner in a foreign land" (Exod 2:22). Yet Moses chose to return from Egypt.

After they have arisen "before one could recognize another" and Boaz urges Ruth that they should keep people from seeing for a while (3:14), Boaz asks Ruth to hold out her mantle so he can fill it with six measures of barley to give to Naomi when she returns to the city. Ruth has no need for "tokens of virginity" (Deut 22:12–31) such as bloody sheets might provide, because she has long since been married. The grain in her mantle is surely a token of fertility, but Ruth explains Boaz's gift in his own words: "You must not go back empty-handed to your mother-in-law" (3:17). Indeed, she does not. Ruth having worked with Boaz's maidens throughout the harvest, and he having already said that "all my fellow townsmen know that you are a woman of worth" (3:11), Boaz would surely "Give her of the fruit of her hands, and let her works praise her in the gates" (Prov 31:31). Naomi's recognition that Ruth's own works include the conception of Obed, which they had worked together to achieve, seems clear from her response. As she instructed at the beginning of part 3, so she instructs and predicts at its end: "Wait, my daughter, until you learn how the matter turns out, for the man will not rest, but will settle the matter today" (3:18). The women have done their work, now the man will do his.

Part 4: At the Gate

Like midwives, mother-in-law and daughter-in-law have succeeded in bringing the child "to the birth" (Isa 66:9): out of the dark fertile ground of close interpersonal relations, conveyed in the intimately conversational narrative, to the gate of the city, a place of public scrutiny, expressed in codified law. Boaz's determination in handling the legitimation of these new relations reflects well on his own daring and resourcefulness as the farer kinsman who goes directly to what he seeks and cleaves to it. "Boaz went up to the gate and sat down there" (4:1); and one after another, the next of kin and ten "men of the elders of the city" come by, turn aside, and sit down in response to his request (4:2).

The legal procedures spell out the terms of the covenant that has already been introduced and achieved in the preceding three chapters (1:8, 2:20, 3:10). Their implications are sharpened now by the fact that the unnamed "next of kin" *chooses* not to "restore the name of the dead to his inheritance," lest he impair his own (4:5–6). So Boaz *chooses*, now before witnesses, to redeem his inheritance "that the name of the dead may not be cut off from among his brethren and from the gate of his native place" (4:10). The people and elders at the gate confirm the greater closeness of the farer kinsman when they respond to Boaz: "We are witnesses. May the Lord make the woman, who is coming into your house, like Rachel and Leah, who together built up the house of Israel" (4:11), naming the youngest first and alluding to terrible conflicts over child-bearing (Gen 29:15–30:24) that have been overcome in Naomi and Ruth's cooperative labor.[7] They intensify their point by adding: "may your house be like the house of Perez, whom Tamar bore to Judah, because of the children that the Lord will give you by this young woman" (4:12). Perez, though second, came out first, as the midwife proved with the scarlet thread, testifying to it in naming him (Gen 38:28–30).

Given the references to Ephrathah and Bethlehem that immediately follow, I wonder if the storyteller also means to remind the listener that Rachel died in childbirth, bearing Jacob's twelfth son, since the pillar that Jacob set upon her grave "on the way to Ephrath (that is, Bethlehem)" is said to be "there to this day" (Gen 35:19–20). It may also be relevant that the pillar marking the grave of Rachel who died bearing the progenitor of the twelfth tribe, is contrasted in the immediately preceding passage of Genesis with the stone pillar at Bethel that Jacob set up to commemorate the spot where God renamed him Israel, saying:

> I am God Almighty: be fruitful and multiply; a nation and a company of nations shall come from you, and kings shall spring from you (Gen 35:11).

---

[7] I am grateful to Professor Galit Hasan-Rokem for pointing out a passage in *Ekah* (Lamentations) *Rabbati* (Proem 24, Soncino trans.) where Rachel and Leah, in a similar reversal of the hostile relationship in Genesis, are represented as working together, thus saving the Israelites from extinction (see Hasan-Rokem).

It is perhaps a more distant possibility that these references to Rachel's death in the course of Benjamin's birth would evoke memories of the Benjaminites' murder by rape of the Levite's concubine from Bethlehem, resulting in the civil war that ended in the extinction of the Benjaminites' women as told in the concluding chapters of Judges (19, 20). The storyteller might be alluding to Saul, who proved to be a barren line as far as Israelite kingship was concerned. So listeners might recognize once again the hazards—death in childbirth, barrenness, rape—amidst which women carried out their own acts of heroism in defying threats to extinguish the Israelites that were usually directed at men, but sometimes resulted in the extinction of women as well.

Part 5: The Birth

After a long gestation and labor, completed in adherence to God's law, the human conception and birth follow in a rush of verbs:

> So Boaz took Ruth and she became his wife; and he went in to her, and the Lord gave her conception, and she bore a son (4:13).

They celebrate the life that comes from loving and cleaving to the Lord, epitomized in the union of Ruth and Boaz, but including the whole community. Pharaoh's daughter chose to adopt a Hebrew child, while paying his mother to nurse him; "and he became her son; and she named him Moses, for she said, 'Because I drew him out of the water'" (Exod 2:10). In this case, Ruth the Moabitess has chosen to become a daughter to Naomi who has chosen to return. Naomi takes Ruth's child to nurse, and

> the women of the neighborhood gave him a name, saying "A son has been born to Naomi." They named him Obed; he was the father of Jesse, the father of David (4:17–18).

Naomi serves as midwife to Ruth—her entrance into the community and her birth of Obed, as Ruth serves as midwife to Naomi's return and regeneration in Obed.

According to Campbell (166), many scholars have assumed that 4:17 might read: "And the neighborhood women called him Benno'am, saying 'A son (*bēn*) is born to Naomi,'" in keeping with such punning elsewhere in the Bible. He sees the second naming of Obed as displacing "the original name, whatever it may have been, with the name needed to get the link to David into the picture." But perhaps Obed is the original, punning name. Women usually bestow these punning names to commemorate the circumstances of a baby's birth. Given the neighborhood women's knowledge of Naomi's former bitterness (1:19–22), Obed ("worker/worshipper") may celebrate the work, the service or devotion to God, that Naomi and Ruth have accomplished together, enabling them to bring fullness out of emptiness.

Giving Birth to Kingship

Betrothal scenes in the Bible evoke God's betrothal of Israel, which is one of the commonest metaphors for the covenant relationship. I suggest that these are not only betrothals, but also conceptions of a people from this union who are both chosen and choosing. These betrothal-conception scenes usually focus on the groom who is God's bride. In Ruth, where the bride seeks her partner, the emphasis is on women's efforts to restore the dead through the living, as it is in the prototypical story to which I think Ruth's story refers, the birth of Moses.

Much of the imagery representing God as both mother and father comes from Exodus.[8] Moses himself is represented as motherly and fatherly, drawing the Israelites out of the Red Sea and feeding them in the desert until a new generation is born. If the Israelites were raised from political infancy to maturity in the wilderness between Egypt and Canaan, they had to be born out of Egypt to begin with. Judging by Moses' farewell addresses in Moab, they had to keep bearing themselves out as well. If they were brought out of Egypt by the strong hand of God, commemorated in the consecration of the first-born, so they bore themselves out of Moab by choosing life. The parallels between these acts of not returning from following in Ruth and Exodus-Deuteronomy seem intended to assert that the house of David will not reproduce Egypt in Canaan because it recognizes God's ultimate sovereignty. Its God-fearing origins are evident in the fruitful relations that Naomi, Ruth, and Boaz have with one another, in contrast to the drought and destruction portended by the fiery brambles in Judg 9:15.

Although the book of Ruth cannot be dated on content alone, it is notable that King Josiah explicitly characterized his reforms as a return to Mosaic practice, including the reinstitution of "the passover to the Lord your God, as it is written in this book of the covenant" (2

---

[8]See Trible (1976:218–21; 1978:31–71) for a discussion of womb imagery in the Hebrew Bible and its association with ideas of compassion; see Camp (24–29) for a discussion of the symbolism of biblical images of mothers, its relationship to "wise women" in 2 Samuel 14 and 20, and to the image of Wisdom as a woman in Proverbs 1–9. The interpretation of the book of Ruth offered here would certainly support their views that female images of creation and nurture are not minor or isolated themes, but central to understanding creativity, humanity, and divinity as depicted in the biblical texts.

Kgs 23:21) and as a rededication to "the words of the law . . . written
in the book that Hilkiah the priest found in the house of the Lord" (v.
24). The writer emphasizes that

> no such passover had been kept since the days of the judges who judged
> Israel, or during all the days of the kings of Israel or of the kings of Ju-
> dah; but in the eighteenth year of King Josiah this passover was kept to
> the Lord in Jerusalem (2 Kgs 23:22–23);

and, likewise, that

> Before him [Josiah] there was no king like him, who turned to the Lord
> with all his heart and with all his soul and with all his might, according
> to all the law of Moses; nor did any like him arise after him (v. 25).

Jeremiah, who presented himself as sent by God "to say, 'Do not
go to Egypt to live there'" (Jer 43:2), prophesied during the reign of
King Josiah, whose adherence to the law he saw as an exception to
the faithlessness of the Israelites. But Josiah was probably not the
only king to portray his lawfulness in this form. Earlier reformer
kings, such as Jehoshaphat or Hezekiah, are likely to have seen themselves not only as David reborn, but also as Moses reborn.

The book of Ruth may convey ideas about the moral and legal
origins of Israelite monarchy; nevertheless, it is not written like the
kingly histories or the laws . The creation scenes in Ruth 1–3 and in
Exodus 1–2 are women's stories in several respects: they are presented from the perspectives of women; they repeatedly draw attention to social connections among women and among men through
women; they emphasize the heroism of women in the face of mortal
dangers unique to women; and perhaps—at least in the case of the
book of Ruth—they are even told by women (see Campbell:22–23). In
keeping with these structural emphases on women, these creation
scenes portray women's work—from their travail to their agricultural
work to their work in connecting people—as being no less fundamental in reproducing Israelite society as men's work, a vision completely
in keeping with the imagery of a God who acts as both mother and
father, while transcending both (see Trible, 1978: 31–71) .

This is why there are so many foreign women in just these well
scenes about conception—Egyptian princesses, Egyptian slaves,
Moabitesses. Perhaps in Ruth they represent the openness of
Judaism, but I suggest they are also meant to say that birth is a social
process like politics. It is (should be) likewise the result of consent;
beyond that, it is the result of women's work, sometimes fixing (Gen
16:2), sometimes "mighty wrestlings" (Gen 30:8), inevitably travail
(compare Isa 66:7–9). The numerous parallels between food and
progeny in the book of Ruth strengthen this possibility. "Like Rachel
and Leah, who together built up the house of Israel" (4:11), so Naomi

and Ruth *created* fullness through work. Their work is cooperative to the point of denying well-known conflicts between women that are emphasized in other accounts. It involves communities as well as households—the elder women who care for Naomi in the town and the younger maidservants with whom Ruth works in the field. The people and elders alike represent the birth of children, ultimately from God, as women's gift to men: "may your house be like the house of Perez, whom Tamar bore to Judah, because of the children that the Lord will give you by this young woman" (4:12).

The book of Ruth turns on contrasts between famine and plenty, death and regeneration conceived in social terms. It evokes recurrent cases involving the actions of women when men failed to come forward, when they got angry like Jacob, saying "Am I in the place of God, who has withheld from you the fruit of the womb?" (Gen 30:2), especially when they killed or were killed. Cooper's (1987) analysis of the laws of mixture may be relevant here. Cooper argues that the biblical restrictions against mixing meat and milk, linen and wool, and wheat and grapes expresses a more basic opposition between killing and promoting life. The first term in each pair is the one found in both the most sacred and the most profane contexts, but in the most sacred contexts only after something has been "removed." In circumcision, the *'orlâ* is the foreskin.

Cooper does not pursue the implications of these parallels, nor can I do that here. I would simply note that Naomi, Ruth, and Boaz, in contrast to Orpah and the nameless next of kin, are unusual in exemplifying the life-giving responsiveness that is said to result when people remove the *'orlâ* inside, around the heart (Lev 26:41; Deut 10:16; Jer 4:4). More often, the contrast is drawn in ways that separate men from women. Nevertheless, if women's unrestrained sexuality is associated with death and men's works with life, as perhaps in Genesis (chaps. 2–3), so in other contexts men's uncircumcised sexuality may be associated with death and women's works with life.[9]

---

[9]These kinds of interdependencies presumably underlie the persistence of dual male-female imagery in Torah and the *sefer Torah* or Torah scroll. Goldberg (1987) analyzes the human attributes of Torah primarily in male terms. His data provides examples of what could be interpreted either as consistently more masculine attributes of the humanity of the Torah or as instances of an historical process of the masculinization of Wisdom/Book that, in scripture at least, is as much (possibly more) feminine as masculine.

Kirshenblatt-Gimblett's (1982) analysis of Western Ashkenazic Torah binders could be interpreted in the same way. While describing (like Ashkenazim) the Torah as a "queen," completely in keeping with the feminine nature of scriptural Wisdom, she shows how Ashkenazim saw Torah binders as binding a newly circumcised boy to the Torah and to the community of believers. Goldberg suggests that the Torah pointer is a phallus and the oral transmission of the Torah from men to boys is a form of male procreation (114–16). However, the central portion

The dialectical imagery of gender in the Hebrew Bible is inseparable from the recurrent questions concerning chosenness and
choosing. While men's works seem focused mainly on building up
lines of first-born sons, women's works seem to be associated especially with events that persistently undercut primogeniture or repair
recurrent and disastrous attacks on firstborn males in favor of relations based on choice, faith, knowledge, *recognition* of what lies beneath veils, skins, or skirts.[10]

Women seem to be represented in the Hebrew Bible as particularly well suited to discerning the wombside or inner face of things,
in distinguishing recurrent lookalikes, for example, "fountains of
living waters" as opposed to "broken cisterns that can hold no water"
or a "slave . . . homeborn servant" as opposed to a worshipper of the
one God, in the servant's song about the woman who looks barren for
not having born vast numbers of faithless, lawless children:

Sing, O barren one, who did not bear;
break forth into singing and cry aloud,
you who have not been in travail!
For the children of the desolate one will be more
than the children of her that is married, says the Lord.
Enlarge the place of your tent,
and let the curtains of your habitations be stretched out;
hold not back, lengthen your cords
and strengthen your stakes.
For you will spread abroad to the right and to the left,
and your descendants will possess the nations

---

of the Torah binder usually depicts marriage and the multiplication of progeny
that is the blessing of the union of men and women. Possibly the Torah binder is
seen as a kind of umbilical cord (though Kirshenblatt-Gimblett does not suggest
this). The feminine regenerative qualities of Torah as queen are conveyed especially clearly in the Simḥat Torah rituals, where the Torah is the bride and the
readers of Deuteronomy and Genesis are her bridegrooms.

Further ethnographic research on the humanity of Torah as conceived in different times and places would be valuable. Prell (1987), for example, analyzes
struggles concerning gender focused on two American Simḥat Torah ceremonies.
She interprets these struggles as the result of male bias in the Hebrew Bible, but
they may have resulted from an historical differentiation of gender roles related
to the embattled circumstances of Jews in the Diaspora (see Kuzmack).

[10]Alter (4, 9, 10) analyzes how the recurrent use of "recognizing" (*hakkēr*)
structures the story of Tamar and Judah in Genesis 38 and links it to the
preceding narrative in which Joseph's brothers (but especially Judah) deceive
Jacob, using Joseph's tunic dipped in goat's blood (Gen 37:32–33). I would
emphasize that the theme of "recognition" reverberates throughout the later
stories in Genesis for example, the stories of Sarah and Hagar, Ishmael and Isaac,
Rachel and Leah (and their paired maidservants), Rachel's twins, Tamar's twins
in the writings of the prophets, and in Psalms.

and will people the desolate cities (Isa 54:1–3).[11]

Beruriah of second century C.E. Palestine, one of the few wise women in Talmudic literature, is remembered for her response concerning these lines, especially her logic that scholars should always "look at the end of the verse" (Gordis:243):

> A certain *Min* said to Beruriah: It is written *Sing, O barren, thou that didst not bear* (Isa 54:1). Because she did not bear is she to sing? She replied to him: You fool! Look to the end of the verse where it is written, *For the children of the desolate shall be more than the children of the married wife, saith the Lord.* But what then is the meaning of *a barren that did not not bear?* Sing, O community of Israel, who resemblest a barren woman, for not having born children like you for Gehenna (TB *Berakhot* 10a).

The singing of women who produce children of faith will confound the cries aloud of women who have been in labor, but not the travail that gives birth to communities of Israelites. All these resemblances turn on the difference between an Israel dedicated solely to God and an Israel "like all the nations," or on the question of how Israel can be "like all the nations" if dedicated wholly to God.

Perhaps it is in keeping with a special association of women with this enduring tension between the seemingness and realness of things that biblical images of women are so strikingly mutable: mothers and daughters (in-law), elder and younger, serving as midwives to one another as in the case of Naomi and Ruth; alternately barren and fertile, desolate and married, as in this passage from Isaiah, referring to different kinds of women and to Women. Ezekiel (chap. 16) relies on this mutability when he moves from one image into the next almost imperceptibly. Jerusalem turns back and forth from a bloody, fertile maiden to a bloody, newborn baby just as the Lord says, clearly speaking of mutable Israelites for whom laws can be fully valid yet wrong:

> When I passed by you again and looked upon you, behold, you were at the age for love; and I spread my skirt over you, and covered your nakedness: yea, I plighted my troth to you and entered into a covenant with you, says the Lord God, and you became mine. Then I bathed you with water and washed off your blood from you, and anointed you with oil . . . (Ezek 16:8–9).

---

[11]Perhaps Ruth's request of Boaz, "spread your skirt over your maidservant, for you are next of kin" (3:9), is also meant to suggest the enlarging and strengthening of the homestead, the "spread[ing] abroad to the right and to the left," which the descendants of the woman who only seems barren will do in these verses from Isaiah.

I have argued that the book of Ruth depicts women's work as essential to creating the Davidic monarchy. The form of the book may express similar contrasts along gender lines between narrative created by repeating words with changed meanings, punning, and other forms of structural ambiguity regarding re-cognition in the broadest sense, and laws intended to establish clear-cut "hedges" (Job 1:10; 3:23). One may come before the other—in this case, women's work comes before men's—but both are finally inseparable.

Conclusion

In the Pabir kingdom of Biu in pre-colonial northern Nigeria, the Maigira, a senior daughter of a previous ruler, was seen as giving birth to kingship during the interval between one ruler and the next. Titled women seem to have played similarly essential roles in dual monarchies throughout Africa. More would be known of their activities had western observers thought differently about the nature of power and politics. Rattray, an early District Commissioner in the Gold Coast, who has provided the best ethnography on Ashanti "queen mothers" that has been published to date, said of his own work:

> I have asked the old men and women why I did not know all this. . . .
> The answer is always the same: "The white man never asked us this;
> you have dealings with and recognize only men, we supposed the Eu-
> ropean considered women of no account, and we know you do not rec-
> ognize them as we have always done" (Rattray:84).

Israelite society is often described as patriarchal, but it is unclear how much of this derives from the scriptures themselves and how much from biblical scholarship and popular understanding. Bird (1974, 1987) and Hackett (1985) provide analyses of anthropological and historical literature on gender that would help to broaden perspectives on biblical material. Comparative ethnographic research would confirm Bird's (1987:339) point that "what is needed is a new reconstruction of the history of Israelite religion, not a new chapter on women." It is not simply a matter of abandoning the concept of patriarchy, inaccurate in most contexts, but of rethinking the nature of society. Melanesian ethnography provides one of the best examples of this process in social anthropology. The Trobrianders living off the northeast coast of Papua New Guinea are famous in world ethnography not only for men's *kula* exchange, described by Malinowski and others, but also for their alleged ignorance of men's role in conception. The "virgin birth" controversy, as Delaney (1986) has convincingly argued, was really an argument about "paternity," the assumption that men alone create the child; women merely nurture it in the womb. As such, it derived far more from western ideas and practices concerning conception than from those of Trobrianders.[12]

Weiner's (1976) reanalysis of the Trobriand case, based on further ethnographic research, incorporates data on women's exchanges at funerals that Malinowski knew about, but ignored. Her analysis provides one of the clearest examples of a case in which women's work is considered to be as essential to the reproduction of social life as men's work. She shows that Trobriand ideas about gender, sexuality, and the reproduction of persons are inseparable from their ideas and practices about the reproduction of society through political-economic means. Trobriand speech has not been analyzed systematically from this perspective; nevertheless, other studies show how linguistic genres, especially forms of direct and indirect speech, are organized along gender lines (for example, Philips et al.).

Delaney argues, on the basis of fieldwork in Turkey, that the monogenetic theory of procreation reflected in the "virgin birth" controversy, in which women bear children, but men alone create them, derives from scriptural sources common to Muslims and Christians alike. The male-female imagery of the Hebrew Bible is strikingly absent from New Testament writing about God, but it is fundamental not only to Mary's virgin birth, but Jesus's feeding miracles and Paul's mission as a whole. The roots of these images in earlier Israelite conceptions about the regenerative powers of women and men and the nature of their transformations during the critical intertestamental period warrant further research.

WORKS CONSULTED

Alter, Robert
	1981	*The Art of Biblical Narrative.* New York: Basic.

Beattie, D. R. G.
	1978	"Redemption in Ruth, and Related Matters: A Response to Jack M. Sasson." *JSOT* 23:55–68.

---

[12]Biblical scholars may be familiar with the beginnings of the "virgin birth" controversy through Leach's (1967) comparison of the Trobriand and Christian cases. Leach did not consider the ethnocentric assumptions about gender that were involved.

Berlin, Adele
1983   *Poetics and Interpretation of Biblical Narrative.* Sheffield: JSOT.

Bird, Phyllis
1974   "Images of Woman in the Old Testament." Pp. 41–88 in *Religion and Sexism: Images of Woman in the Jewish and Christian Tradition.* Ed. Rosemary Radford Ruether. New York: Simon and Schuster.

1985   "The Place of Women in the Israelite Cultus." Pp. 397–419 in *Ancient Israelite Religion. Essays in Honor of Frank Moore Cross.* Ed. Patrick D. Miller, Jr., Paul D. Hanson, and S. Dean McBride. Philadelphia: Fortress.

Camp, Claudia
1985   *Wisdom and the Feminine in the Book of Proverbs.* Sheffield: Almond/JSOT.

Campbell, Edward F., Jr.
1975   *Ruth: A New Translation with Introduction. Notes. and Commentary.* AB 7. Garden City, NY: Doubleday.

Carmichael, Calum
1979   *Women, Law and the Genesis Traditions.* Edinburgh: Edinburgh University Press.

Cohen, Ronald
1977   "Oedipus Rex and Regina: the Queen Mother in Africa." *Africa* 47:14–30.

Cooper, Samuel
1987   "The Laws of Mixture: An Anthropological Study in Halakhah." Pp. 55–74 in *Judaism Viewed From Within and From Without: Anthropological Studies.* Ed. H. E. Goldberg. Albany, NY: State University of New York Press.

Daube, David
1956   *New Testament and Rabbinic Judaism.* London: Athlone.

1959   "Concessions to Sinfulness in Jewish Law." *JJSt* 10:1–13.

Delaney, Carol
1986   "The Meaning of Paternity and the Virgin Birth Debate." *Man* 21:494–513.

Derrett, J. Duncan M.
  1971   "Virgin Birth in the Gospels." *Man* 6:289–93.

Goldberg, Harvey E.
  1987   "Torah and Children: Symbolic Aspects of the Reproduction of Jews and Judaism." Pp. 107–30 in *Judaism Viewed From Within and From Without: Anthropological Studies*. Ed. H. E. Goldberg. Albany, NY: State University of New York Press.

Gordis, Robert
  1940   "Beruriah (Valeria)." P. 243 in *The Universal Jewish Encyclopedia*, vol. 2. New York: Universal Jewish Encyclopedia.

Green, Barbara
  1982   "The Plot of the Biblical Story of Ruth." *JSOT* 23:55–68.

Hackett, Jo Ann
  1985   "'In the Days of Jael': Reclaiming the History of Women in Ancient Israel." Pp. 15–38 in *Immaculate and Powerful: The Female in Sacred Image and Social Reality*. Ed. Clarissa W. Atkinson, Constance H. Buchanan, and Margaret R. Miles. Harvard Women's Studies in Religion Series. Boston: Beacon.

Hasan-Rokem, Galit
  1987   "'My Sister's Voice': Female Symbolism in Lamentations Rabbati" (ms.).

Hillers, Delbert R.
  1969   *Covenant: The History of a Biblical Idea*. Baltimore, MD: Johns Hopkins University Press.

Kirshenblatt-Gimblett, Barbara
  1982   "The Cut That Binds: The Western Ashkenazic Torah Binder as Nexus Between Circumcision and Torah." Pp. 136–46 in *Celebration: Studies in Festivity and Ritual*. Ed. V. Turner. Washington, D.C.: Smithsonian Institution.

Kuzmack, Linda
  1976   "Aggadic Approaches to Biblical Women." Pp. 248–56 in *The Jewish Woman: New Perspectives*. Ed. Elizabeth Koltun. New York: Schocken.

Leach, Edmund
1967 "Virgin Birth." *Proceedings of the Royal Anthropological Institute*, 1966:39–49.

May, Harbert G. and Bruce M. Metzger
1977 *The New Oxford Annotated Bible with the Apocrypha*. Revised Standard Version, containing the second edition of the New Testament and an expanded edition of the Apocrypha. New York: Oxford University Press.

McCarter, P. Kyle, Jr.
1980 *I Samuel. A New Translation with Introduction Notes and Commentary*. AB 8. Garden City, NY: Doubleday.

Niditch, Susan
1979 "The Wronged Woman Righted: An Analysis of Genesis 38." *HTR* 72:143–49.

1985 "Legends of Wise Heroes and Heroines." Pp. 445–63 in *The Hebrew Bible and Its Modern Interpreters*. Ed. Douglas A. Knight and G. M. Tucker. Philadelphia, PA: Fortress and Chico, CA: Scholars.

Philips, Susan U., Susan Steele, and Christine Tanz (eds.)
1987 *Language, Gender and Sex in Comparative Perspective*. London: Cambridge University Press.

Prell, Riv-Ellen
1987 "Sacred Categories and Social Relations: The Visibility and Invisibility of Gender in an American Jewish Community." Pp. 171–93 in *Judaism Viewed from Within and from Without: Anthropological Studies*. Ed. H. E. Goldberg. Albany, NY: State University of New York Press.

Rattray, Robert S.
1923 *Ashanti*. Oxford: Clarendon.

Rauber, D. F.
1970 "Literary Values in the Bible: The Book of Ruth." *JBL* 89:27–37.

Sasson, Jack M.
1979 *Ruth: A New Translation with a Philological Commentary and a Formalist-folklorist Interpretation*. Baltimore: Johns Hopkins University Press.

Trible, Phyllis
1976 "Depatriarchalizing in Biblical Interpretation." Pp. 217–40 in *The Jewish Woman: New Perspectives*. Ed. Elizabeth Koltun. New York: Schocken.

1978 *God and the Rhetoric of Sexuality*. Philadelphia: Fortress.

Weitzmann, Kurt
1971 "The Illustration of the Septuagint." Pp. 201–31 in *No Graven Images: Studies in Art and the Hebrew Bible*. Ed. Joseph Gutmann. New York: Ktav [orig. pub. in 1952/53].

Walzer, Michael
1985 *Exodus and Revolution*. New York: Basic.

Weiner, Annette B.
1976 *Women of Value Men of Renown: New Perspectives in Trobriand Exchange*. Austin, TX: University of Texas Press.

14. On Feeley-Harnik's Reading of Ruth
Edward L. Greenstein

Gillian Feeley-Harnik's reading of Ruth is rich in association, illuminating diverse Biblical passages by viewing them in a mutually clarifying light. It is, however, more than exegesis, as it identifies the redemption of Israel itself through what many will see as a redemption of Israel's women from long and entrenched traditions of patriarchal interpretation. Feeley-Harnik finds in the resounding revolution of Israel in Egypt (cf. Walzer) as well as in the quiet manipulation of Israelite life that one finds in the Book of Ruth a revolution in the Biblical tradition: women take the initiative to insure the survival and success of the Hebrew people.

Feeley-Harnik locates the story of these radical women most prominently in the narratives of Exodus 1–2 and Ruth. She might have drawn a parallel between the stories only thematically, in terms of their underlying structural concerns alone. In both stories the act of redemption is crucially initiated by heroes who are women. But the ends of the stories, or their aftermaths, also correspond. The lesson of the exodus, as she reads it, is that Israel should never return to Egypt. In establishing the monarchy, Israel may have done just that. To mitigate this tension—or, to formulate it in good structuralist fashion, to resolve the apparent contradiction—the Ruth narrative reassures that David's background gives reason to hope that his monarchy will not entail a return to Egypt but rather a journey back to Judah, the land of milk and honey. It is not for nothing that Naomi and Ruth return to and reclaim possession of territory in *Bêt-Leḥem*, "The House of Bread." The story of Ruth constitutes, then, not merely a parallel to the exodus but an answer to one of its potential and undesirable consequences.

Clearly Feeley-Harnik's is a feminist reading, one which goes so far as to identify the female with the Biblical and the male with the historical order that the Bible attempts to upset. She states:

> While men's works seem focused mainly on the building up of lines of first-born sons, women's works seem to be associated especially with

events that persistently undercut primogeniture or repair recurrent and disastrous attacks on firstborn males in favor of connections based on choice, faith, knowledge, *recognition* of what lies beneath veils, skins, or skirts.

As Miller (1977) has shown in a cogent structuralist analysis of Genesis 37–Exodus 20, dissimulation, the repeated demonstration that things are not what they appear to be, is a most basic Biblical theme. To claim that Biblical women monopolize that special perception that sees beyond the immanent is to claim too much. But it is truly remarkable that within a presumably patriarchal world, certain Biblical women, like Sarah, Rebecca, the mothers of Moses and Samson, and Naomi, to name a few, break stereotypical expectations and display a perspective in sharp alignment with that of the deity.

It should be noted, with Fewell (1987) and others, that feminist readings of the Bible come from different places. Feeley-Harnik's reading reminds me both in some of its particulars and in its general tone of the hermeneutics of Phyllis Trible. Trible (1978, 1984) approaches Scripture with a sense of commitment and an interest in interpreting Biblical narrative toward feminist concerns. Along those lines, one might adduce yet another feature of the Ruth narrative in its support. In his folklorist commentary on Ruth, Sasson (1979) argues that Ruth went out of her way to pursue Boaz, not merely chancing upon his field but seeking it out. Similarly, her first meeting with Boaz, like the memorable night on the threshing-floor, resulted not from sheer providence, but from Ruth's assertiveness. In this instance, Ruth deviates from the folktale scheme delineated by Propp (1977), which Sasson was in fact attempting to identify in Ruth. (For critiques of Sasson's application of Propp, see Greenstein [1981:204–5], Niditch [1985:456], Milne [1988:esp. 144–54].) One could, nevertheless, adopt Sasson's interpretation to underscore a feminist reading: the unusual initiative taken by the woman Ruth subverts the traditional folktale conventions.

Moreover, if one adopts this type of positive feminist exegesis of Scripture, one might suggest a possible ramification in Jewish post-Biblical developments. Feeley-Harnik's overall thesis is that women have a role as important as men in (re)producing Jewish society. In the Mishnah, the code of rabbinic law composed around 200 C.E., women are treated for ritual reasons as somehow less than a full person—or more precisely as an anomalous category or problematic case (cf. Neusner:esp. 267–72; Wegner). At the same time, one finds for the first time (explicitly) in the Mishnah (Cohen) that Jewishness is transmitted by the mother rather than the father. Might this represent structurally a measure to maintain equilibrium in the distribution of importance between men and women in the Mishnah?

While appreciating the strength of the type of feminist reading Feeley-Harnik performs, we should acknowledge the alternative feminist critique that finds the Bible hopelessly androcentric. In studying the same betrothal type-scenes that Alter (47–62) and Feeley-Harnik do, Fuchs (1987; cf. also 1985) shows them to be expressions of male domination. Even in the Ruth narrative women are socially significant only as an instrument to produce sons and preserve inherited property. (For a different sort of feminist critique of Ruth, see now Fewell & Gunn.) The fact that the fate of Ruth as well as the unredeemed property of her late husband Mahlon are decided in an all-male forum reinforces the traditional division of functions between men and women: the public belongs to men, women are confined to the private (cf. Trible, 1982:182). Neither Naomi nor Ruth are present at the town's gate when the official proceedings are conducted. They remain at home.

Indeed, perhaps on account of its thoroughly male character Feeley-Harnik omits any discussion of the quasi-levirate procedure. In so doing, however, I fear she may be missing the most central concern of the body of the narrative. As Niditch (1979) has perceptively explained, the levirate institution functions to provide a social niche for an otherwise anomalous person—"the young childless widow." Somewhere between an unmarried virgin daughter and a widow with sons, the young childless widow, like Ruth, or Tamar, with whose story ours is intertextually related (see Fisch), must find a household in which to live. The levirate accomplishes that objective. But it achieves something else, too.

It insures the preservation of a man's name in the title to his property. It is toward this end that the action of the Ruth narrative moves. Somewhat ironically the story of Ruth immortalizes two women, Naomi and Ruth, who achieve their distinction by immortalizing the name of Naomi's late son and Ruth's late husband, Mahlon. That is the extraordinary *ḥesed*—act of devotion—for which Boaz praises Ruth on the threshing-floor (Ruth 3:10). Because he, like Onan before him, refuses "to establish the name of the dead on his estate" (Ruth 4:5, 10), the relative who is first in line to redeem the estate, the *gōʾēl*, is denied a name by the narrator (cf., e.g., Trible 1982:184; Campbell 1975:141–43). He is called *pĕlōnî ʾalmōnî*—"So and So."

The nature of So-and-So's refusal has perplexed many readers, so it may be worthwhile to explain at least how I understand what's going on. My interpretation is close to that of Sasson. Boaz presents the sale of the estate in one of two ways. According to Sasson (119–36), who reads the *ketiv* of the text in Ruth 4:5, Boaz offers for sale the field alone. He himself declares his intentions of marrying Ruth—reading *qānîtî*, "I am acquiring" Ruth the Moabite as a wife. If one reads the *qere*, as I incline to do (cf., e.g., Campbell:146), Boaz stipulates that whoever redeems the estate must also marry Ruth—reading *qānītā*, "you will acquire" Ruth as a wife. Then, either way, the son born to Ruth is accounted not to his biological father but to his legal father, Mahlon. That son will inherit Mahlon's estate. In that event, So-and-So would lose the full price he paid for the field. That is what he means when he says (Ruth 4:6): "lest I ruin my own estate." He would be diminishing his own estate by using some of it to purchase Mahlon's property. So-and-So chose money over *ḥesed*, but Ruth chose *ḥesed* in marrying Boaz over a younger man (Ruth 3:10).

In order that the suspense introduced on the threshing-floor work, it is critical to understand that in the end Ruth was only symbolically but not literally impregnated by Boaz. I quite agree with Feeley-Harnik that the grain Boaz heaps into Ruth's apron betokens fertility—which had been suggested already in the classical *Midrash Zuta*—but it is a future fertility, not a present one. The text of Ruth 4:13 is clear. Only after Boaz had properly removed So-and-So from the picture, and only after the couple Boaz and Ruth received the blessings of the town council, do we read: "Then he took, Boaz did, Ruth, and she became to him a wife; then he went in into her (i.e., he had intercourse with her); then he gave to her, YHWH did, pregnancy, and she bore a son." The sequence of events is delineated by the chain of *waw*-consecutives. It would have been entirely improper and outright dangerous for Boaz to have impregnated Ruth prior to acquiring the legitimate right to marry her and redeem the property. Without the estate of Mahlon in his possession, there would have been no reason at all for Boaz to have married Ruth. Indeed, it would have spoiled the plan to immortalize Mahlon's name.

At this point I would like to return to the parallel that Feeley-Harnik has drawn between the narratives of Ruth and Exodus 1–2. Although I recognize certain thematic associations, as I mentioned above, I myself would not press the parallel. I do not bring different Biblical passages into association unless I find between them similar constellations of wording and/or similar names—or similar plots. I would, with Fisch (1982), for example, connect together the stories of Lot's daughters, Judah and Tamar, and Ruth, as they share quite a number of plot elements.

On the other hand, Feeley-Harnik does well to emphasize the role of women in redeeming the Hebrews in Egypt (cf. also Ackerman:95). In fact, one could further strengthen this reading by comparing the Moses birth story with its well-known parallel, the Akkadian Legend of Sargon (cf. Lewis:esp. 263–66). There, a mother abandons her infant son and exposes him in a river. It is a man, Akki the Water-Drawer, who rescues the boy and raises him as his own. In Exodus, of course, women observe a constant watch over baby Moses and a woman—an Egyptian woman, no less—and her female cohort save the boy.

Finally, I would note that although Feeley-Harnik's reading may be said to uncover implicit feminist tendencies within Biblical Israel, it does not meet the standards of historical anthropology that Feeley-Harnik (1982) herself has so lucidly outlined in her essay, "Is Historical Anthropology Possible?" In order to ground structural anthropological conclusions in a particular social and historical matrix, one must control one's reading through reference to what is otherwise known about a society's life. Thus, for example, in order to examine what he calls the mystification of problematic women in Genesis, Wander (1981) used studies of kinship patterns among conservative bedouin in modern times as an admittedly uncertain control on his interpretation. Feeley-Harnik would seem to bypass the anthropological control she has elsewhere so eloquently advocated. Is this because she assumes that we share a consensus view on what ancient Israel was like? Or is it perhaps because she understands her present analysis to be a useful feminist reading the perennial value of which transcends any specific historical circumstances?

WORKS CONSULTED

Ackerman, James S.
    1974   "The Literary Context of the Moses Birth Story (Exodus 1–2)." Pp. 74–119 in *Literary Interpretations of Biblical Narratives*. Ed. Kenneth R. R. Gros Louis et al. Nashville: Abingdon.

Alter, Robert
    1981   *The Art of Biblical Narrative.* New York: Basic.

Campbell, Edward F., Jr.
    1975   *Ruth.* AB 7. Garden City, NY: Doubleday.

Cohen, Shaye J. D.
    1985   "The Origins of the Matrilineal Principle in Rabbinic Law." *AJS Review* 10:19–53.

Feeley-Harnik, Gillian
    1982   "Is Historical Anthropology Possible? The Case of the Runaway Slave." Pp. 95–126 in *Humanizing America's Iconic Book: Society of Biblical Literature Centennial Addresses*

1980. Ed. Gene M. Tucker and Douglas A. Knight. Chico: Scholars.

Fewell, Danna Nolan
1987   "Feminist Reading of the Hebrew Bible: Affirmation, Resistance, and Transformation." *JSOT* 39:77–87.

Fewell, Danna Nolan, and David M. Gunn
1988   "'A Son is Born to Naomi!': Literary Allusions and Interpretation in the Book of Ruth." *JSOT* 40:99–108.

Fisch, Harold
1982   "Ruth and the Structure of Covenant History." *VT* 32:425–437.

Fuchs, Esther
1985   "The Literary Characterization of Mothers and Sexual Politics in the Hebrew Bible." Pp. 117–136 in *Feminist Perspectives on Biblical Scholarship.* Ed. Adela Yarbro Collins. Chico: Scholars.

1987   "Structure and Patriarchal Functions in the Biblical Betrothal Type-Scene." *Journal of Feminist Studies in Religion* 3:7–13.

Greenstein, Edward L.
1981   "Biblical Narratology." *Prooftexts* 1:201–208.

Lewis, Brian
1980   *The Sargon Legend.* Cambridge, MA: ASOR.

Miller, Alan W.
1977   "Claude Lévi-Strauss and Genesis 37–Exodus 20." Pp. 21–52 in *Shiv'im.* Ed. Ronald A. Brauner. Philadelphia: Reconstructionist Rabbinical College.

Milne, Pamela J.
1988   *Vladimir Propp and the Study of Structure in Hebrew Biblical Narrative.* Sheffield: Almond.

Neusner, Jacob
1980   *A History of the Mishnaic Law of Women. Part Five: The Mishnaic System of Women.* Leiden: E. J. Brill.

Niditch, Susan
1979 "The Wronged Woman Righted: An Analysis of Genesis 38." *HTR* 72:143–149.

1985 "Legends of Wise Heroes and Heroines." Pp. 445–463 in *The Hebrew Bible and Its Modern Interpreters.* Ed. Douglas A. Knight and Gene M. Tucker. Chico: Scholars.

Propp, Vladimir
1977 *Morphology of the Folktale.* 2nd ed. Rev. Louis A. Wagner. Austin: University of Texas.

Sasson, Jack M.
1979 *Ruth: A New Translation with a Philological Commentary and a Formalist-Folklorist Interpretation.* Baltimore: Johns Hopkins University.

Trible, Phyllis
1978 *God and the Rhetoric of Sexuality.* Philadelphia: Fortress.

1982 "A Human Comedy: The Book of Ruth." Pp. 161–190, 314–317 in *Literary Interpretations of Biblical Narratives,* Vol. 2. Ed. Kenneth R. R. Gros Louis with James S. Ackerman. Nashville: Abingdon.

1984 *Texts of Terror: Literary-Feminist Readings of Biblical Narrative.* Philadelphia: Fortress.

Walzer, Michael
1985 *Exodus and Revolution.* New York: Basic.

Wander, Nathaniel
1981 "Structure, Contradiction, and 'Resolution' in Mythology: The Treatment of Women in Genesis 11–50." *JANESCU* 13:75–99.

Wegner, Judith Romney
1988 *Chattel or Person? The Status of Women in the Mishnah.* New York: Oxford University Press.

15. ETHICS IN CONFLICT:
SOCIOLOGICAL ASPECTS OF ANCIENT ISRAELITE ETHICS
Robert R. Wilson

ABSTRACT

Recent studies of ancient Israelite ethics have given little attention
to the components of Israel's moral world. Although these components
are difficult to describe with precision, comparative studies of ethical
and legal systems can help the interpreter to isolate three important influences on Israelite ethical perceptions. These three influences—traditional norms, law, and prophecy—existed throughout Israelite history,
but the relative importance of the three varied throughout the national
life of the people and within the different groups that made up the society. A clearer understanding of these influences can provide interpreters
with a more sophisticated understanding of the ways in which ancient
Israelites actually made moral decisions and can thus make an important contribution to the study of biblical ethics.

I. Recent Study of Ancient Israelite Ethics

Although biblical scholars have thoroughly explored most
aspects of ancient Israelite religion, they have generally neglected the
study of Israel's ethics. To be sure, studies of Old Testament theology
have occasionally included a brief discussion of Hebrew ethical
thought, but full-scale monographic treatments have been rare
(Bruce, Mitchell, J. M. P. Smith, Hempel, van Oyen). However, in recent years this situation has begun to change, and scholars have once
again taken up the question of biblical ethics in a serious way.

Credit for this revival of interest in Israel's ethics should probably
go to Brevard Childs, who included in his survey of the current state
of biblical theology an essay on the neglect of ethics by biblical theologians (1970:123–38; cf. 1985:51–91, 204–21). According to Childs,
New Testament scholars and ethicists have occasionally dealt with
biblical ethics or with the use of the Bible in making contemporary
ethical decisions, but specialists in Hebrew Bible have generally

avoided considering the ethical dimensions of their material and have not related their work to modern believers seeking biblical guidance for living the moral life. To remedy this situation, Childs proposes that scholars begin the task of exploring Old Testament ethics by considering the central ethical problem of the Bible itself: knowing the will of God. This task is a difficult one, for while Israelite tradition maintains that God's will can be known, the Bible contains many expressions of what God's will actually is. Some of these expressions are in conflict with each other, a fact which causes difficulties when modern communities of faith seek biblical help for discerning God's will in the present. Childs can find no simple solution to this problem but suggests that the full range of biblical witnesses to God's will must be taken into account when contemporary ethical issues are explored. Such a comprehensive use of biblical material will not provide definitive answers to modern moral dilemmas, but will at least define the boundaries within which answers might lie.

Since Childs' call for a reconsideration of ethics in ancient Israel, two major monographs on the subject have appeared, and more are promised for the future. In *Bible and Ethics in the Christian Life* Bruce C. Birch and Larry L. Rasmussen focus on the hermeneutical issues raised by Childs and provide a useful survey of the way in which the Bible has been used by ethicists. On the basis of this survey, the authors suggest that modern communities of faith can most fruitfully use the Bible as a source of moral laws, "stories, symbols, images, paradigms, and beliefs" that can help to build moral character (104). This suggestion further develops the theological issues raised by Childs but leaves unanswered a whole host of interpretive questions concerning the applicability and even the morality of individual biblical laws, stories, and beliefs.

A more detailed study of these issues is provided by Walter C. Kaiser, Jr., in *Toward Old Testament Ethics*. However, rather than deal with all of the possible biblical influences on modern ethical behavior, Kaiser concentrates on the problem of interpreting God's direct moral commands as they are reflected in Israelite law. After distinguishing ancient Israel's moral law from its ceremonial and civil law, Kaiser argues that all moral laws have an underlying principle which can be used to derive ethical guidelines not explicitly included in the original law. Although not everyone will agree with Kaiser's attempt to isolate Israel's moral law or with his analysis and elaboration of the law's underlying principles, he has at least called attention to the importance of considering the role of law in Israel's system of ethics.

In spite of the recent revival of interest in ancient Israel's ethics, it is important to note that little energy has been expended on historical

and sociological investigations into the ways in which moral decisions were actually made during the biblical period. For the most part
recent scholarly attention has focused on the issue of how the Bible
might be used to shape the moral life of modern communities of
faith, and there has been no comprehensive study of the role that
ethics played in the biblical period itself. There have been a few
preliminary studies of specific ethical issues and some consideration
of the hermeneutical dimensions of the problem (Barton; Knight,
1980, 1982, 1985; McKeating), but historians of ancient Israel have
produced nothing comparable to Wayne Meeks' recent study of the
moral world of the early Christians. In this work, Meeks traces the
various forces that helped to shape the moral perspectives of the first
Christians, analyzing in turn the ethos and structure of the Greek
polis, the influence of Greek and Roman ethical thought, the ethical
traditions of the Hebrew Bible, and the moral thought and practice of
the emerging Christian community. All of these factors, in varying
proportions, played a role in molding ethical thought and in
determining moral action. Ethical decision making, then, should be
understood not as the mechanical application of abstract laws or
theological principles to a moral dilemma but as the choice of a
course of action in the light of the various social and cultural
components of an individual's moral universe.

Meeks' way of conceiving the study of early Christian ethics is
valuable precisely because it is able to integrate the historical, sociological, and conceptual aspects of moral decision making. By focusing
on the dynamic processes involved, he is able not only to provide a
more detailed description of an important part of early Christian life
but also to provide a clearer understanding of what might be involved in using the Bible ethically in modern communities of faith.
Clearly his approach would also be useful in the study of ancient Israelite ethics, for an investigation of the components of ethical decision making would greatly enrich our knowledge of the way in
which Israelite society actually worked. However, any investigation
of the moral world of ancient Israel faces some formidable difficulties
which should not be minimized. First, while Meeks could rely on extensive textual material outside of the New Testament in order to reconstruct the social structure of the *polis* and to describe the classical
moral tradition, the historian of ancient Israelite ethics is confined
primarily to evidence found within the Hebrew Bible. To be sure, ex-
trabiblical texts from Syria, Palestine, Mesopotamia, and Egypt can
supply evidence on moral perspectives in the nations surrounding Israel, but the influence of these perspectives on Israelite perceptions
remains to be demonstrated, at least during the preexilic period.
Furthermore, even if foreign ideas could be shown to have influenced
the moral world of certain individuals or groups in Israel, there is no

way to determine how widespread this influence was. For the most part, therefore, the historian of Israelite ethics must rely on information provided by the Hebrew Bible, which unfortunately is silent on many of the issues that the historian would like to investigate.

Second, while Meeks could deal with a relatively homogeneous group, namely middle-class urban Christians living in Hellenistic cities, the historian of Israel's ethics must deal with a wide variety of groups spread throughout the social structure. Unlike early Christians, early Israelites were not all of one type, and it may well be that the moral world of the king and the royal court was different from the moral world of the priesthood, which in turn was different from the moral world of the wealthy landowner or the slave. In any given period, then, a number of moral worlds have to described in order to present a comprehensive picture of Israelite perceptions.

Third, while Meeks could focus his attention on the first hundred years or so of the church's growth, the historian of Israelite ethics must reckon with almost a thousand years of Israel's history. During that time there were several major alterations in the social structure, and it is necessary to assume that social, political, and religious developments also brought about changes in the way that people saw the moral universe. A description of Israelite ethics must therefore include a historical dimension in order to paint an accurate picture.

Finally, Meeks was able to describe two of the components of the early Christian moral world as fixed influences: the classical moral tradition and the Hebrew Bible. In contrast, the historian of Israelite ethics must take into account the development of a canon of authoritative traditions during the period being studied. Thus, for example, in early Israelite history there seem to have been several law codes, each of which was considered an authoritative guide to ethical behavior by the particular group that cherished and preserved it. However, after the compilation and canonization of the Torah, the composite law code was presumably considered binding on all Israelites and had to be taken into account in making ethical decisions. Precisely how this complex process worked is unclear, but it must have been a factor in the history of Israelite morality.

II. The Components of Israel's Moral World

Meeks' study of the early Christian moral world illustrates the enormous complexity of that world and the complicated ways in which its components interacted with each other. This situation seems to be a feature of most societies and is likely to have existed in ancient Israel as well, a fact which would make any analysis of the Israelite moral world both difficult and somewhat artificial. However, such an analysis is also a helpful tool to use as an aid to understanding the dynamics of moral decision making, and it may be safely employed so long as its heuristic character is recognized.

At the risk of great oversimplification, then, three important components of ancient Israel's moral world may be isolated for analysis. First, all Israelites acknowledged certain customary behavioral norms that were part of a traditional view of the social and physical worlds, although these norms may not have been the same within all segments of the society. These norms or mores were usually accepted without question and were the primary ground for moral decision making. They were rarely articulated systematically or even discussed, except when they were challenged or when discussion was necessary in order to resolve disputes. They are therefore extraordinarily difficult to study, especially at a distance of two millennia. However, they have left traces in biblical literature, particularly in the narratives, poems, and proverbs that express ancient Israelite views of reality. Some of these expressions are quite individualistic and undoubtedly reflect the values of relatively small groups within Israelite society. In this category would fall texts such as the Priestly creation narrative (Genesis 1) or the Priestly version of the Exodus (Exodus 1–15), which testify to a cosmos having a fairly rigid hierarchical structure, presided over by a single, all-powerful deity, who is in absolute control of the world and its history. Similarly, the group that produced and preserved the Deuteronomic History and the Book of Deuteronomy had views on the nature of monotheism, election, and the structure of the state that stressed a conditional, covenantal relationship between God and Israel and supported a state that would rob the king of much of his political power. In the same way, the core of the Book of Proverbs is literature which reflects the relatively well-to-do world of property owners and government officials (Kovacs).

The commonly accepted norms held by various Israelite groups are most visible in literature coming from a fairly late period in Israel's history. In this period the divergent views of the various priestly groups, the Deuteronomic groups, and the wisdom writers reached their classic forms. In this period, too, the literature attests to the existence of rival groups with conflicting value systems, as Paul Hanson and others have recently noted (Hanson:215–381; M. Smith; Plöger). The roots of these conflicts seem to lie not only in differing theological stances but also in fundamentally divergent views on the nature of reality and Israel's role within that reality. These differing perceptions must have issued in differing ideas on appropriate behavior, although the details of these ideas are difficult to describe with any specificity. It is even more difficult to delineate the ethical norms that might have been held earlier in Israelite history, even though these norms were probably more widely held than were those of the postexilic period. The narrative literature dealing with Israel's early history suggests a stress on the importance of the nuclear and extended families as the basic social unit and on the necessity of maintaining harmony within the family structure. Fairly strict views on marriage, parental authority, and ownership of property also seem to have been a basic part of the commonly held worldview, and there seems to have been a basic acceptance of Israel's characteristic belief that God was specially related to the people in some way and was active in history on their behalf (de Vaux:3–61; Wolff:157–229). These fundamental perceptions of reality had clear implications for ethical behavior and seem to have persisted throughout the biblical period, although they were increasingly challenged as the postexilic period approached.

The primary domain of these foundational norms was the family, where each new generation absorbed the commonly held views of society and of appropriate social behavior. The moral formation of the young probably took place informally as well as formally. Children were able to deduce group values by watching their elders make decisions, discuss problems, and adjudicate disputes. More formal instruction may have also taken place, probably through the use of stories, instructions, and proverbs reflecting the family's fundamental values. (Note, for example, the emphasis placed on formal ethical instruction in Deuteronomy 6–11).

The second primary component of Israel's moral world was law, which operated in the society at different levels and with varying degrees of influence. In recent years anthropologists have provided a number of detailed studies on the role of law in society in general and in societies having structures similar to that of ancient Israel in particular (Pospisil, 1971, 1978; Nader and Todd; Bohannan; Gluckman, 1955, 1965; Gulliver). Although the relevance of some of this material for the study of ancient Israel has recently been questioned (Rogerson, Fiensy), it can often be helpful when it is used judiciously. In societies organized on the basis of kinship, as was early Israel, legal authority resides in kinship groups or lineages. In nuclear or extended families, the power to enforce the group's traditional laws rests with the lineage heads, who are usually able to maintain social stability within their lineages by imposing settlements in legal disputes and by meting out punishment when laws are violated (cf. Genesis 16, 38; Joshua 7). When several large lineages are involved in a dispute in which no living person is able to impose a solution, then inter-lineage negotiations must take place in an attempt to reach a settlement which is considered just by everyone involved. In societies which operate in this way, law is usually customary and coincides with the society's commonly held ethical norms. If the society is to remain stable, then legal disputes must be resolved in accord with group perceptions of what is just and right.

However, law can under certain conditions develop in a way that eventually brings it into conflict with the society's traditional norms. This sometimes happens, for example, when lineage-based societies become monarchical states or when they are controlled by a foreign government which has the right to impose law. In the former case, the state normally begins by using the threat of military force to enforce the society's traditional ethical norms and customary laws (Bellefontaine). However, states tend to develop peculiar interests of their own and become particularly concerned with regulating relationships between the people and the state in addition to regulating interpersonal relationships. In such cases state law is likely to come into conflict with customary law or commonly held ethical norms, and social unrest may result (see 1 Kings 11–12). In the case of control by foreign powers, there is also likely to be civil strife if the law being imposed clashes with local perceptions of what is right and just.

In addition to possible conflicts between customary and state law in monarchical societies, special interest groups within a society may be in a position to impose their own laws within the sphere of social life which they control. The most common example of this phenomenon is the promulgation of ritual law by priestly groups, which are able to exercise total control over the cult. Such laws may or may not conflict with customary law, or they may simply be additional laws unrelated to the society's ethical perceptions (Albertz).

The final component of ancient Israel's moral world is prophecy. There has been much discussion in the scholarly literature concerning the relationship between ethics and prophecy, but this discussion has usually focused on the prophets as purveyors of ethical norms or on the ethical views of the prophets themselves (Davies). Similarly, the relationship between prophecy and law has been discussed, but scholarly attention has usually focused on the question of whether or not the prophets grounded their oracles in Israelite law and in the covenant to which the law was related (Phillips). However, to date there has been no thorough investigation of the way in which law, ethics, and prophecy related as part of the same social system. As in the case of law, prophecy has also been the subject of much anthropological study, and this comparative material suggests that prophets may have played a variety of roles in shaping Israel's moral perceptions (Wilson, 1980:21–88).

By definition prophecy is a process in which an individual becomes a channel of communication between the human and divine worlds. The divine message that the prophet delivers is in human speech, which is of course influenced by his personal history and the setting in which he works, but the basic contents of the message cannot be predicted. Prophets can therefore play a variety of roles within the social structure. At one extreme, the prophet's message may support traditional ethical norms and help to maintain the stability of the social structure. However, on the other end of the spectrum, the prophet may call for major changes in the society and thus provide a direct challenge to commonly held perceptions and generally accepted law. In this case the prophet becomes a source of instability and conflict within the society and can cause serious problems for people who want to take prophecy seriously as a part of their moral world. When prophecy contradicts established law or social custom, then they must choose one at the expense of the other. The result is likely to be conflict and social unrest.

Because of the tendency of prophecy to lead toward social instability, not all societies tolerate prophets as part of the social system, and even in Israel, where prophecy was a recognized institution, some groups did not recognize prophetic authority precisely because of its potentially dangerous effects. The conflicts between prophets and the northern kings are well documented (1 Kings 13–2 Kings 10) and finally led to the violent overthrow of the Omri dynasty. Similarly, in the tense final days of the siege of Jerusalem, government officials tried to suppress prophecy because they feared that it would lead to political anarchy (Jeremiah 29). On the other hand, one Israelite group, the people who preserved the Deuteronomic traditions, made a provision for the prophet in their ideal state and built into the political system the possibility that prophetic revelation might contradict previously authoritative laws and ethical norms (Deut 18:9–22). Even though the Deuteronomists did impose some limits on the freedom of prophetic speech (Deut 13:1–5), their acceptance of prophecy and law as equally authoritative led to ethical dilemmas which were difficult to resolve (see Jeremiah 26).

III. Ethical Systems in Conflict

The three major components of Israel's moral world interacted in various ways throughout the nation's history. In the period before the rise of the monarchy, primary emphasis was probably on traditional norms and customary laws, which were decisive in making ethical decisions. Consciously formulated laws may well have existed, but there is no evidence of a comprehensive legal structure that unified groups above the level of the extended family or the village. In some groups, particularly those whose traditions finally crystallized in the Deuteronomic History, prophecy may have also been a part of the moral world, but its influence in relation to customary law is unclear.

This situation began to change with the rise of the monarchy. At that time three tendencies began to be visible, and all three had an important impact on Israel's moral perceptions. First, the creation of a monarchical state set the stage for conflicts between royal law and customary law, although evidence for the actual existence of such conflicts is in fact scarce (1 Samuel 11–12; 1 Kings 11–12, 21). It may conceivably be that the state in fact left most legal matters to local lineages and only rarely came into conflict with them. Second, David's establishment of Jerusalem as the religious capital of the country was accompanied by the formation of an official priesthood, which soon began to develop its own laws pertaining to the cult. These laws impinged on the general population only insofar as they mandated the general performance of certain rituals, but they were otherwise morally neutral and did not conflict with customary ethical norms. Finally, during the preexilic period prophecy arose as a major influence on moral behavior. On the basis of the prophecies that have been preserved, it appears that many of the prophets challenged existing perceptions and often came into conflict with the official views of the state. Prophecy would therefore have been a source of social instability and would have confronted the general population with major moral dilemmas when the prophets' words conflicted with group perceptions and state laws (see 1 Kings 18, for example).

During the exilic and postexilic periods, additional changes took place in Israel's social structure, and these, too, had their impact on the people's moral world. First, the Davidic monarchy was not reestablished, but Israel was ruled by a whole succession of foreign rulers, beginning with the Babylonians and Persians. These rulers seem to have imposed their own civil law on Israel, and this law must have increased the level of conflict between state law and customary law (note, e.g., the conflicts described in Daniel 1–6). Second, prophecy seems to have been discredited as an active force capable of shaping ethical perceptions. In its place the prophetic literature provided a fixed influence on ethical thinking, along with law, narratives, and proverbs. Third, when the power to regulate their own civil law was taken away from the Israelites, the only law that remained in their hands was religious law. The various priestly groups, by default, thus became the primary custodians and interpreters of law. However, because priestly interests tended to be somewhat specialized, religious law ran the risk of neglecting the people's everyday ethical concerns (note, e.g., the complaints of Malachi). Finally, the growing body of authoritative literature that we call the canon began to play an increasing role in the process of shaping Israel's moral world. Traditional ethical norms, as shaped by the biblical tradition, became the primary grounds for making ethical decisions, while state law and direct prophecy declined in importance. This situation persisted until the strong influence of Hellenism caused both Jewish and Christian moral perceptions to develop in new directions.

WORKS CONSULTED

Albertz, Rainer
1984 "Täter und Opfer im Alten Testament." *Zeitschrift für Evangelische Ethik* 28:146–66.

Barton, John
1978 "Understanding Old Testament Ethics." *JSOT* 9:44–64.

Bellefontaine, Elizabeth
1987 "Customary Law and Chieftainship: Judicial Aspects of 2 Samuel 14.4–21." *JSOT* 38:42–72.

Birch, Bruce C., and Larry L. Rasmussen
1976 *Bible and Ethics in the Christian Life.* Minneapolis: Augsburg.

Bohannan, Paul
1957 *Justice and Judgment among the Tiv.* London: Oxford University Press.

Bruce, W. S.
1909 *The Ethics of the Old Testament.* 2nd rev. ed. Edinburgh: T. & T. Clark.

Childs, Brevard S.
1970 *Biblical Theology in Crisis.* Philadelphia: Westminster.

1985 *Old Testament Theology in a Canonical Context.* London: SCM.

Davies, Eryl W.
1981 *Prophecy and Ethics.* Sheffield: JSOT.

Fiensy, David
1987 "Using Nuer Culture of Africa in an Understanding of the Old Testament: An Evaluation." *JSOT* 38:73–83.

Gluckman, Max
1955 *The Judicial Process among the Barotse of Northern Rhodesia.* Manchester: Manchester University Press.

1965 *The Ideas in Barotse Jurisprudence.* New Haven: Yale University Press.

Gulliver, P. H.
1963   *Social Control in an African Society*. London: Routledge & Kegan Paul.

Hanson, Paul D.
1986   *The People Called*. San Francisco: Harper & Row.

Hempel, Johannes
1964   *Das Ethos des Alten Testaments*. 2nd ed. Berlin: Alfred Töpelmann.

Kaiser, Walter C., Jr.
1983   *Toward Old Testament Ethics*. Grand Rapids: Academie.

Knight, Douglas A.
1980   "Jeremiah and the Dimensions of the Moral Life." Pp. 87–103 in *The Divine Helmsman: Studies on God's Control of Human Events*. Ed. James L. Crenshaw and Samuel Sandmel. New York: Ktav.

1982   "Old Testament Ethics." *Christian Century* 99/2:55–59.

1985   "Moral Values and Literary Traditions: The Case of the Succession Narrative (2 Samuel 9–20; 1 Kings 1–2)." *Semeia* 34:7–23.

Kovacs, Brian W.
1974   "Is There a Class-Ethic in Proverbs?" Pp. 171–89 in *Essays in Old Testament Ethics: J. Philip Hyatt. In Memoriam*. Ed. James L. Crenshaw and John T. Willis. New York: Ktav.

McKeating, Henry
1979   "Sanctions against Adultery in Ancient Israelite Society, with Some Reflections on Methodology in the Study of Old Testament Ethics." *JSOT* 11:57–72.

Meeks, Wayne A.
1986   *The Moral World of the First Christians*. Philadelphia: Westminster.

Mitchell, Hinckley G.
1912   *The Ethics of the Old Testament*. Chicago: University of Chicago Press.

Nader, Laura, and Harry F. Todd, Jr.
1978   *The Disputing Process—Law in Ten Societies.* New York: Columbia University Press.

van Oyen, H.
1967   *Die Ethik des Alten Testaments.* Gütersloh: Gerd Mohn.

Phillips, Anthony
1982   "Prophecy and Law." Pp. 217–32 in *Israel's Prophetic Tradition: Essays in Honour of Peter R. Ackroyd.* Ed. Richard Coggins et al. Cambridge: Cambridge University Press.

Plöger, Otto
1968   *Theocracy and Eschatology.* Richmond: John Knox.

Pospisil, Leopold J.
1971   *Anthropology of Law: A Comparative Theory.* New York: Harper & Row.

1978   *The Ethnology of Law.* 2nd ed. Menlo Park, CA: Cummings.

Rogerson, J. W.
1986   "Was Early Israel a Segmentary Society?" *JSOT* 36:17–26.

Smith, J. M. Powis
1923   *The Moral Life of the Hebrews.* Chicago: University of Chicago Press.

Smith, Morton
1971   *Palestinian Parties and Politics That Shaped the Old Testament.* New York: Columbia University Press.

de Vaux, Roland
1961   *Ancient Israel: Its Life and Institutions.* New York: McGraw-Hill.

Wilson, Robert R.
1980   *Prophecy and Society in Ancient Israel.* Philadelphia: Fortress.

1983a   "Enforcing the Covenant: The Mechanisms of Judicial Authority in Early Israel." Pp. 59–75 in *The Quest for the Kingdom of God: Essays in Honor of George E. Mendenhall.* Ed. H. B. Huffmon et al. Winona Lake, IN: Eisenbrauns.

1983b   "Israel's Judicial System in the Preexilic Period." *JQR* 74:229–48.

Wolff, Hans Walter
1974   *Anthropology of the Old Testament.* Philadelphia: Fortress.

16. COMMENTS ON ROBERT WILSON
John Middleton

These comments are those of a social anthropologist and not of a historian of religion. I take a main aim of anthropology to be that stated by the great French scholar Marcel Mauss: to understand the means used by the members of a society to conceptualize experience. Another way of expressing this would be to understand and analyze the society's moral imagination, in its social and historical context. The study of "ethics" fits precisely this definition. And I see ethics as being without any essential or comparative meanings unless seen as part of the set of beliefs and practices of a given society at a given time in its history. Ethics form part of the conceptualization of experience in the sense, first, of defining social and moral categories and the boundaries between them, that comprise a social structure; and secondly, defining the proper relationships and the modes of behavior associated with them within and across these boundaries. These categories and boundaries are socially and historically made constructs; they are perhaps always seen by the people themselves as given and sanctioned by their gods, but social constructs they remain and so should be understood.

I come therefore to the questions of what are the particular social and moral categories constructed by a society (and they vary from one society to another), who constructs them, who validates and legitimates them, who sanctions them, and how all these things are done. I try to answer these questions here with particular reference to what Robert Wilson has mentioned in his paper as three components of ancient Israel's moral world: certain customary basic social norms; law, intergroup disputes and their settlement, royal and priestly codes; and prophecy, which may lead either to the conservation of a society or to its change, the latter being considered by its rulers as political anarchy.

Let me first consider the forms given to the moral world (or set of moral worlds) by a particular people. All societies construct a moral universe, or map, and despite the many cultural differences of content and of symbol, these would seem to have certain common elements of basic structure. I suggest that the most basic, whichever society we are talking about, whether of the past or of today, is a distinction in both space and time between what in many present-day African cosmologies, at least, are referred to as the "inside" and the "outside" (or by similar terms). The former is the sphere within which are the basic social groupings and networks of relations, bound together by authority, often by genealogy, often by forms of non-commercial exchange of goods and spouses, the recognition of obligations such as assisting at rituals of many kinds, and so on. All are relations based on the recognition of a shared morality, and the members of the "inside" are, in Durkheim's words, members of a single moral community and a church. The size and composition of this moral community may vary in both space and time, and there may be several levels of such relationships within a given society at any given period. The "outside" is the converse, the sphere of power uncontrolled by those who live in the "inside," the sphere of the natural, the wild, the inhuman, the animal, and of the unknowable and unpredictable powers of Divinity in all its many guises and manifestations. The same *schema* may be made in time, from the viewpoint of any given "now." In this dimension is stated the difference between history and myth, between time and non-time, between present and flawed society and an original Eden. There are many idioms, metaphors, and symbols used for such *schemata*, different for each of the many thousands of societies in the world. Yet some such pattern seems to be a universal one, and it makes sense of the world around one and the present and the past in which one lives. Essentially the "inside" is the sphere of the good, the ordered, the social, the moral, and is often symbolically associated with men. The "outside" is associated with evil, the unordered, the asocial and amoral, and the antisocial and the immoral, often with certain cardinal points and in many societies with women. The boundary between is the area of the ambiguous, anomalous, and the uncertain.

From much modern ethnographic evidence some such *schema* provides a frame with which to look at the questions that Robert Wilson has raised. Sometimes this is a simple matter of ethnographic comparison and probability. For example, among the ethnographically famous Nuer and also in early Israelite society, relations within the "inside" are or were sanctioned by ritual, domestic and lineage authority, and many informal sanctions. Relations at the edge or near the boundary with the "outside" are controlled by sanctions such as the feud (a highly formalized and controlled use of limited force) and associated with rules of exogamy and endogamy and often with notions and accusations of magic, the miraculous, witchcraft and sorcery and other expressions of an ambiguous morality. Relations with groups beyond, in the sphere of the "outside," are seen as expressed in sanctions such as warfare and the exercise of apparently divine power as expressed in epidemics and outside conquest which are regarded as intrusions of external power across the boundary which act upon those dwelling in the "inside" as all guilty of common sins. For any particular society the boundary between the categories is always changing, although ordinary people may be unaware of this until it is, as it were, too late. The boundary is rarely exactly the same in all social and historical situations in any given society. And it is permeable: both deities and spirits, and some kinds of human beings, can pass from one to the other sphere and back again. Some people, such as witches, are traitors, the enemies from outside who have secretly entered the "inside" and must be sought out and removed. The categories are typically expressed in myth and cosmology as being in space and in time, but essentially they are moral.

However remote and otiose is the High God of a particular society, certainly it is usually accepted that refractions of Divinity can and do cross the boundary at their own will (or at that of God for whom they act as messengers and agents). In the ethnographic literature these are given various terms by anthropologists who try to translate the essential meanings of the indigenous words used. They are called gods, deities, divinities, spirits, angels, or other terms, most of which when written with a capital letter refer also to the High God; and some, at least "spirit," may also occupy a living human being as sign of his or her divine creation and also of his or her temporality on earth, in the "inside." There may be many kinds and different levels of them, such as the Nuer Spirits of the Above and Spirits of the Below, and often their relations with ancestors are often unclear, ill-defined, or interchangeable. All may be contacted in various guises, since all are suprasensible and at various places (shrines, altars, etc); and they enter the existence of human beings by possession and may appear among them at masquerades, in forms of animals, and so on.

Conversely, living beings may cross into the "outside," to the realm of divine power, and then return: the priest, the prophet, diviner, medium, shaman, miracle worker, oracle worker, and so on, and of course at times kings, as sacred beings. A crucial point is that those spirits and humans who cross the boundary, or who are associated with or live along it and beyond it, are everywhere given various attributes (of character, behavior, and often appearance) of symbolic inversion. These attributes are many, but the universal ones are those used in a given society to make a being or event or place sacred, whether permanently or merely temporarily and situationally. The attributes are those of anomaly and ambiguity, and, by being so considered in terms of cosmological categories, they are powerful, miraculous, beneficial, and dangerous. In cosmologies the "inside" is typically defined by its boundaries in these terms, as well as more simply in terms of space and time. This cosmological boundary is never fixed, but is ever-moving, flexible, and uncertain, especially during periods of great ethnic and cultural movements, amalgamations, or conquests, when there are always new contacts with strangers, the formation of new patterns of economic exchange, marriage, and forms of descent and kinship. The history of early Israelite society is one of continual changes of these kinds, and so we would expect, as we find, that symbolic notions of the "boundary" are found throughout the Bible. To cross the boundary, to confuse it, to ignore it, is everywhere associated with the breaching of taboos. Breaching of the basic cosmological and behavioral codes, which are "mapped" in terms of the *schema* I have been describing, may be seen as the breaking of taboos and in terms of the sicknesses, avoidances, and punishments associated with them. The breaking of moral rules of behavior and of taboos leads to many kinds of ritual performances, to sacrifice, and purification with the temporary destruction of the impure *persona* and its cleansing and return in the purified form that it had before. All these actions may be carried out by priests, diviners, and seers. To do this does not usually involve bringing a divine message but does typically involve the practitioner moving symbolically to the "outside" and back into the "inside," and it may include forms of possession as symbolic ways of so doing. These moral (and physical since the physical may be a visible expression of the moral) purifications of individuals, groups, and places involve all manner of anomalous, sacred, inverted beings, persons, and events.

So we come to prophets. Robert Wilson has already written a most valuable commentary on prophets in both ancient Israel and as reported in modern ethnographic accounts in his book *Prophecy and Society in Ancient Israel.* He pointed out there some important points that I think are too often forgotten. One is that with all the confusion and effort to distinguish in the literature between the various kinds of religious intermediaries (priest, prophet, diviner, medium, seer, and so on) we may easily forget the fact that we are really discussing functions, which may in one society be divided among different personages and in another allotted to a single personage. We must therefore distinguish between the functions. His second point follows: that these functions are defined culturally by any given society and at any given period in its history. Intermediaries have "support groups" that play certain historical and social roles, so that we need to look carefully at the prophets' "constituencies." In other words, prophets are social institutions and not aberrant and idiosyncratic persons. Of course a society will normally, as with all forms of religious intermediaries (including kings), give them certain specific symbolic attributes. One of our dangers is the ethnocentric one of accepting these symbolic attributes as being descriptions of their actual historical behavior. That is, if a person is accepted after his or her death to have been a prophet (if an "ordinary" message later turns out to have been morally and politically effective and so "true"), then later memories and documents may describe his or her behavior as having the conventionally prescribed and stereotypical inverted symbolic features that define a prophet. These symbolically inverted features are commonly regarded as including charismatic authority (the inverse of properly constituted bureaucratic authority), possession, and particular forms of speech; and there are many more that Wilson did not mention in his paper, such as dress, gesture, food habits, and others.

In his book he rightly warns of the dangers of too great a reliance on the notion of charisma. As he says, the "gift from God" is also a "gift from society." But I would like to say something about some of the other mechanisms and idioms of intermediation. One is possession. As Wilson pointed out in his book, this should be distinguished from trance; and another confused term is "ecstasy." Trance is dissociation from the everyday world, but it need not be a part of the crossing of the boundary by a religious intermediary. Possession is different: it involves both the possessing agent and the possessed victim in crossing the boundary. And it may be induced by various means. We need not here worry about matters such as central and peripheral possession, which have been considered in his book and elsewhere. But one aspect of intermediation has perhaps not much been considered. This is the central notion, as I see it, of "truth." Let me give an example. The Lugbara of Uganda hold that a main task of an imaginative man or woman (and I use the word imaginative as they do for someone who is morally and cosmologically aware) is to seek Divine truth, which was according to their myths lost to humans when they separated from God after the beginning of the world. Priests are the repositories of this truth, although they are unable to express it in words, and the other intermediaries seek it and bring back bits of it to their adherents and clients. This becomes the essential function of the prophet, who acts as a Divine mouthpiece to tell the living of this truth, the truth that gives the power to construct and to re-form moral categories and boundaries and so society itself.

We come here to another central mechanism or idiom of intermediation, the speech of prophecy and its interpretation. Wilson pointed out that prophets, in varying historical situations, can play two roles. They may appeal to tradition in the sense of giving a divinely inspired message to discard modern things and to return to the old gods and the values that they sanctioned. Prophets may do this particularly in times of rapid social change that ordinary people do not want. Or they may do the opposite. As he has written, they may preserve or they may revive, and these messages are perhaps always taken by those who hear them to be much the same. It is surely difficult to find an example of any prophet who really suggests a blueprint for a new heaven and a new earth. It is simply beyond human experience to do so, and the prophetic blueprints are always those of a primordial past as it is stated in myth as being devoid of the imperfections and impurities of today. The Utopia of the future is the Eden of the past, whatever the idioms actually used: equality, moral perfection, proper hierarchy of gods and men, and so on. The ideas and inspiration for them are thought to come from the "outside" from which the prophet fetches them, in this case an outside defined in terms of time rather than of space.

The speech of prophecy is based on this point. I admit to ignorance of the vast body of Biblical interpretation of the speech forms and writing forms used by the Hebrew prophets. But they would appear to have the quality of masking the human identity, or the humanity, of the speaker or writer who is seen as merely the mouthpiece of Divinity. There are several idioms that may be used in prophetic speech, which may be placed on a continuum that runs from everyday speech, to forms of formal, ritual, intoned, and sung speech, to glossolalia, with increasing use of complex metaphor, hidden and secret references, and so on. The same would seem to be so of written messages, with a continuum from bureaucratic writing, to ordinary style, formulaic style, poetry and to perhaps total unintelligibility. I suggest that the more radical is the message in the sense of recommending or commanding greater departure from presently accepted values and behavior, the nearer will be the speech form to glossolalia (and perhaps the written form to poetry). Only Divinity can create new categories, and the nearer to Divinity in this sense is the prophecy the more powerful is its message and the speech in which it is uttered.

Finally, the message is so powerful and thus so dangerous that only speaking in "tongues" is safe to the hearers. Here lies one of the functions of a prophet's interpreter, the go-between between prophet and society, who is a powerful figure whom we all too often ignore, seeing him or her as merely some kind of impresario. I should add here a word on the importance of considering the interpretation of prophecy. As in myth, this is done not by the speaker as such but rather by the audience (even where there is an interpreter), each member interpreting the message according to his or her understanding, aspirations and fears, that is, to his or her social and historical position. We come back to the social context of the prophet and the prophecy. He or she is judged successful or a failure according to the interpretations later made of the message, the support or threats in it to the politically and socially powerful or potentially powerful, and to the action taken upon it by the adherents of the prophetic movement.

D. REFLECTIONS ON THE HEBREW BIBLE AND FOLKLORE: A CONCLUSION

The remarks of five commentators serve as a fitting conclusion to this volume, reviewing major methodological issues and debates evoked by the papers and responses and challenging us to open and explore further avenues of inquiry. Trajectories from oral to written and from written to oral are major emphases of the commentators as they refer to the "refolkafying" or "reoralization" of the biblical tradition (Long; Mills), or to the way in which literary traditions never fully succeed in self-canonization (Nagy), or to the fact that a group of scholars may form its own oral tradition in the process of shared discussion and interpretation (Mills). The commentators remind us of the importance of appreciating the biblical writers' own messages, multivocalic and layered as they are, and the actual cultural, historical settings in which these writers participated in the tradition as composers or collectors or preservers. They address the challenges faced in reconstructing these ancient worlds (Coote; Mills) and of knowing how the composers themselves viewed issues of oral versus written. What, for example, were the sources of ancient authors' authority to produce written texts (Nagy)? At the same time, we are urged to be self-conscious in examining the sources, settings, and motivations of our own responses as readers (Long; Mills).

17. REFLECTIONS

Robert A. Oden, Jr.

A genre much in evidence during the conference was that of personal storytelling—appropriately so for a conference whose title includes the word folklore. As I was consistently pleased throughout with all I have begun to learn (and, with that, regularly reminded of how little I know), I am loath to abandon this genre. Hence, I, too, would like to relate a couple of tales, both narratives of encounters in my own past with the discipline of folklore studies.

These tales I want to preface by reading briefly from a newspaper. This newspaper account, which comes from the April 30 edition of the *Boston Globe*, may provide us with an up-to-date footnote to Frank Cross' comments on brothels and safe-houses in his response to Yair Zakovitch's paper on Joshua 2. You will recall that Cross argued that there was some reason to suspect that the spies knew what they were doing when they lodged with Rahab. The article from the *Globe* tells us that Massachusetts state troopers discovered a fugitive from the Maine State Penitentiary hiding in a large boarding house inhabited by "a large number of women dancers." I suspect that the newspaper is here utilizing a common euphemism and hence that this fugitive, too, knew what he was doing when he chose his particular refuge.

But to my stories. The first is a story about one in a series of most interesting and revealing, for me, conversations I had with an extraordinarily gifted folklorist called Stuart Blackburn. Blackburn, who works chiefly on Tamil material from south India and who now lives in Berkeley, was my colleague at Dartmouth for four years. Our conversations, partly prompted by a course we taught together, centered on what he as a folklorist saw as his chief task and on what I as a student of the religion of ancient Israel saw as mine. I think it is fair to say that our discussions revealed that I was much more impatient to leap, probably too hastily, to questions of meaning and significance than was he, while Blackburn envisioned a larger share of his own task to be the careful collecting and sifting of materials before such questions were raised.

For example, I recall vividly our initial conversation after his return from an extended stay in India. "How did it go and what did you find?" or some words to that effect, I said first. His reply was framed in delight: it had gone very well, and he had come upon several new versions of the set of Tamil traditions upon which he was working. After congratulating him, I then turned to a series of questions which revealed, again, my place as perhaps a perduringly literal-minded exegete: "what do the new versions mean?," "how do you now look at your collection of Tamil traditions in new ways?," and "what difference do these newest versions make?" His response, if I read it correctly, was essentially this: it is far too early to ask, much less to answer, such questions; but important new evidence has been found, and that ought to be seen as the accomplishment of chief importance.

This story I tell partly because it turns out to be a coincidental appendix to Robert Coote's remarks (below). Coote notes, among other observations, that there may well be other sources of material of potential importance for biblical scholars to which we have attributed little or no significance. A part of the personal gain to me from my conversations with Stuart Blackburn was to raise the same question. Are there materials from Syria-Palestine in whatever era which we biblical scholars have overlooked to our own peril? Susan Niditch (to whom we owe the idea and the execution of the conference and thus to whom I am ever more grateful) on page one of her *Underdogs and Tricksters*, notes that folklore scholarship sets itself three tasks. The third of these is, to be sure, "questions about meaning, function, and context," but this third set of questions arises only along with questions of description and of composition and transmission. And these latter questions are most adequately answered only in the context of searching for relevant and analogous material wherever it may be found. Given what Coote has to say, I will speak no further to this point, except to add to his comments my own and hearty second.

My second tale goes back further still, and is thus even more in keeping with the personal reminiscences related by other participants in the conference. Twenty-three years ago, I was an undergraduate enrolled at the same time in a course taught chiefly by Albert Lord on folklore and in a Greek course taught by Leonard Muellner, who is now a professor of classics at Brandeis University. In the latter course, my introduction to reading the Iliad in Greek was coupled with an introduction to oral literature in the broadest sense and hence to the importance of oral formulae. So, too, Professor Lord's course gave to all enrolled a heavy dose of the place of oral formulae in the epic tradition more generally.

My initial reaction to both these courses was something like wild excitement, as my undergraduate roommates might ruefully remember. All those years of puzzlement at reading continually about horse-taming Hektor, and well-grieved Achaeans, and (of course) the wine-dark sea and rosy-fingered dawn were now happily resolved. No longer did I have to shrink and apologize in the presence of non-classicists who pilloried Homer and others for relying so heavily on those tired clichés. It was not that Homer nodded; it was rather and happily that Homer stood in a proud tradition of oral epic-making.

However, my pleasure and excitement did not sustain themselves. Indeed, by some point in midyear, I had turned deeply anti-folkloristic and anti-formulaic, for the following reason. What was happening, especially among my fellow undergraduates in the Iliad course, was that a brief and plainly incomplete acquaintance with folklore studies seemed to provide many students with a license to shirk much responsibility toward reading the text with any care. Any textual point upon which I wished to build some model for reading a particular book or section in the Iliad was quickly dismissed as merely the result of some oral poet's momentary need and therefore as of no interpretive significance whatsoever. I remember in particular trying to build some case around the slight but intriguing differences between a speech Agamemnon had delivered and the version of that speech as relayed by Odysseus to Achilles in Book 9 of the Iliad. Those differences, most students in the course insisted, were of no use as evidence in supporting any reading about the character of Odysseus, for example, because the differences were in a sense the accidental and inevitable by-product of the way in which poems like this were produced.

Now, as the academic year progressed and as all of our understanding of oral composition techniques advanced, everyone in the course realized that the folkloristic model for the composition of the Iliad most certainly did not demand that we ignore distinctive signs in the text, as many of us had initially concluded. A presumed oral setting for the composition and delivery of the Iliad did not mean that one could write a sort of glib algebraic formula such that written literature was to oral, traditional literature as the sophisticated was to the unsophisticated.

And this leads me to my final comment, or perhaps my final series of questions. Might it not be the case that some of the comments made in the past few years, especially those by biblical scholars and literary critics, reveal an unhappy reliance on just this ultimately unsustainable formula? Might it not be true that many of us have assumed that the written is to the oral as the careless is to the careful? I would, then, want to ask of folklorists if I am correct in assuming that this formula is radically wrong—if I am right in having concluded that oral, traditional literature can be and often is at least as carefully crafted and textually intricate as are the productions of individual, writing authors. If I am right, if the glib formula is the result only of an incomplete reading of folklore scholarship, then the apparent dichotomy between subtly sophisticated written literature and quickly tossed off oral literature disappears. And that means we can both read the Bible as a palimpsest, as a collection of community material composed and transmitted over generations and centuries, and still read the Bible with the utmost concern for every nuance in the text.

18. REFLECTIONS
Joseph Falaky Nagy

I wondered for a whole year why Professor Niditch invited me, a Celtic folklorist, to a conference on the Hebrew Bible. I'm still not sure, but I know that I have certainly learned a great deal, and that the conference has provided an experience for which I am very grateful. Among the things I have learned is that Biblical scholars, like other scholars working with archaic texts, are very curious and even anxious about a "seen-through-a-glass-darkly" oral tradition (or traditions) that thrived alongside or even despite the literary tradition, the products of which Biblical scholars study. I have also learned that in a milieu of such competing media, a literary tradition never quite succeeds in its attempts to canonize itself, since the ongoing oral tradition inevitably affects the bearers and producers of the written word. In performing their labors of composition and redaction, the Biblical literati were, it would seem, by no means sealed off from the world of oral discourse—even, I gather, as it exists in Near Eastern and Jewish traditions today. (I mention in passing that the exciting prospect of illuminating the literature of an ancient people by means of comparison with the modern "folklore" of their heirs beckons in medieval Irish studies as well. Here, too, we have a body of texts from a bygone era that was produced in conscious counterpoint to a still-living oral tradition, with which the literary process engaged in a shifting, synergistic relationship through the centuries.)

I was also intrigued by the point so well made in Robert Culley's paper about the importance of our appreciating the significance (in the literal sense!) of the composite nature of Biblical texts. I agree that compositeness does not rule out the possibility of consistent—even "traditional"—meaning in either the parts of a text or their sum. Hence, we should be wary of smugly analyzing a literary composition into its supposed components, tracing these off to various sources, whether literary or "folkloric," and thus ignoring the array itself, which may have all kinds of interesting paradigmatic and syntagmatic features. Perhaps this is the point that the anthropologist

Edmund Leach was trying to make in his impish excursions into the Bible. No matter what else we choose to do with it, a text (or a collection of texts) deserves to be examined as a whole.

There were some notions underlying some of what was said at the conference that, I think, deserve challenging and testing. One of these was the assumption that in the process of the translation of form or content from the oral mode into the literary, the capacity for subtlety of expression increases. I am troubled by this implicitly aesthetic judgment, as, I suspect, most folklorists would be. In texts collected from virtuosic oral performers, one can find as much "discriminating art" as can be found in any literary text.

A quite different assumption that emerged occasionally was the idea that in the shift from oral to literary expression, there is an inevitable loss of immediacy—of the vital rhetorical give-and-take between performer and audience which gives flavor and meaning to the performance in the oral settings—or, that writing engenders a kind of homogenization of expression. Yet, while a written text does become a thing unto itself in some respects, it only has existence and meaning insofar as it is pitched at, and appreciated by, an "audience." Furthermore, although writing may make it easier to establish and maintain a theological or ideological party line, it also allows, as many scholars have noted, for greater self-consciousness and retrospective thinking—on the part of both author and reader—about the process of transmission from oral to literary. The reality—or conceit—of transmission haunts many early literary corpora, in a variety of manifestations. Why, the medieval Irish literati (for example) wondered aloud in their writings, should the written text have any kind of authority over the spoken word, of which the written is supposedly a record? And why should the spoken word be written down at all? In light of John Middleton's useful reminder of the "inside"/"outside" model of society and social behavior, we should assess the extent to which Biblical writers may have felt, and expressed, that they or their literary activities were "marginal" in the face of what at some points in their culture's history must have seemed a monolithic oral tradition. Were they really so confident of being on the "inside" of the proper, authoritative channels of communication? And how did they themselves conceptualize the oral tradition? In what ways did this conceptualization positively or negatively inform their sense of their own written tradition?

There are, of course, passages in the Bible that shed light on these matters. Carole Fontaine and Claudia Camp proposed in their paper that the story of Samson as told in Judges offers a literary analysis of an oral performance situation and an oral genre (riddling). Galit Hasan-Rokem sees in the opening chapters of Genesis not just the story of how the world came into being but also, and perhaps more importantly, the *aition* of language. These are instances of the self-consciousness of the Hebrew literary tradition.

Let me go further. What are we to make of the shifting portrayal in Exodus of the process whereby the Commandments were inscribed on stone tablets? Did God himself write them, or did Moses take dictation? And, in the acts of destroying the first copy in his fury at the Hebrews and then obtaining another, is Moses (and the scribal tradition he represents) demonstrating the endurance or the vulnerability of the written text? Is Moses' destructive impatience really with the medium of writing? I am tempted to connect his behavior at this important juncture in the history of communication between God and man with the sentiments expressed in Eccl 12:11–12: "The sayings of the wise are like goads, and like nails firmly fixed are the collected sayings which are given by one Shepherd. My son, beware of anything beyond these. Of making many books there is no end, and much study is a weariness of the flesh." It's not easy being a writer, or even a reader, especially in the face of a powerful oral tradition.

Or, there is the remarkable contrast in the Book of Daniel between the fate of Nebuchadnezzar and that of his son, Belshazzar. Nebuchadnezzar experiences a portentous vision, which he tells as a first-person narrative, and the prophet Daniel tells him what it means. After these key verbal performances, the king undergoes the life-changing rite of passage that was foretold to him in his dream. He goes mad, runs off into the wilderness where he lives like an animal (far from the written word!), and returns enlightened. There is in medieval Irish tradition a famous wild man named Suibhne, who becomes wild as a result of a curse laid upon him by a saint, whose book he had attempted to destroy. A side effect of Suibhne's bewilderment is a newfound ability to compose poetry, through which he both commemorates and laments his skittish life. It has been proposed that Suibhne was modelled to an extent on the figure of the maddened Nebuchadnezzar—a modelling that, I propose, reflects the Irish literati's perception of an ideology of oral performance at work in the story of the Babylonian king. That the power of speech is indeed a topic of Daniel 4 would seem to be confirmed by the contrasting story of Belshazzar, which immediately follows. This arrogant king, so caught up in "cultural affairs," receives a warning, as did his father, but Belshazzar's comes in writing, which the prophet Daniel, now turned reader, deciphers for him. This terse written message leads to no rite of passage, but only Belshazzar's sudden death—reported abruptly in the text, in contrast to the expansiveness of Nebuchadnezzar's account of his dream. Is there perhaps a connecting strand between this pair of stories and the tradition of thought represented in Paul's words in 2 Cor 3:6: "The written code kills, but the spirit gives life"?

No doubt there is much work that could be done on these self-reflective passages in the Bible. But if this is all old hat to Biblical scholars, I beg your indulgence.

19. REFLECTIONS
Burke O. Long

In thinking about the above papers and our discussions of them, I was struck by how frequently something like the phrase "artful ambiguity" was actually uttered or, if not spoken, would have served to describe what was being talked about in various analyses of Biblical texts. I recall particularly the papers by Zakovitch, Fontaine and Camp, Alter, Hasan-Rokem, and others where this seemed to happen.

Asking whether the phrase, or even the sentiment behind it, is justified when applied to Biblical literature would be an appropriate question, and one that might send us along the byways of source and redactional analysis, the *culs de sac* of original author's (redactor's) intention, or scales of aesthetic value accepted by authors and readers. These trails are less important to me right now than asking about hermeneutical strategies which "artful ambiguity," that phrase with cunning appeal, might bundle together and protect.

What does "artful ambiguity" defend, or perhaps hide from view? We might speculate about our modern fascination with ambiguity; our making an aesthetic virtue of it; our suspicion of the overly determined; our resistance to any hegemony of reading that delegitimates difference. On the other hand, "artful ambiguity" may hide a theory of art that requires the unitary, a notion that coherence after all is preferable to incoherence, more pleasurable and beautiful, even if the aesthetic pleasure of coherence is found in a balance of multiple meanings. Invoking the Bible's "artful ambiguity" might grow out of a continuing need to justify reading the Bible at all, especially in the academy of critics, now that the religious impulse which empowered Biblical study from the beginning may no longer be taken for granted.

Perhaps the phrase simply served us as a rhetorical device to legitimate our explorations of pluriform readings of the Bible. On the one hand, someone might attribute a purposeful open-endedness to a Biblical writer (even we translate this to mean an implied author or

redactor). On the other hand, the phrase might warrant the exploitation of undecidability (in our reading, or in the text, depending on the
theoretical niceties that might be assumed). "Artful ambiguity" may
allow for a theory of high, but mysterious, art at one extreme, and a
deconstructionist notion of texts and readers divided against themselves at the other extreme. We heard something of the former during
the past two days, and little if anything of the latter. Simply put, the
phrase "artful ambiguity" justified pluriform readings among us, and
allowed us to imagine that we were getting along together.

In a sense that's what the conference was all about, or at least that
it turned out to be less about folklore than a celebration of multiform
readings of the Bible, each one seemingly developed within its own
set of conventions, questions, and rules of interpretation. It was a
feast of sorts, and I believe that pluriform readings were entered into
with extraordinary tolerance. They were resisted with remarkably
few public, but many private, outbursts as though it were uppermost
in our minds to observe some code of scholarly civility.

It strikes me that "artful ambiguity," because it may be symp-
tomatic of so much, deserves further reflection and clarification. But
it's the resistance to pluriform readings that interests me right now,
those moments when ambiguity in a text was disallowed, or when
tolerance for difference among readings broke down. Recall, for example, some of the public signs of resistance: the Zakovitch/Cross
repartee over "my *peshat*, your *midrash*." Or the Camp/Fontaine exchange with members of the audience over the allowable translation
for a particular verb.

Now these occasional ruptures of surface tension suggest an agi-
tation running beneath the calm waters, a problem that may need
some reflection. I believe a number of unexamined and unresolved issues may lurk here, perhaps boiling down to a question of locating
authority for reading. We didn't take much time to identify and acknowledge the vested interests that may be expressed in one reading
or another, or in one reading being defended against another, or intimated as a standard for another. What are the limits to allowable
ambiguity that a text might present us with, and at what point do
conventions of interpretation—methods if you will—disguise arbi-
trariness?

It seems to me that these issues could bear discussion. Why? Because the exercise of self-acknowledging analysis about these matters
may help us to understand more of what went on at that delightfully
stimulating conference. I would hope it might lead us to see more
deeply where and how connections can be made between the Bible
and folk-lore, or rather between Biblical scholars and folklorists, each
among its variant kind, and across the species divide.

A second observation grows out of thinking about this phrase, "artful ambiguity." In case after case, and especially in our favorite case, the story of Samson, speakers or respondents exposed ambiguity in the story, examined it, disambiguated it into a rich catalog of intention, or if not intention certainly some kind of social or literary function open to our scrutiny. The question that arose for me in all of this discussion was this: have we really been dealing in these cases with folklore? With folktale? With proverb? Or have we been exploring together something that is already, or maybe always was, literature produced and honed by a literate, book-producing segment of an ancient culture?

Of course, the distinctions between literature and folktale are not always clear or necessarily easy to state. And the debates about oral and written materials, their distinctive styles, if any, and the interrelationships between them, have consumed major amounts of scholarly energies. Generalizations, if valid at all, are difficult to sustain across cultural and linguistic lines. Even the very definition of folklore seems uncertain, or at least has a history like everything else.

In view of the rich discussion among professional folklorists on these matters, it strikes me as odd that we heard relatively little about them. Given the reality that most of our presentations were particular readings of a written Biblical text, long transmitted among the "folk" of our own cultures, and among the educated "folk" in the academy, I simply wonder how important the study of folklore as a distinct discipline of inquiry really was to the conference. Some of the main lecturers obviously saw the Bible with eyes accustomed to observing non-Biblical materials or societies-as-text. One presenter, Robert Alter, in effect threw away folklore into a dustbin of discarded, unrecoverable materials. For him the Samson tale was a forever lost folkloristic substance melted down and recast, a substance newly created into "an exacting, subtly discriminating art." How, and in what ways, is the study of folklore as practiced today important for Biblical interpretation?

On the other hand, certain lectures, particularly those given us by the Israeli scholars, suggested a rich and long-lasting interaction between folk culture and the sorts of literate, learned interpretation that collections of midrashim and talmudic elaboration represent. And where would one place a modern midrashist, such as Elie Wiesel, who in a sense shows us the vitality of the Bible as a book out of, and living in, a folk culture?

Perhaps in this area we might find bountiful folkloristic harvest that could serve as a model for the study of other communities of people who read the Bible. In Jewish cultures, we might investigate anew how the Bible lived through elaboration in legend and popular interpretation, how its ambiguities (artful or just plain puzzling) were resolved and deposited in collections of interpretation, e.g., midrashim; how complex social realities turned inert text into a book belonging to a particular "folk," should we say, the rabbis; how this vital stuff of living from the Bible became books, and then, in further transformations of study and teaching, how it took on a new form in a discourse as modern, and as ancient, as Elie Wiesel's *Messengers of God*.

This focus on communities of interpretation broadly understood as a subject for the folklorist and Biblicist to study, the various "folk" of reading (and maybe just knowing a culturally filtered and interpreted Bible without actually reading it)—this focus might extend to Christian and Muslim communities, too. Although collections of midrashim are not associated with such cultural groups, one might study the substance of the matter. We need to investigate systematically the relation between Bible, a book of the folk, and the interpretations that are generated and persist through weavings of folklore and more tightly controlled "scholastic" readings of the same book. In short, what might a cooperative effort among folklorists and Biblical scholars produce in understanding how the Bible has been, and is, appropriated in various cultures? This line of inquiry de-ethnicizes study of the Bible, brings it into the realm of living folk traditions, and opens onto cross-cultural study of scriptures. Here we touch the wider concerns of comparative history of religions, and perhaps glimpse one way to integrate the study of Bible more fully into the paradigms of study that are commonly assumed in non-sectarian university environments.

20. REFLECTIONS
Robert Coote

I appreciate the critical and hermeneutical remarks that have just been made. The questions raised are indeed important ones. I wish also to raise a question, but a sort of ethnographic rather than critical question. It's a genuine question in the sense that I only have an inkling of an answer myself. I hope someone here might have something to say about it.

I liken our situation to a person who is trying to figure out what the picture on a 500-piece jigsaw puzzle looks like when we only have 15 pieces of the puzzle to go on. The picture of the puzzle is, as it were, the body of folklore possibilities out of which biblical literature emerged. What does the whole picture look like, not just the tiny part I am able to glimpse through the Bible? That is a question we in biblical studies are always up against. I think Dan Ben-Amos' way of expressing it was perhaps the most elegant at the conference, but I think it's an important reality for all of us: how to conceive of the wider traditional and conceptual landscape in which the individual compositions we have to study took shape. How do we cope with the lack of evidence that classical form criticism may not have taken seriously enough?

I wonder whether there isn't a body of material that is currently largely neglected but that might be quite useful to our work. I am thinking of collections of narrative lore, proverbial lore, customary practices, and reminiscences thereof from Palestinian villages in the nineteenth and early twentieth centuries. Much such material was published by Western travelers, diplomats, missionaries, medical missionaries, entrepreneurs, philologists, anthropologists, and historians. To call most of this material ethnography might be to overstate its value, or at least the accessibility of its value. There is not a whole lot published. (Are there collections of unpublished material of this sort somewhere?) But there is much of value available nevertheless. I have not done a careful study of what is available. Some of you probably know more about what is available than I do.

There is the question of how this material is to be used, how we are to assess its value. For example, someone here may know something about Tewfik Canaan, a Palestinian whom Albright apparently met in Jerusalem or elsewhere in the country and persuaded to write up his knowledge of Palestinian folklore. How did this come about? What is the value of this material from a critical standpoint? A great deal of it was published in the old *Journal of the Palestine Oriental Society*, which ceased publication 50 years ago or more. Some of it was published in *BASOR* later on. I know this stuff exists, and I have read most of it, but I don't know its status, its true value. Questions come up like: how we are to use such material critically. Under what circumstances was it collected? Though I have no reason to doubt Canaan's reliability, I actually have no idea about it myself. About some of the collectors there can be no doubt, but that may not be true of all of them. Are there other Palestinians in the group? Canaan was the only one I could name, but there may be others.

And then there are the Europeans and Americans, of which there were a whole lot. Philip Baldensperger comes to mind, but he's just an example. Baldensperger apparently grew up in Palestine and lived there most of his life. His daughter was a life-long resident of Artas south of Bethlehem and lived into the 1920s there. How reliable is his material, much of it published in *PEFQ* and in his book *The Immovable East*? This is very interesting material, if it can be used. What is required for its critical use? The same question applies for these pieces and bits of lore available to us: what is the relation between these and what actually the folklore landscape of Palestine looked like?

What folklore was in Palestine in the nineteenth century C.E. may have been different from what folklore was in the biblical period. But from a comparative perspective there is probably something of value here. While we don't have Gustav Dalman's studies for folklore from the period he gathered information in Palestine (although Dalman himself includes considerable lore, and much of what he provides has been neglected), there is much published in *ZDPV*, *PEFQ*, and other journals. I think also of documents like Stumme's *Neuaramäische Märchen und andere Texte aus Maʿlula*, published around 1910 or 1915. Why do we see so few references to material like this? Is it because it is not good material, or because it has been decided already that it is not germane to the questions of folklore and biblical study, or because we just don't know about it? Probably the answer is different for each source. Should not data of this broad and general kind be of interest to us?

21. DOMAINS OF FOLKLORISTIC CONCERN:
THE INTERPRETATION OF SCRIPTURES
Margaret A. Mills

Torah is fixed, but it is permissible and indeed, necessary to unfix it orally, for otherwise who would understand it? (Bruns:29).

The overall function of the oral Torah has been to infuse with dynamism and vitality the religious message of the written Bible, the arrested spoken Word with a capital W. Its effect is to have enabled Scripture to maintain its impact until now on the mind and life of the believing Jew. And the same conclusion applies, mutatis mutandis, to the role of Scripture and Tradition among the scions of Judaism, Christianity and Islam (Vermes:94).

This varied and vigorously contested symposium has served to highlight the considerable variety of approaches to the study of folkloristic features *in* the Hebrew Bible, their detection and interpretation. What is equally fascinating to me, however, is its lack of attention to a complementary set of problems which, I think, if undertaken, could shed light on the enterprises here represented and move them ahead, and that is the presence of scripture in oral tradition down to the present day (Graham). Let me hasten to add that I am not advocating a simple equation between folklore and oral tradition: one area of exploration whose necessity has been illustrated by the proceedings is the definition of those two concepts, for present and wider purposes. The variety of offerings in this symposium reflect, among other things, a lack of consensus over such definitional issues, though the problem of consensus was somewhat obscured because definitions were not made explicit.

A consistent note in all the presentations is a consciousness of and concern to take into account canonical scripture's oral prehistory. Albert Lord, in a comment during the discussion of the first pair of papers (his own and Culley's), rightly directed our attention to the need for better understanding of the actual processes of transition from oral (multi-variant) to written (canonical) form. As he pointed out, this is a crucial and fascinating dimension, but a highly elusive one in part because our information about the social context of the production of these texts is so slim. Professor Lord, his colleagues, and students, who have labored in the vineyards of the oral-formulaic theory, certainly can attest to the trickiness of arguing from text form, content, and style to try to specify social processes of textual production. (Vermes wisely examines texts not so much for formal evidence, but for their own observations on textuality and text production. But the process of canonization especially, for obvious political reasons, has a pronounced tendency to cover its own tracks.) More generally, we have not resolved for ourselves the question of what a "transitional" text is, either formally or in terms of production, and it is likely that transition processes between oral and literary verbal arts, and the texts produced by such processes, vary as much as the literacy practices and literacy environments which are coming to light through the ethnographic study of literacy (Scribner and Cole; Street, with bibliography; Graham; Baumann; and especially Vermes). In any case, the fact that investigations of text-generative processes removed in time and space are fraught with pitfalls, should not totally deter us from framing at least the questions implied by that line of inquiry, as long as we also recognize the necessary indeterminacy of our own answers to such questions, and resolve not to substitute generalizations when, as will happen for historical or other reasons, the desired ethnographic specificity eludes us.

But beyond the archeology of knowledge (I use Foucault's phrase advisedly here), one great area of interest which ought to be addressed in the sort of intellectual context established by this symposium, is scripture's perpetual *return* to oral currency, and the processes of "re-oralization," if I can call it that, called for by the very nature of scripture as a peculiarly authoritative kind of text, as words to live by in the profoundest sense. While scripture's claim to authority is profound, one might say elemental, its actual interpretations in context—its re-oralizations—are by nature vigorously multivocal and contestive. They are also often communicated face-to-face in small groups (congregations) who are negotiating for shared meaning and cohesion. The process of scriptural re-oralization, generative not only of interpretations but of the believing community itself, is the process of folklore par excellence (Ben-Amos). Given that oral Torah was by no means an amateur enterprise (Vermes:93), the study of scripture seems to be a usefully problematic field for re-examining the relationship between "oral" and "folk" knowledge.

I would invite the symposium participants to consider ourselves, for the sake of present argument, as a folk group in Ben-Amos' sense, who for reasons very worthy of exploration have chosen to engage orally over scripture—in our case to try to arrive at certain kinds of consensus, not so much about what this or that piece of text means (though some contributors have certainly tried for that level of specificity as well), but also more broadly, for a consensus about some of the *ways* scripture makes meaning—particularly those ways most closely related to other folk processes, visible in living traditions where we can observe the social contexts and uses of such productions. Two caveats pertain here: first, these texts are just as laconic about the processes of their own production as they are about intended interpretations, and we must avoid facile parallelisms between present social practice and ancient textual artifacts (cf. Lavie, concerning the politics of present-day Israeli constructions of Sinai desert nomadism as a nostalgic reinvocation of Biblical social conditions, a dubious ethnography). I submit that we are not only contemplating such processes of meaning-making, we are, in ways peculiar to our own community's sociolinguistics, simultaneously engaging in processes like those which we are trying to study.

I am not, however, about to assert that our interpretive processes closely resemble in their particulars those of "oral Torah" (Vermes), nor that mere reflexive exercises can resolve the indeterminacies of historical ethnography just described. The diversity of believing (and skeptical) communities represented in the symposium itself makes this group a rather anomalous scriptural community, and intellectual procedures certainly vary with time and place. But I think it would be useful to uncover, insofar as possible, the pervasive patterns of the unsaid within the discourse of this symposium, for some of that unsaid is a matter of tacit agreement among the group, while other aspects of it are integral to the very interesting disagreements we have articulated among ourselves. In approaching the lacunae of Biblical texts, this group has generally assumed that much of what is not explained (and is now cryptic to us) in scripture was self-evident to its audience around the time the texts were canonized, as part of a rich substrata of unspoken understandings about social organization: that the laconic quality of scripture is some of the strongest evidence for its debt to folklore. There is a hidden implication here, however, which is probably best aired and then avoided, and that is the sense of distance that arises if we attribute the incomprehensible and foreign (to us) in scripture to folklore, and thereby put folklore and folk processes at an impenetrable distance by our own definition.

Folklore may well be "behind" the text of scripture both in time and in implicature, but that is not to say that all the ways scripture engages folklore are to be located in the remote, pre-canonical past. Seeking folklore as the distant, as the social history only of Biblical times, bypasses the important issue of communal relations to the text now. Why is this dimension not being explored here? What sort(s) of understandings of the Bible, and of folklore, underpin a lack of interest in modern scripturally-based communities? Our own tacit "making strange" of the scripture-community relation seems to me to *be* one such "folklore," i.e., that folklore (with regard to scripture) is something that other people did, elsewhere and long ago. This tacit assumption operates as an agreement not to consider our own operations as a community of interpretation, distancing ourselves from an "other" called "folk" in its intellectual processes.

To test the implications of the generalization that the unsaid and now-cryptic in scripture was consensual, tacit, largely folk knowledge to its compilers, we might profitably have a look at our own "unsaids." Some such unsaid has been a major factor in just about every presentation here: the shared methodological issue, in each case, is, *how* is this scriptural text laconic, and therefore not self-explanatory, and how shall we fill in the gaps? This goal we share both with the scholarly perpetuators of "oral Torah" and with nonscholarly believers of all persuasions. Ordinary people, as well as scholars, are forever filling in these gaps with interpretation and elaborated ritual enactments designed to foreground those among the potential meanings of the text which they are taking as primary (Mills:90; Kane; Brandes; Lawless 1983, 1987; Briggs 1986, 1988: chap. 5). The openness to interpretation of complex symbolic texts is certainly not news to any of this symposium's participants, but the workings of negotiated interpretation in small groups, including our own, responding to the laconicness of scripture, have been left out of the purview of our discussion.

For instance, the phenomenon of multivariant existence, the sine qua non of oral tradition, is acknowledged in various ways by most contributors here, but our hypotheses about what variant status might mean to our interpretations, vary considerably. The question of variants must not be made the stalking horse for assertions of "what was *really* going on" between, e.g., Samson and his in-laws, or Rahab and the spies. "Really" assumes an authoritative version (or interpretation), and that's against the rules of oral variation. Especially, if the variant status of a text is to be sought in part in the particulars of its language (and this does seem basic: "We base our method on the assumption that one can reveal the meaning of the text only be paying full attention to every detail of its form and by persistently searching for the meaning of every word in its context"; Zakovitch, above), we cannot assert that the absence of a certain kind of statement indicates censorship, unless variants exist to confirm for us that what we think has been suppressed, actually did exist elsewhere in the tradition. It is not within the rules to assert that Rahab herself tipped off the king about the spies' presence in her house in Joshua 2, unless one is willing either to show a coeval variant to demonstrate that possibility, or else to tell one's own variant (thus becoming a noncanonical, but perfectly respectable "folk" interpreter of the tale).

I also would insert a word of caution about "*the* meaning of the text" (Zakovitch, above). Implicit assumption of monovocality is probably more dangerous than the explicit variety. Thus when Culley juxtaposes a series of five (plus two) disaster-as-punishment stories and observes, "punishment comes but it is less clear when, why and to whom," we must consider the impact on our interpretive processes if our goal is a single "why": *the* point to be taken from five-plus-two rather contradictory-seeming tales, for us (as analysts rather than believers), may be that this is exactly the sort of irresolvable complexity that keeps the text of scripture as a whole open, because it keeps the relationship of human and Divine also disturbingly but vitally open. Culley's challenging assemblage of texts for comparison poses another (here not directly confronted) question: on what scale is coherence and/or schema to be sought in scripture? On what grounds, and to what ends? Culley has posed as our task "how best to grasp the nature of the Biblical text, in all its complexity," but this, too implies another question, one of audience and context: "best" for whom, for what purpose? As Culley himself aptly reminds us, "the relationship between performer and audience is vital," but how are we to construe that question reflexively, with regard to our own activities? This latter question is one we should be answerable for, as a specialized audience methodologically equipped and responsible to articulate its interpretive goals.

We scholars, like other audiences, interpret partly by imposing certain expectations for connectedness and mutual coherence on different "sets" (as we see them) of narratives, or of the whole, as "the Word of God." Here we can contrast Ben-Amos's historically-inclined perspective on the disaster narratives with Culley's literarily-inclined one, and contemplate our own mixed motives in choosing interpretive fields. I am also uneasy about making generalizations about proprietorship and audience in a folk-narrative corpus without specific ethnographic information on the performance of the lore. Hence, Zakovitch's generalizations about "men's stories" and "women's stories" are tantalizing but ethnographically unsubstantiated, Walt Disney's personal vision notwithstanding. Stone, whose work Zakovitch cites, is by contrast quite cognizant that we can only discover whose stories are whose, by direct observation and inquiry within the community or communities of performance. If certain Biblical stories "belong" to men or women, that seems discoverable by research within scripture-using communities. That stories "about women" can carry different significance for different audiences is well demonstrated by Feeley-Harnik's (above) rereading of the Book of Ruth in response to earlier interpretations.

Robert Alter's approach to "Samson without Folklore" may be operating, according to his definition, "without folklore," but this is largely because he has tacitly defined strategic word-plays and verbal intricacy as non-folkloric. In this he diverges sharply from perspectives which are integral to contemporary folkloristics, developed through the close examination of oral texts by Hymes, Tedlock, and their interlocutors. Hymes and Tedlock—notwithstanding their serious methodological differences—have both shown how individual words (and for Tedlock, even intonations and other para-linguistic phenomena) operate architectonically and interpretively in subtle patterns within the fabric of oral narrative performance.

Alter may inherit this difficulty with the folklore/literature nexus from a generation of "folklore and literature" scholars described by Wilson (1988), who have preoccupied themselves with atomistic "folklore in literature" detection, according to a now-outmoded evolutionary view of folklore, which obscures the far more interesting and productive question of folklore *as* literature. And like Zakovitch, Alter occasionally gives weight to words that are not there, e.g., when he traces the pervasive theme of seeing in the story of Samson but finds it absent during Samson's encounter with Delilah, and observes, "no seeing is indicated, but perhaps by now it may be implied" (Alter, above). Not to indulge in literary overinterpretation of the unsaid, perhaps seeing is not mentioned in Samson's first encounter with Delilah, because he is, at that early point, well on his way to being blinded by her. Not my point or Alter's point, but the juxtaposition of them is instructive on the indeterminacy of interpretations of silence (unless, perhaps, the silences can be shown to be patterned, best done in contrast of other formulations of "the same story" rather conservatively defined).

Another largely unstated, but very interesting counterpoint in these proceedings is the alternation between Bible-centered readings, which endeavor to make scripture make the most possible sense from within itself and especially to make it define its own social domain and practices of interpretation (implicitly respecting its status as a unique document for believers), and more broadly comparatist, "nonethnocentric" readings such as those of Lord and Bynum which, without denying the particularities of scriptural content, seek a level of generalization sufficient to draw it into juxtaposition with other world literatures, only some of which have or have had scriptural status. The two perspectives here seem to have a modus operandi based on only the most oblique and nominal recognition of their crossed purposes, while in the process, neither engages directly the point that scripture in its life as socially contexted and employed text is multivocal, that readings are not only multiple, but usually ethnically and sectarianly proprietary and contestive. African-American interpretations of the Egyptian and Babylonian captivity narratives, in a rich array of religious discourse from sermons to songs, spring to mind in this regard. If we take up David Bynum's challenge, in his commentary on Alter's paper, to consider scripture in reference to "the whole ethnographic background," how would each of us define that background? Not identically, I would wager. The symposium seems to have engaged in a decorous degree of contest over interpretations, while mostly avoiding overt recognition of the constitutionally contestive nature of the material under study.

Robert Wilson's observation (above) that "specialists in Hebrew Bible have generally avoided considering the ethical dimensions of their material, and have not related their work to modern believers seeking biblical guidance for living the moral life," is well taken. While one can readily understand scholarly reluctance to arbitrate matters of faith and interpretive moves based on them, yet it is interesting that many scholars, like believers (modern and not), in their respective ways, seem to have been preoccupied with the recovery of an Ur-text of unambiguous meaning and also, though for different reasons, seem to be trying to reconstruct some kind of primordial authoritative voice in scripture, the difference being scholars' lack of attention to scripture's engagement with life as presently lived.

The political power of scriptures as supremely authoritative texts is such that various authorities, spiritual and intellectual, are constantly trying to close the texts (to "defolk" them) via "authoritative" interpretation. In this regard, Dan Ben-Amos's observation about the "flattening" of oral texts in written redactions is instructive, but we must also note that multivocality is restored in re-oralization, when the source text is reinterpreted for diverse purposes, in diverse contexts. All interpreters recognize that scriptural text is authoritative in special ways, but nonexpert believers repersonalize it unself-consciously. I would reiterate that we scholars normally repersonalize, too, but that the politics of scholarship tend to veil that repersonalizing function from our own gaze. For instance, it is debatable what cogency or cogencies an ambivalent and ironized view of Israelite intelligence operations might have had for the compilers of Joshua 2 (Zakovitch, above), but the cogencies of such a reading for Israelis and many others in our own day are rich to contemplate.

Regarding Ben-Amos's point offered in response to Culley's paper, on the theocentric reading of disaster tales as punishments, and the general transformation of historical events to scriptural narratives, I would go a little further, to say that stuff—events—*becomes* history only by virtue of being susceptible to ideological interpretation. These narratives *are* history because they *can* be read as punishment narratives. Disaster events not readable in that way would not become sacred history, since sacred history is basically a moral discourse in its social use and interpretation, however cryptic its words (cf. Wilson, above). The enigmatic qualities of scriptural texts have been tantalizingly explored in this symposium—Samson's firefoxes spring to mind—and we seem no closer now than when we started to definitive explanations for why some of these stories were and are worth the telling. That being the case, I would like to direct our energies not to the project of superseding and avoiding "folk" readings of the Bible (by the construction of different types of interpretive authority which we hope will prevail), but instead to understanding those very folk processes of understanding. "Vernacular Bible literacies" (plural) are worthy of folklorists' attention (and I hope also of that of theologians), not even primarily as a way to explore pre-canonical oral spirituality, but as social processes in their own right.

We must also ask ourselves, fairly, are we ourselves "just another folk" when it comes to reading the Bible? It is not just reflexive self-preoccupation that induces me to suggest that we need a better articulated sense of ourselves as a reading community. Alter, Culley, and Zakovitch (all above) each use somewhat different tacit concepts of variants in oral tradition, and corollary procedures, for the understanding of folkloric elements in scripture in ways that at certain points become either misleading, self-contradictory, or simply flabby. If these problems with definition are emanating from folklore-based methodology, then the interpretive exercises we undertake in a symposium of this kind should help Biblical scholars to test and critique folklore's method, not just limp along with it. We *are* equipped to be a particularly reflexive, self-aware community of readers. From the point of view of the ethnography of literacy (or better, the ethnography of the oral-literary interface), we should be very easy to study, because we engage in so much meta-commentary about our own modes of understanding. But even if our methods are more highly elaborated, articulated, and contested, we are nonetheless a reading community among reading communities all in various ways defending their rights of interpretation, and our own search for authoritative interpretive procedures can be seen as a time-honored and folk-ratified enterprise.

Thus, the intense and exciting intellectual exchange of the symposium can be seen not only as a scholarly interpretive exercise, but also as an exercise in re-oralization. The question then arises: why *do* we do this face to face? To *close* the texts, or to open them? I would opt for the latter. The scripture we study is, on abundant current evidence, living text. The other major product of face-to-face interpretation is the creation of community, and at the conference at Professor Niditch's instigation, we have made a very promising step toward the creation of a dialogue, and a community, integrating historians of religion, literary scholars of scripture, and folklorists. Let us so work together that no group claims the last word.

WORKS CONSULTED

Baumann, Gerd (ed.)
    1986   *The Written Word: Literacy in Transition.* Oxford: Oxford University/Clarendon Press.

Ben-Amos, Dan
    1972   "Toward a Definition of Folklore in Context." Pp. 3–15 in *Toward New Perspectives in Folklore.* Ed. A. Paredes and R. Bauman. Austin: University of Texas Press.

Brandes, Stanley
    1983   "The Posadas in Tzintzuntzan: Structure and Sentiment in a Mexican Christmas Festival. *JAF* 96:259–80.

Briggs, Charles
    1986   *Learning How to Ask.* London and New York: Cambridge University Press.

    1988   *Competence in Performance: The Creativity of Tradition in Mexicano Verbal Art.* Philadelphia: University of Pennsylvania Press.

Bruns, Gerald
    1982   *Inventions: Writing Textuality and Understanding in Literary History.* New Haven: Yale University Press.

Foucault, Michel
    1972   *The Archeology of Knowledge.* Trans. A. M. Sheridan Smith. London and New York: Harper Colophon.

Graham, William
    1987   *Beyond the Written Word: Oral Aspects of Scripture in the History of Religion.* London and New York: Cambridge University Press.

Hymes, Dell
    1981   "In Vain I Tried to Tell You." *Essays in Native American Ethnopoetics.* Philadelphia: University of Pennsylvania Press.

Kane, Steven M.
  1974   "Ritual Possession in a Southern Appalachian Religious Sect." *JAF* 87:293–302.

Krupat, Arnold
  1987   "Post-Structuralism and Oral Literature." Pp. 113–28 in *Recovering the Word: Essays on Native American Literature.* Ed. B. Swann and A. Krupat. Berkeley: University of California Press.

Lavie, Smadar
  1988   "Notes on the Fantastic Journey of the Hajj, His Anthropologist, and Her American Passport" (paper delivered at the American Anthropological Association annual meeting, Phoenix, AZ).

Lawless, Elaine
  1983   "Shouting for the Lord: The Power of Women's Speech in Pentecostal Religious Service." *JAF* 96:434–59.

  1987   "Piety and Motherhood: Reproductive Images and Maternal Strategies of the Woman Preacher." *JAF* 100:469–78.

Mills, Margaret A.
  1987   "Oral Tradition." Pp. 87–92 in *Encyclopedia of Religion,* vol. 11. Ed. M. Eliade et al. New York: MacMillan.

Nelson, Kristina
  1985   *The Art of Reciting the Qur'an.* Austin: University of Texas Press.

Scribner, Sylvia, and Michael Cole
  1981   *The Psychology of Literacy.* Cambridge, MA: Harvard University Press.

Street, Brian
  1984   *Literacy in Theory and Practice.* London and New York: Cambridge University Press.

Tedlock, Dennis
  1983   *The Spoken Word and the Work of Interpretation.* Philadelphia: University of Pennsylvania Press.

Vermes, Geza
1987   "Scripture and Tradition in Judaism: Written and Oral Torah." Pp. 79–96 in *The Written Word*. Ed. G. Baumann. Oxford: Oxford University/Clarendon Press.

White, Hayden.
1981   "The Value of Narrativity in the Representation of Reality." Pp. 1–24 in *On Narrative*. Ed. W. J. T. Mitchell. Chicago: University of Chicago Press.

Wilson, Willam A.
1988   "The Deeper Necessity: Folklore and the Humanities." *JAF* 101:156–67.

CONTRIBUTORS

Robert Alter teaches in the Department of Comparative Literature, University of California, Berkeley. A scholar of Western literature who has in recent years turned his attention to the prose and poetry of the Hebrew Scriptures, he is the author of *Fielding and the Nature of the Novel*, *A Lion for Love: A Critical Biography of Stendhal*, *The Art of Biblical Narrative*, *The Art of Biblical Poetry* and *The Pleasures of Reading in an Ideological Age*.

Dan Ben-Amos is a member of the Department of Folklore at the University of Pennsylvania who has worked extensively in Jewish folklore with a special interest in classical texts. The author of scores of major articles on folklore methodology such as the classic "Toward a Definition of Folklore in Context," and of two books, *Sweet Words: Storytelling Events in Benin* and *Folklore in Context: Essays*, he has also edited *Folklore Genres* and co-edited *In Praise of the Baal Shem Tov: The Earliest Collection of Legends about the Founder of Hasidism* (with Jerome R. Mintz) and *Folklore: Performance and Communication* (with Kenneth S. Goldstein). He is currently a key participant in the preparation of an abridged and annotated edition of *Mimekor Yisrael: Classical Jewish Folktales* by Micha Joseph bin Gorion.

David E. Bynum, who taught in the Slavic Department at Harvard University for many years and served as curator of the Milman Parry Collection, went to Cleveland State University in 1982. A professor in the Department of Modern Languages, he continues his life-long work, translating and interpreting the oral literature of the South Slavs represented in the Parry Collection. The author of numerous articles on South Slavic literature and folklore, he is the author of *The Daemon in the Wood*.

Claudia V. Camp is Associate Professor of Religion at Texas Christian University. The author of *Wisdom and The Feminine in the Book of*

Proverbs and of a variety of other publications, Camp's work explores the social-historical, literary, and theological dimensions of the female imagery in Proverbs and other "wisdom" literature. Her current research focuses on the figure of the strange woman in the Bible.

Robert Coote is Professor of Old Testament at San Francisco Theological Seminary. The author of *Amos Among the Prophets* and co-author of *The Emergence of Early Israel in Historical Perspective*, Coote's research deals with prophecy, the social world of ancient Israel, and biblical poetry.

Frank Moore Cross is Hancock Professor of Hebrew and other Oriental Languages at Harvard University. His interests and numerous publications span the 2nd millennium B.C.E. to the first century C.E. He has made seminal contributions to the discussion of relationships between Canaanite and Israelite religions and to the study of the Dead Sea Scrolls in *Canaanite Myth and Hebrew Epic* and *The Ancient Library of Qumran and Modern Biblical Studies*.

Robert C. Culley has taught in the Faculty of Religious Studies at McGill University since 1964. He has edited four issues of *Semeia* for the Society of Biblical Literature and has been an active contributor to American and Canadian scholarly biblical societies. He is the author of numerous articles and two major books, *Oral Formulaic Language in the Biblical Psalms* and *Studies in the Structure of Biblical Narrative*. He is currently preparing a monograph on "Action in Biblical Narrative."

Gillian Feeley-Harnik joined the Department of Anthropology at Johns Hopkins University in 1983 after several years at Williams College. Her major field work and research interests have been in the social organization, religion, and political economy of Madagascar, sub-Saharan Africa. While most of her publications deal with Madagascan culture, Feeley-Harnik also works in comparative religion, her recent book, *The Lord's Table* being an excellent example of her comparative and cross-cultural work.

Carole R. Fontaine is Associate Professor of Old Testament at Andover-Newton Theological School, where she has taught since 1979. The author of *Traditional Sayings in the Old Testament: A Contextual Study* and of numerous articles on proverbs, Job, and ancient Near Eastern wisdom literature, she is currently completing a new book entitled, *Holy Torch of Heaven: Goddesses, Queens and Ordinary Women in the Ancient Near East*.

Edward L. Greenstein is Professor of Bible at the Jewish Theological Seminary of America, where he has taught since 1976. Coeditor of the *Journal of the Ancient Near Eastern Society* and Associate Editor of *Prooftexts*, a major journal in Jewish literature, Greenstein has published actively in biblical studies and on ancient Near Eastern languages and literatures. Author of *Essays on Biblical Method and Translation* and coeditor of the reference book, *The Hebrew Bible in Literary Criticism*, he edits *Semeia Studies*.

David M. Gunn is Professor of Old Testament at Columbia Theological Seminary in Decatur, GA. The author of numerous articles on biblical narrative, oral tradition in the Bible, and literary criticism of the Old Testament, David Gunn has written two major books, *The Story of King David: Genre and Interpretation* and *The Fate of King Saul: An interpretation of a Biblical Story*. He is currently preparing a work for the Oxford Bible Series on "Old Testament Narrative."

Galit Hasan-Rokem is Chair of the Department of Jewish Folklore, Hebrew University and Associate Editor of the international journal *Proverbium*. She is the author of *Proverbs in Israeli Folk Narratives: A Structural Semantic Analysis* and of numerous articles on proverbs, proverbs in folktales, and other areas of folk discourse. Born in Helsinki and having studied at the University of Helsinki and at Hebrew University, Professor Hasan-Rokem has an interest in Scandinavian folklore as well as in Israeli and Jewish materials.

Burke O. Long is Professor of Religion at Bowdoin College. He has been editor of the "Sources for Biblical Study," an important translation project of the Society of Biblical Literature, since 1977 and has also served on the editorial boards of the *Journal of Biblical Literature* and *Semeia*. The author of *The Problem of Etiological Narrative in the Old Testament* and *1 Kings with an Introduction to Historical Literature* and numerous articles, his research interests are in ancient historiography, modern literary approaches to the Bible, and the anthropological and sociological study of Israelite religion.

Albert Bates Lord is Arthur Kingsley Porter Professor of Slavic and Comparative Literature Emeritus at Harvard University. An eminent scholar of oral literature who works in Slavic, classical Greek, and Germanic materials, Lord is the author of *Serbo-Croatian Folk Songs* (with Bela Bartok), *Serbo-Croatian Heroic Songs*, and the well-known classic work *The Singer of Tales*. Professor Lord is currently completing a sequel to this groundbreaking book.

John Middleton, who taught for many years at the University of London, joined the Yale faculty in 1981. An anthropologist whose field research has been among the Lugbara of Uganda, the Swahili of Zanzibar and Kenya, and the Akan of Ghana, Middleton is the author of many seminal books and articles including *Lugbara Religion: Ritual and Authority among an East African People*, *The Lugbara of Uganda*, *The Study of the Lugbara: Expectation and Paradox in Anthropological Research*, and the editor of several valuable anthologies such as *Myth and Cosmos*, *Gods and Rituals*, *Magic*. *Witchcraft and Curing*, and *Studies in Social and Cultural Anthropology*.

Margaret Mills is Associate Professor of Folklore at the University of Pennsylvania. She has done field work in Iran, Pakistan, and Afghanistan, Afghan oral literature being her primary area of research and publication. She is the author of the article on "Oral Tradition" in the *Encyclopedia of Religion* (ed. Mircea Eliade) and co-author of "Iranian *Sofreh*: From Collective to Female Ritual" in *Gender and Religion: On the Complexity of Symbols* (Beacon, 1986). She teaches courses in "Myth," "Epic and Romance," and other basic areas of folklore in addition to more specialized courses in orality and literacy and ethnic dimensions of folklore.

Roland E. Murphy, O. Carm., is George Washington Ivey Emeritus Professor of Biblical Studies (Duke University). He has served as editor-in-chief, and as a member of the editorial board of the *Catholic Biblical Quarterly* (1959-65; 1977-84) and as president of both the Catholic Biblical Association and the Society of Biblical Literature. A well-respected scholar of the biblical wisdom tradition, Father Murphy is one of the co-editors and contributors to *The New Jerome Biblical Commentary* (1990), and is the author of many works including *Psalms, Job* (Fortress, 1977); *Wisdom Literature* (Eerdmans, 1981); and *Wisdom Literature and Psalms* (Abingdon, 1983).

Joseph Falaky Nagy has taught in the English Department and the Folklore and Mythology Program at UCLA since 1978 and is currently Chair of the Program. He is the author of *The Wisdom of the Outlaw: The Boyhood Deeds of Finn in Gaelic Narrative Tradition* (University of California Press, 1985), which was awarded the Chicago Folklore Prize. He is completing a translation of the *Colloquy of the Ancients*, a treasure-trove of medieval Irish oral and learned lore. His primary areas of scholarly interest include the "interface" between literary and oral traditions, and the nature and function of myth in various cultures.

Susan Niditch is Associate Professor of Religion at Amherst College. She is the author of *The Symbolic Vision in Biblical Tradition, Chaos to Cosmos: Studies in Biblical Patterns of Creation,* and *Underdogs and Tricksters: A Prelude to Biblical Folklore.* Her current research project is a study of Israelite ethics of war.

Robert A. Oden, Jr., taught in the Department of Religion, Dartmouth College for over a decade, having served as chair. He has recently accepted a position as Headmaster of the Hotchkiss School in Lakeville, Connecticut. The author of *Studies in Lucian's De Dea Syria* and numerous articles in biblical and ancient Near Eastern literature, his new book, *The Bible Without Theology,* is a major critique of normative biblical scholarship.

Edgar Slotkin is Professor of English and Comparative Literature at the University of Cincinnati where he teaches folklore and Celtic Studies. He is the author of many articles in these fields and the co-translator of *A General Rhetoric* by Group μ. He is the Secretary/Treasurer of the Celtic Studies Association of North America.

Robert R. Wilson has taught at Yale University since 1972 and is currently the Chairman of the Department of Religious Studies. His major works include *Genealogy and History in the Biblical World, Prophecy and Society in Ancient Israel,* and *Sociological Approaches to the Old Testament.* He is currently working on two new books, "Approaches to Old Testament Ethics," and a commentary on the Book of Kings.

Yair Zakovitch teaches in the Department of Bible, the Hebrew University, Jerusalem. He is the author of *The Life of Samson—Judges 13–16* (in Hebrew) and a forthcoming commentary on Ruth. He has published numerous articles and reviews in all the major international biblical journals, and is currently working on a new commentary on the Song of Songs.

GENERAL INDEX

INDEX OF CHARACTERS

Index of Biblical Citations

INDEX OF AUTHORS